SHARED PARENTHOOD

A Handbook For Fathers

Johanna Roeber

CENTURY
LONDON MELBOURNE AUCKLAND JOHANNESBURG

First published in 1987 by Century Hutchinson Ltd
Brookmount House, 62–65 Chandos Place,
Covent Garden, London WC2N 4NW

Century Hutchinson Australia Pty Ltd,
PO Box 496, 16–22 Church Street, Hawthorn, Victoria 3122, Australia

Century Hutchinson New Zealand Limited,
PO Box 40-086, Glenfield, Auckland 10, New Zealand

Century Hutchinson South Africa (Pty) Ltd
PO Box 337, Bergvlei, 2012 South Africa

Typeset by Rowland Phototypesetting Ltd,
Bury St Edmunds, Suffolk

Printed and bound in Great Britain by
Richard Clay Ltd, Bungay, Suffolk

British Library Cataloguing in Publication Data
Roeber, Johanna
Shared parenthood: a handbook for fathers.
1. Pregnancy   2. Childbirth   3. Parenthood
I. Title
618.2'00240431   RG525

ISBN 0-7126-0724-2

About the Author

Johanna Roeber is a qualified family therapist and antenatal teacher with three children of her own. She was the author of *Exercises for Childbirth* with Barbara Dale, which was published by Century in 1982.

Contents

To Alex Pollock, Sheila Kitzinger and my children Anya, Adam and Rebecca Suschitzky with my love and thanks.

Acknowledgements

This book has taken time to come into being. Its conception was easy, but the pregnancy, labour and birth have been challenging! Fortunately I have been helped and sustained by many generous people who allowed me to draw upon their strengths when my spirit was flagging (in alphabetical order) – Katrina Bruce, John Claxton, Sue Cohen, Barbara Dale, Elizabeth Fenwick, Lizzy Hibbit and all the midwives at St Mary's Hospital, Sheila Kitzinger, Ray Kreedy, Simon Lichtenstein, Frances Lincoln, Sandra Lousada, Tony Lycholat, Dr Maberley, Catherine Mackwood, Levana Marshall, Clare Mitchison, Jim Obelkevich, Mr David Painton, Pippa Rubenstein, Graham, Sue and Tom Samuel, Judith Schott and all my colleagues at the N.C.T., Melody Weig, John Webber who was particularly helpful, and to all those men who talked about the experience of becoming a father with me – my thanks to you all.

Introduction

Why have I, a woman, written a book for men – particularly those men who are in the process of becoming fathers? A quick answer would be that I'm fascinated by the father–child relationship because I did not have the opportunity to experience it myself. My father abandoned my mother and myself when I was still a baby, and because I did not grow up with the daily familiarity of my own father I have never taken such a presence for granted and have always searched to understand the phenomenon of fathering. My loss affected me profoundly and even today feels like an empty space in my inner world. But perhaps this privation propelled me into action: if more men were convinced of the value to themselves of their fathering role there might be fewer children cut off from this essential relationship. It is undeniably true that children need their fathers – I am also convinced that those same fathers need their children, as I hope to demonstrate during the course of this book.

In many ways giving birth to our three children and sharing the early relationship they had with their father was a powerfully healing experience for me. I often said to myself as I watched my husband with our daughter, 'So that's what it's like. . . .'

And later on it seemed inevitable that I became an antenatal teacher and family counsellor working with couples preparing for birth – the birth of their baby and the birth of themselves as parents. It was during the course of my work that I realized how often a man's personal feelings and needs are ignored, while subtle pressure is exerted upon him to keep out of the mainstream and stay in his traditional role as a supporter to the pregnant woman. Men in that environment often do not find the support and encouragement they require to negotiate dynamically the transition into fatherhood. If 'getting it right' in the early stages is vital for mothers to feel confident and competent in their new role, surely the same must be true for fathers?

The men I have met through my work have shown me that becoming a father is just as much a voyage of personal exploration and demands an equal amount of creativity as becoming a mother demands of a woman. In many ways preparation for fatherhood is a more complex undertaking because the man does not have the public recognition, nor the daily reminder of the baby growing within his body. A man's involvement during pregnancy and in the early postnatal period is necessarily more diffuse than his partner's; it is she who carries, bears and then often enjoys the intense intimacy of breastfeeding her baby. Because men are in a real sense bystanders to the physiological process of pregnancy and birth, it is understandable, given the mores of our society, that many feel distanced or even alienated from this undeniable and inexorable act of creation. Too often when the baby is born a father feels himself to be outside the 'magic' circle which encloses the mother and child. This fragile link should not be accepted as normal or healthy, as anyone concerned with promoting the closer involvement between fathers and their children will agree.

In our society until recently, too many fathers have remained on the periphery of childbirth and childrearing. But there are welcome signs that attitudes are changing. During the interviews I did while preparing this book I was struck by the number of fathers who look for, and expect to achieve, a more intimate involvement with their babies than they themselves had experienced with their own fathers. These men are not satisfied to hover on the sidelines of family life. They know, as well as I do from my own personal lack of good fathering, just how vital their presence will be. But what many of them do not discover until they become more active is that this involvement not only ensures the child's healthy development, it also gives the father an ideal opportunity to evolve a complete and whole personality of his own.

However, a man does not become a father in a vacuum. The baby's mother plays a crucial and powerful role in his evolution as an active participant within the family. Those couples who seek a new approach to family life find that the changes and shifts in emphasis bring new, unexpected challenges. Men and women who look towards shared parenting will need courage to open themselves to the psychological challenges and practical upheavals that this closer involvement between father and child entails. Not only will the couple's relationship 'suffer a sea change into something rich and strange' but also the structure and nature of family life, and their working world as well.

This book is dedicated to all those couples and their children who seek a closer understanding of this new style of parenting – I hope it will be useful. There is no one way to be a 'good enough' parent; there is only the on-going opportunity to give of one's best – only you and your child can discover what that may be.

Give me my infant now
Te-whaka-io-roa

Where are the hands and feet
That Tiki made? Gone with the gods.
Yes, O my children's mother!
Speak, and let me know
That I shall soon an infant see,
And priests shall stand before
The Ahu-rewa altar, where,
With incantations, they shall chant
To bones of those of ancient days,
And taunt the earthquake god.
Yes, Yes, my children's mother,
Give me my infant now,
That, dandling it upon my knees,
My joy may be complete –
That I no more may feel
A want and ache not yet appeased.

Anon.
From the Maori (trans, unknown)

Chapter 1

Making shared parenthood a reality

Some of today's parents no longer accept that 'biology' is destiny and have evolved their own style of sharing the everyday care of their children. Opening the door to shared parenthood inevitably leads to a two-way traffic: the man comes in and develops his relationship with his child – the woman goes out and explores more of her own needs. Both seek to meet their own personal requirements while continually searching for the best for their child, rather than following a pre-ordained pattern.

Couples who want to explore the possibility of shared parenthood need determination to reassess old stereotypes and courage to create their own solutions. Fathers very soon realize that their role is a matter of personal choice – they do not have to accept the dogmatic laws of nature, instinct or tradition. All men have the ability to care for their baby singlehanded – men can 'mother' just as well as women can 'father', given the need, or the desire to do so. The real issues are rather different. First the man has to be very clear that fathers are not just stand-ins for mothers. Next he has to accept a less conventional interpretation of a father's role. And then he has to evaluate what he will gain from the experience against what he will have to relinquish. Finally, and probably most crucially, he has to establish a mutually supportive relationship with a partner who will wholeheartedly contribute to the reality of shared parenthood. Recent research in Australia by Graeme Russell confirms that the strongest identifiable influence when embarking on shared parenthood is that the father chooses it of his own free will, because he and his partner have a less stereotypic view of fatherhood and parenting. Other factors may be the woman's commitment to her work, and the man's personality which naturally inspires him towards parenting. However he may be unemployed, and therefore unlikely to continue this level of involvement longer than is absolutely necessary. The pressure to conform with traditional parenting practices is very strong, and unless a couple have equally strong personal convictions they often find the conflict too much for them. Men can be made to feel less masculine and women to feel bad mothers if they opt out of traditional parenting roles and cross into each other's worlds. So it is essential that both partners feel secure enough to develop and express all levels of their personalities. Research seems to indicate that it is those couples who are already pursuing a more 'egalitarian' partnership, who then opt for shared parenthood as a continuation of their already established lifestyle.

With the birth of a baby a couple are themselves born as parents. It is the beginning of a lifelong relationship with the child. Couples may separate but one cannot divorce a child, although sadly large numbers of fathers do lose contact with their child if the couple separate. With the arrival of his baby the man has a choice about the depth and scope of his involvement which to an extent can be a continuous process of evolution for the rest of his life. Motherhood is more urgent in its demands – when her baby is born a woman has no choice but to begin her career as a mother. During the early postnatal weeks a father who has made time to be at home has the opportunity to ease himself gradually into parenting and to explore the possibility of eventually taking a full share in the care of the baby. In their book *Earth Father–Sky Father*, Arthur and Libby Coleman describe those couples who share the care of the baby, while continuing to work outside the family as 'dyadic' parents – willing to sacrifice some aspects of their individuality and modify usual gender differences. This may sound easy, but in fact it demands a great deal of psychological work for even the most committed and compatible couples to adjust to the demands of this style of parenting.

The decision to try shared parenting is a very personal one, and will obviously depend upon a variety of circumstances. Economic necessity is cited as one of the biggest barriers for most of the fathers I spoke to. Men's earnings are usually higher than women's and this reinforces the traditional family structure. Or where a couple is used to both partners working, having a baby may actually compel a father to take on more, not less work to compensate for the loss of the woman's income. A father is expected to provide material support for his family and most men take pride in their capacity to do so. If he has time left over to be with his child and partner so much the better, but this is not seen as an absolute necessity for either his or their well-being. Many men spoke wistfully of wanting to spend more time with their family. They all recognized the importance of a deeper involvement but felt trapped in the traditional pattern by economic pressures. However they all felt they had achieved a higher level of contact than their own fathers had demonstrated. But the bills have to be paid, and until couples negotiate some fundamental changes in our attitudes to work and child care, the economic alibi will continue to mask the deeper barriers and maintain the traditional parenting arrangements.

Women have always suffered the same problem in reverse – they are often 'allowed' to work if it does not interfere with their husband's or child's welfare or contentment. In effect many women do two full-time jobs, desperately trying to juggle the demands of motherhood and a career. However, shared parenting is not in itself a way of solving these problems, and couples who reject traditional parenting roles may initially have the feeling that they are jumping out of the frying pan to end up in the fire! But their choice is a dynamic one, full of promise for the future. To become 'dyadic' parents takes courage. Inevitably it also means a willingness to confront both the economic and psychological demands of this new way of life which in turn leads to new, unconventional solutions to the age-old challenges of child rearing.

ADJUSTING TO THE DEMANDS OF SHARED PARENTHOOD

To organize shared parenting both partners need to be equally immersed in childcare and their outside pursuits. Couples have to be flexible and receptive, able to negotiate on every level of their lives. There is a need for a high level of thoughtful awareness towards each other, and in the early stages it seems as if nothing can be taken for granted. Normal family life lurches from one 'crisis' to the next. Couples who share parenting become more sensitive to each other's and the children's changing needs, and more aware of the different stages of family growth which make these crises inevitable. Russell's recent study of couples who were trying shared parenting in Australia found that the first six months were the most difficult and stressful. After that couples felt their dual roles helped their relationship and they began to see definite benefits emerging.

Practical irritations are often cited as an initial cause of conflict when parenthood is shared. Women complain that men's housework is not up to standard; men often feel that women fuss unduly.

Discipline can be another issue. Mothers are likely to be concerned that the fathers are too 'soft' on the children, but this problem diminishes the more time the father spends as primary caregiver. The longer he takes full responsibility the more likely he is to accept the need for sensible control. More complex are the shifts in the balance of the traditional affectual ties between parent and child. For example, if a child turns more to his father for comfort even when the mother is present, she may feel hurt, displaced and even hostile towards her partner. The universal problem endemic to child care – lack of time to spend together as a couple – is also a concern in shared parenting. Women are often physically exhausted, particularly if they try to maintain the role of 'super-mum' and carry on as traditional home carers as well as everything else. In this context it is interesting to note that men are more likely than women to insist on their personal need for free time away from childcare. Perhaps women are more prone to guilt than men, more likely to feel grateful to their partners for their 'help' and to renounce their own needs. Russell also found that fathers who stayed at home with their baby also craved some romanticism in their lives. They wanted the woman to bring them flowers or a bottle of wine at the end of a hard day looking after the children. It seems that the women were not so good at remembering this, although they appreciated being on the receiving end themselves!

A man who has an interesting and demanding career may also feel frustrated and isolated in his role as a full-time father. Incomprehension, lack of support from colleagues or anxiety about the future can create feelings of conflict even when the decision has been reached willingly or from a deeply felt conviction. But for couples who make the step into 'dyadic' parenting the long term benefits outweigh the difficulties and give both partners a richer understanding of each other's problems. Because of the shared commitment parents have to spend more time talking to each other and giving mutual support. In several countries studies have been carried out which show that the more a father voluntarily entered into family life, the happier everyone was, and the more satisfied both partners were with the marital relationship.

On a practical level, parents who share their role enjoy the more even distribution of responsibility in the home. And the continual communication means fewer disagreements over childcare practices and a higher level of mutual toleration. In the Australian study of shared parenting 82 per cent of couples agreed that it was the fathers and children whose relationship benefited most. Fathers that I have talked to confirm this view: 'In the beginning I was very nervous about whether I could cope as well as my wife. But you just have to get on and try. Now I feel Cara is easy, she really knows me and her mother, she has two people she can trust equally well. I think the benefits are fantastic. And I really understand about housework now, I'm much more tolerant than I used to be.'

TRADITIONAL ROLES

The traditional view of parenting is that men work and women have babies, that because men do not have wombs or breasts it is obviously a 'waste' of their time – or even mildly eccentric – for them to be actively involved with babies and childcare. Boys, emulating their fathers, grow up believing that work outside the home is the only acceptable work for a man. In return, or perhaps in retaliation, women invest their power in their unique biological ability to bear babies and nurture them with their breasts. Meanwhile society reinforces the traditional belief that this is the 'best' way to organize baby care and family life. These social and economic pressures collude with men's and women's profoundest unconscious fears, that if parenthood is really shared it would mean a loss of personal identity and chaos. For a man to involve himself in baby care, enjoying the nurturing, caring side of his personality, invokes a deep fear of diminished masculinity and for some men this represents an insurmountable barrier. It may also seem safer for women who, on the whole, enjoy being mothers, to remain defined by their motherhood, while men continue to define themselves first and foremost by their work.

The real danger of this model is that it limits both freedom of choice and the possibility of negotiation as and when individual needs change. Inevitably the underlying conflicts we all have between what is perceived as 'masculine' and 'feminine' become that much more firmly entrenched and inflexible.

For those who are willing to try, baby care represents a unique opportunity for personal growth. Those men who stay at a distance from their babies in the early months miss the chance to discover their own capacity for caring, nurturing and responding intensively to another's needs. Finally, if as a couple you do not explore alternatives to the traditional patterns you risk excluding each other and depriving yourselves and your baby from deeper relationships within the family and of a richer experience of life.

MOTHERHOOD AS A POWERBASE

Women who focus too exclusively upon motherhood are in danger, as many have found to their cost. By overdeveloping their obvious 'feminine' traits they often become unwittingly trapped into 'professional' motherhood and neglect the rest of their personality. But perhaps women have other reservations about truly sharing this part of their lives with men. Do they intuitively recognize the danger of losing the only power in society they have ever really gained for themselves? Perhaps this is why a number of women are reluctant to encourage men to enter more fully into childcare as anything other than 'helpers'. Listen to a group of these women discussing their menfolk's talent for babycare – they often seem almost jubilant in recounting the men's comic ineptitude. This prejudice is very similar to some men's ritualized reluctance to believe in any woman's capacity to drive a car – 'woman driver' is always an acceptable insult for any idiot of either sex on the road.

IS THERE A PATERNAL INSTINCT?

Is there some innate quality – the maternal instinct – which women possess but men lack? Russell's study found that 51 per cent of mothers and 71 per cent of fathers believed in maternal instinct. These fathers tended to see their own role starting much later in the child's life, after infancy. Even so, 60 per cent of mothers felt that their husbands, too, had the ability to care for infant children, but only 34 per cent of the men agreed.

A large part of the mythical 'maternal instinct' seems to be bound up with the mother's ability to feed which in the past was so vital for the baby's survival. Recently in America, Ross Parke investigated fathers' nurturing qualities and, specifically, how well men bottle-fed their babies. It was found that the fathers were just as successful and sensitive as the mothers, apart from the fact that they smiled less. But then it is said that woman always smile more than men!

Everywhere, all women are brought up on the myth of maternal instinct, expected to be intrinsically capable of being 'good mothers' enriched by their motherhood. Men, on the other hand, seldom grow up with the idea that they too will one day use their 'mothering' skills, let alone be enriched by doing so. Many men discover almost by accident when they have a child just how neglected that part of their personality has been until then.

So why is it that, given that they too have all the innate qualities necessary, men do not participate more in the care of their babies? Practical obstacles, so often given as the reason why men remain at a distance are really a smoke screen for what has aptly been called the 'male dilemma'. Watching the close bond between the mother and the child from the sidelines can distort the father's feelings of care and transform them into jealous resentment of the powerful relationship in front of him. Some experts believe that these feelings of exclusion then painfully reactivate the man's own early infantile conflicts. Without a determined effort to resolve these often deeply hidden fears, the ensuing helplessness simply reinforces the very situation which perpetrates the conventionally distant relationship between father and child.

If we look around us we will probably agree that this exclusion of fathers from infant care has not made for a comfortable society for men or women. Because men leave all the early infant care to women, it is with and through women that babies of both sexes learn to develop those 'affective bonds and diffuse multifaceted, ongoing personal relationship to caretakers for physical and psychological growth' (Ingham) without which they cannot develop normally. This tradition where men are mothered by women and women by themselves is not so restricting for girl babies; although it too has grave long-term implications for repetition in each successive generation of mothers. But female domination of infant care has long been recognized as a potential hazard, leaving boys at a distinct disadvantage where emotional and psychological development is concerned. Difficulties in developing a harmonious inner sense of maleness, rather than a stereotype representation is the result of deprivation of an everyday, close and intimate knowledge of a real father. While this aspect of male development remains unappreciated by both sexes men will continue to be relegated to the second division of parenting. Here fathering is seen as hardly more than 'mother's little helper' or as a holiday treat for the children. Neither concept is honest or calculated to ease tension between the sexes or get fathers clamouring to enter into an intimate dialogue with their children. If men who are becoming fathers do not resolve to participate actively in the care of their infant, they risk continuing the pattern which has created areas of painful conflict within most men – and trapped most women in the role of dominant caregiver.

SOME WIDER IMPLICATIONS

'I didn't know how I'd be as a father – I knew more how I didn't want to be. My own father was away such a lot, I don't think we ever really got to know each other. The one thing I was really set on was that my kids should know me, for better or worse . . .'.

'Good enough' fathering (like mothering) should ideally be every child's normal daily experience. A father's presence should be taken for granted in the child's view of the world. Some men fear that if they climb down from their work pedestals they will simply become surrogate mothers, losing their male identity. This is just not the case, as any baby or toddler knows. When a man takes over the 'mothering' role it has a distinctively different flavour. Fathers tend to approach even routine childcare chores with an open mind, often transforming them into exciting 'happenings'. Men tend to be more physical with their babies, often more verbally demanding, stretching the child's methods of communication. They frequently spend more time playing – a vital part of every child's physical and emotional development. Men seem to regard their babies as miniature adults and this invariably gives the child a very different perspective on life. It is interesting that when a man takes over full responsibility for the baby, the difference between what is seen as maternal and paternal care gradually merges. However, for most employed fathers, snatching time when and where they can, it is the quality of the time spent together which is important and not the number of hours. The father's focused involvement enriches the child's everyday experience of life and stimulates his intellectual and physical development.

THE RISK OF SEX STEREOTYPING

With notable exceptions traditional fathers have been more interested in their sons' development than their daughters'. Recent research observing fathers in hospital delivery rooms confirms just how early this interest begins. Men consistently make more effort to communicate and stimulate their male newborns, and tend to maintain this higher level of involvement with them. Men (and women) have a strong intellectual drive towards sex stereotyping which goes into operation the moment their baby is born and sometimes even before. Fathers instinctively hold boy babies in a position which gives more eye-to-eye contact, thus stimulating the baby's intellectual development. Both parents see girl babies as fragile and more 'cuddly' – they naturally hold these 'delicate creatures' close to their bodies where the baby cannot see anything but the parent's chest! All babies learn through imitation; if you put your tongue out to a baby even a few days old, he will do the same. Fathers seem instinctively to provide this kind of interaction with their boy babies, perhaps because of every man's anxiety that his son should grow up a secure male, a 'chip off the old block'. But they often unwittingly neglect to give their daughters similar opportunities to develop their full potential. It may need a conscious effort to redress the balance and become just as involved with your daughters; this will be easier if you are aware of the vital importance of your role.

Several studies show that girls do better academically if they have an interested father. And a startling number of successful women in all walks of life admit to having a strong link with their fathers, who either directly or indirectly gave them inspiration. But boys and girls need both parents to develop rounded personalities. A father who nurtures and encourages his son's 'maleness' can also show him that a man's nature can have a softer, gentler side. His daughter can develop her female identity with, and through, her mother, but also needs her father's support and recognition to develop her full potential.

CHILDREN NEED FATHERS

Anyone who has grown up totally without a father's care and attention knows the devastation this can create. Those who have had the good fortune to experience a father – however unsatisfactory – have some roots from which their own ability as a parent can grow. Lack of committed fathering can cause a cycle of deprivation which can settle over several generations. Lack of paternal interest means that boys and girls suffer emotional hardship and tend to under-achieve at school. Research done as long ago as the 1960s linked absent fathers in early childhood with children who were more likely to become involved in delinquent or antisocial behaviour around adolescence.

Unfortunately babies often arrive at the most difficult time in a man's career. He may be struggling to establish his career, or in these days of high unemployment, just hang on to the job he has. The conflict this creates is often just as heartbreaking for the father, missing the time with his baby and wife, as it is for them being alone. However some men do have the choice and they still absent themselves from the fathering role, often justifying the lack of time spent with their families by the fact that they are better providers. On the whole they are deluding themselves – a second car or a holiday abroad is far less important than a Dad regularly sitting at the tea table.

Children need fathers. They need them at all ages and they need them to be available and accessible at odd moments during the day or night and not 'by appointment only'. One grandfather spoke wistfully of his gradual realization of lost chances after his son had died at an early age. 'Looking back I think our relationship had the ecstasy of a few close encounters, but the sadness of many lost opportunities . . .' I have heard these sentiments reiterated in many ways, by too many men, not to realize that today's fathers are determined to diminish those regrets, and increase the joys when their turn comes.

FATHERS NEED CHILDREN

Most men assume that one day they will become fathers. They accept that it will naturally occur as part of marriage, but they seldom consider the extent to which they will choose to become emotionally involved with their child. Unfortunately boys are not often brought up to see fatherhood as a central part of their adult lives. And it is not until the decision to start a family has been taken that men will give the subject much thought. But the opportunity for development that can come about as a direct result of becoming an involved father should not be missed. Here every man has the chance to explore the instinctual, caring and nurturing side of his personality; and in so doing to attain the harmonious balance within himself that is everyone's aim. In the evolution of the father–child dialogue there is the unfolding of a new life with all its excitement and unpredictability. The surprisingly intense pleasure of this process is enjoyed by both participants in the relationship – as a father you will receive as much bounty as you give.

FATHERING AT SECOND HAND

Traditionally the father–child connection is filtered through the mother. This arrangement effectively reduces the depth and scope of the relationship – father becomes a back-seat driver. Acceptance of this style of fathering is risky; it can both confirm the man's uncertainty about his own ability to be an involved father and deny him the possibility of discovering any alternative styles for himself. Finally, because most of the child care is done by women, prospective fathers can legitimately be vague about their own eventual involvement and maintain a 'wait and see' policy of fathering. Sadly this hesitant attitude may mean a father misses the chance to establish a close bond with his infant at an early time when circumstances are most favourable.

LOOKING AHEAD

During the pregnancy practical details of baby care may seem very remote. It is hard to imagine your future life with a baby. As one father told me, 'Seeing myself as a father beforehand was like trying to imagine what falling in love would be like before it happened for the first time – I just couldn't do it!' But early in the pregnancy is the time to start thinking about your paternity leave (see page 168), planning your work–home commitments and, most important, talking to your partner about what kind of sharing you both envisage. Fathering does not take place in a vacuum and your partner will strongly influence how much you actually put your ideas into practice. You will need her vote of confidence in your capacity to care for the newborn. This may not be immediately forthcoming and may be complicated by her own anxieties if she does not feel secure about her own mothering skills. In which case you may have to wait until her self-confidence has increased and her trust in you is established before becoming more fully involved yourself (see Ambivalence about sharing, page 159). And, as with everything to do with babies, there is an absolute need for both parents to remain flexible, so be aware when the time comes that any plans you make will also have to meet with your baby's approval too!

MATERNAL BONDING

Ever since birth has become primarily a hospital-based experience, researchers have increasingly turned to mothers and babies as objects of interest and enquiry. In America in the 1970s babies were routinely taken away from their mothers at birth. The research that Klaus and Kennell did at that time showed that mothers' involvement with their babies was greatly enhanced and lasted well into the postnatal year if they had some peaceful, uninterrupted time together directly after the birth. What they did together was termed 'bonding' and as a newly discovered event it was given wide publicity. Nobody noticed that it had only become necessary to define this perfectly natural exchange because of insensitive hospital procedures in the first place! From then on everyone developed clear expectations of mothers' initial contact with their newborns. If 'bonding' is good for the baby, parents become anxious, guilty, or feel let down if they do not seem to be feeling, or doing things in the prescribed way. In fact 'bonding' is very much like falling in love – sometimes it happens instantly, sometimes slowly at first, only later becoming more intense. No one would dream of saying which is the 'right' way to fall in love; or dare predict the outcome of a relationship by how it began.

DO FATHERS 'BOND' TOO?

It did not take long for the spotlight on maternal bonding to widen. Did fathers 'bond' too, or not, and if they did, how and when? Initial studies tended to measure men against the 'maternal' yardstick. This has been largely rectified, and since the mid-1970s research in Britain, the United States and Australia has come up with some interesting observations about this unique process. In the labour room, for example, fathers were observed to be excited and preoccupied – 'engrossed' – with their newborns, and to do all the things mothers do. Father, too, will count fingers and toes and instinctively talk to the baby in the high-pitched voice which is easier for babies to hear. But the father's presence at birth, although universally seen to enhance the mother's positive experience of giving birth, does not in itself produce sustained father–infant involvement over the following eighteen months.

This rests more heavily on the kind of relationship and work structure the couple are already pursuing. It is also strongly related to the father's personality. These personality types can be divided into four main groups according to Brian Jackson's study in 1984 of 100 Bristol fathers. Of these 20 per cent were called 'reluctant'. This type of man pushes the pregnancy and birth to one side and tries to cling to the traditional roles of man at work/woman at home. He may also have strong fears and distaste for what he imagines to be a 'bloody' process. The second 20 per cent are called the 'observer' type; they have the 'wait and see' philosophy and try to maintain their distance by demystification – 'women have been having babies for hundreds of years and what's all the fuss about?' However, in favourable circumstances the 'observer' usually edges closer after the birth to the third group, the 'sharers'. This was by far the largest group, some 50 per cent of the survey. They could be called modern fathers, following a policy of close involvement and interest before and after the birth. Finally the last 10 per cent of fathers found themselves called 'totally identified'. These men were 'stunned and fascinated' by the whole process. They often experienced physical symptoms themselves (couvade) and recognized it. They were happily in tune with themselves and their need to express the side of their personality which having a family would facilitate.

All this is fascinating but I would caution anyone from putting themselves too firmly into any of these categories. Your baby will relate to you innocently and lovingly and your style of fathering will evolve as you live it.

Bonding has become an emotive word which often creates anxiety in expectant parents. It is worth remembering that many men and women do not feel at all close to their babies at birth, or for several weeks afterwards. Gradually, over a period of time their loving feelings intensify, often developing as the baby himself becomes more responsive. Do not be alarmed if either of you feel neutral about your baby in the beginning. However, do talk over any anxieties you have with your partner and then it is far better to spend more time relaxing with your baby and stop worrying about whether you are 'bonded' or not.

'BONDING' BEGINS DURING PREGNANCY

Fathers are at a disadvantage when it comes to forming links with their baby before birth because they do not have the constant physical reminder that the mother has. Yet it is during the pregnancy that the process of 'bonding' is getting under way. You need to be convinced that your relationship with your baby is essentially unlike any other – after the birth you and your baby will work out the details together. Beforehand your caring attention to your partner is also nurturing the baby by creating a loving environment to receive him. You could try talking to your baby; after all, studies show that babies can hear towards the end of pregnancy. Massaging your partner's abdomen not only feels good to her, it also makes contact between you and the baby. Feeling the movements as he kicks and moves around, perhaps responding already to your voice and touch, are just some of the ways you can begin to relate to each other before birth.

'Hello, I'm your Dad and you're my baby', was the way one father I talked to had welcomed his son into the world. He went on to describe his feelings like this, 'Well yes, of course I was pleased, over the moon really, glad it was over at last. There he was, a bit squashed looking, but definitely a baby! Yes it did feel special, but it was all amazing really. I looked first thing to see if he was all right. But I didn't feel all gooey, not like I'd been told, that came gradually after we'd got home. At the time I think I was relieved more than anything, but then over the next few days it really came home to me. I kept saying to myself, "I'm that baby's special person – I'm a Dad" – that felt great.'

That father's normal but unecstatic first meeting with his son is not at all atypical; many mothers feel the same. Research in Britain since the 1970s tells us that most men do report intense emotions just after the birth, some of which are related to greeting their child. Fathers that I talked to told me of emotions ranging from 'pleased' to feeling 'over the moon'. While some men weep openly and are 'high' at the birth and for several days afterwards, others feel calm and collected, gradually becoming more intensely attached as the relationship with their baby is established.

FATHERS WHO NEED TIME

Not all men find it easy to be attentive and involved with the pregnancy. These rather reserved men, who were not in the majority have been called by different researchers, 'observer' fathers. Although during the pregnancy they keep their distance and appear to take up an almost ritualized detachment, I have found this often masks underlying fears and anxieties. These men are reluctant to confront their anxieties and compound their discomfort by refusing to attend antenatal classes or expose their worries. These men seem to need time and privacy to adjust to their new role, particularly, it has been noted, if they felt unready for fatherhood. This air of detachment, seen as unusual these days when many fathers are highly involved, is often painful for both partners who suffer their discomfort in isolation. The man's refusal to attend public events connected to the pregnancy such as antenatal classes may make the mother feel very vulnerable, or even rejected. These women often worry that this lack of interest might continue after the birth. In fact in my experience this rarely happens.

BECOMING INVOLVED

And that is the key word, involvement. The necessary thinking and planning for your family's future should start early in pregnancy. Research, and common sense, have shown that the more supportive and interested a father is during pregnancy the more the mother (and her baby) enjoys pregnancy, childbirth and the first weeks of family life. Being supportive is most fathers' normal response to pregnancy; planning to be an active participant during pregnancy and after the birth is the next step. But as there is no long tradition of fathers sharing the daily care of their babies, it is really up to each couple to formulate their own ideas, and then put them into practice.

Even if you have no very clear image of the kind of father you want to be, you are probably fairly sure that you do not want to model yourself completely on previous generations. A first-time father was emphatic when he told me, 'I felt pretty certain I was different from my own father. I had my own ideas, or I'd concocted them from a few other men I knew. I thought a lot about it, I had worries too; how could I be a "good" father when I felt that my own father wasn't any good. I felt as if I had to start right from scratch, all up to me!'

During this period of exploration it is easy for an expectant father to be deflected by adverse comments from friends, colleagues or older members of the family, based on prejudice about male incompetence in infant care. Try not to be discouraged. Ross Parke says of his research into all aspects of fathering: 'In my studies of fathers and newborns I have consistently found fathers are just as responsive as mothers to infant signals such as sounds and mouth movements.' Ideally every man needs contact with other fathers who can show him what fatherhood can really be like, and describe the very tangible rewards of a close father–infant relationship. But although patterns in child rearing are rapidly changing, these involved, competent fathers are still comparatively rare. A man wishing to make changes in his family of origin's definition of fathering will have to look into himself (with his partner's support) rather than relying on outside role models to supply the answers.

FINDING YOUR OWN WAY

Begin the process of becoming a father by getting as closely involved in the pregnancy as possible – fathering begins at conception. Next you have to believe that you do have the capacity to father in whatever way suits you (and your baby). Try not to allow traditional child care patterns to deter you or undermine your self-confidence. By challenging any ambivalent feelings you or your partner may have about breaking down old barriers of what constitutes 'good' or 'bad' parenting, you will move towards defining your own individual style of mothering or fathering. Sometimes the more flexible approach of shared parenting provokes a disturbing initial response; not only within the couple's relationship but also from outside observers who perhaps do not have the courage to try this more flexible approach themselves.

THE PART YOUR BABY PLAYS

So what about the other person in this relationship – the baby? A satisfying dialogue depends to an extent upon some reciprocal response to fan the flame of involvement. And babies, even from the same family, can be totally different from the minute they are born. Parents of crying or unhappy babies tend to feel responsible and guilty if their baby is unresponsive to their efforts to comfort him. Research done in the United States by Marshal Klaus and John Kennell has highlighted the crucial part the baby plays, right from the start, and demonstrated this capacity for affecting the depth of his parents' feelings for him.

A newborn who is not drugged, and is therefore alert and highly responsive at birth, inevitably attracts more attention and gives more in return – the family 'bonding' process is easily and pleasurably established. Fathers (and mothers) tend to react more positively to physically attractive and responsive babies than to those unfortunate infants who cry persistently and cannot be comforted, or to those who simply look less appealing. This means that parents of premature babies, or those with other problems need extra support and encouragement to overcome the shock of their baby not looking and behaving as they had expected.

TIME TOGETHER AFTER BIRTH

A hospital labour room is hardly the ideal place for your first meeting with your baby. However this is where the majority of fathers do welcome their child for the first time. If everything is normal you should insist on having time alone together as a family as soon as possible after the birth. Many fathers feel awkward and inhibited handling their baby if the medical staff are watching. They all seem to know and do everything that much better and more competently. But your baby needs you to hold him – your touch, your smell and voice are the essential ingredients for his sense of security. Never mind if you do things slowly; after the trauma of birth your baby needs quiet words, and gentle holding to help him relax into his new life. 'Bonding' is a family love affair, it extends the ways in which you can all express care and tenderness for each other. You can nurture your baby just as successfully as your partner, given the time and the opportunity to practise the necessary skills. So make sure that you have enough privacy and time together with your baby in the hospital, and later at home to establish your relationship.

In the first days after the birth everyone in a new family needs extra love and support from each other – and lots of encouragement from outside as well. The only thing you cannot do is breast feed, and even then if your partner expresses milk you can feed your baby with a bottle. (See Postnatal Practicalities, page 168.) And your presence and loving support are absolute necessities if the mother and baby are to establish and enjoy their feeding relationship. Research confirms what every contented, relaxed mother and baby clearly demonstrate: the father's care and appreciation, especially in the first few weeks after the birth, turn a lot of hard work into a satisfying and positive experience. This gives the family a firm and stable base upon which to grow.

THE ROLE OF FAMILY AND FRIENDS

The wider family network and friends all play their part in helping to establish the family 'bonding'. The baby's grandparents are particularly significant for both parents. Even where the relationship has not been a particularly easy one, the birth of a baby can have a strengthening effect, drawing the generations together to share pleasure in the newest arrival. This can have special significance if grandparents can be supportive to the new parents in ways which enhance the couple in their new role. It also seems that many men find the need to draw closer to their own fathers after the birth of a child, which delights both generations.

A newborn baby is increasingly more interesting and more enchanting every day, and even those who are unhappy or fretful have some calm moments to be enjoyed. Sharing the pleasures and inevitable frustrations of life with a newborn can be the best but also the most challenging time for a couple. But whatever happens, your baby will be there waiting for your particular attention to respond to – all you have to do is give of yourself; your baby will show you what to do next.

Chapter 2

Fathers and health care

When a woman wants to become a mother it is assumed that her health is important; enquiries and advice will be available at every turn to ensure she stays well. Unfortunately less attention is given to the prospective father, who receives little encouragement to take care of himself. Before you have a child, living a high-cholestrol, high-stress life is your own affair; but once you are a father all that changes, after all you will want to be alive and well for as long as possible for your own and your family's sake. So you too should review your lifestyle and take positive steps to maintain your general health as part of preparing for parenthood. I found that many expectant fathers do spontaneously give up smoking, cut down on alcohol or take up regular exercise in a spirit of commitment towards creating a secure future for their family. As this father told me, 'I started jogging every day, actually I got a bit fanatical, but I felt like I was getting fit for the baby. I didn't want to be a fat slob! Yes, it felt like part of my duty to be in good shape – like providing a good home.'

Recognizing the value of preventative medicine is important where family welfare is concerned; pre-conceptual care encourages *both* parents to make sure they are in the best possible health before conception takes place. Unless your partner has had difficulty conceiving, or keeping the pregnancy, you will probably not have given this aspect of 'baby care' much thought. Most people assume that any adjustments in their lifestyle need begin only after conception, and then perhaps will only affect the mother. But pre-conceptual care followed by a sensible lifestyle are both parents' responsibility. Try thinking of yourselves as a 'pregnant couple' whose baby has a right to expect two vigorous parents. It is really very simple – a healthy couple will have a better chance of producing a healthy baby and then coping with the demands of family life after the birth.

If you are one of the minority of couples who carefully plans each pregnancy, then ideally pre-conceptual care should begin at least three months before you plan to conceive, and although it focuses mainly on your partner's health, your own is essential too. If you are healthy, you will produce good, vigorous sperm. And if both of you have thoughtfully prepared for conception the fetus will have optimum conditions right from the start. If you are planning to conceive in the near future it makes sense to discuss with your partner the eating, working and relaxing habits which dominate your lifestyle; stress factors and the possible influence of environmental pollution will also need examination so that appropriate corrective measures can be taken at this early stage.

Once the risks are recognized every parent tries to protect the developing fetus from possible harm. However it seems that the vast majority of couples conceive by 'accident'; they are simply unaware of their baby's existence during the first weeks of its life. Parents who then read about the potential hazards to the developing fetus during its early weeks may become extremely anxious about having unintentionally damaged their baby. But as it is virtually impossible to avoid everything that might pose a threat, it is wise to cultivate a sensible and optimistic attitude, while looking for ways to increase safety in the future.

NUTRITION: WE ARE WHAT WE EAT

There are clearly established links between maternal dietary deficiency and problems connected with fetal development. The baby is nourished by the placenta, which in turn is directly dependent upon the mother's diet for its essential nutrients. It is well known that the babies of women who have poor diets, lacking adequate protein, vitamins and minerals, are at risk. These mothers are also more likely to experience difficulties conceiving, during pregnancy and after the birth.

Although in our affluent society it may seem unlikely, many women have such erratic eating habits that they are badly nourished without realizing it. Our culture encourages women to aspire to a particular body image – usually a thinner one. But many women find the only way they can control their food intake and achieve this is by getting on to an alternating diet-binge roundabout. To tell these women to eat 'sensibly' when they wish to get pregnant may not be sufficient. Most people believe their eating habits *are* sensible – and so they may be for someone who is not also nourishing a baby. A woman who is over-concerned about weight gain may find it a problem to increase her food intake, or alter her eating habits. She may need loving support to overcome her anxieties; unconsciously confusing becoming 'fat' with the normal body changes of pregnancy. If you can give her loving appreciation of her new maternal outline this will help to reassure her that she is still attractive. It is also helpful to understand what is the necessary intake of essential nutrients during pregnancy and lactation and which foods provide them. There are many good books on the subject (see Further reading, page 213).

Large doses of vitamin supplements during early pregnancy are inadvisable unless prescribed by your doctor, although a basic mineral and vitamin supplement will do no harm. There is a school of thought that feels our food is so lacking in nutrients these days, and our lives so stressed that these supplements are necessary to maintain good health. However, supplements are always an extra; far better to encourage your partner to respond to her body's instinctive demand for food and allow her natural appetite to guide her now.

ALLERGIES

Any couple who themselves suffer from an allergy, or who have parents who have eczema, asthma or hay fever should take preventative measures to protect their baby after the third month of pregnancy when the baby's immune system develops. A Canadian study has recently found that excluding dairy products, eggs, peanuts and fish during pregnancy will reduce the likelihood of the baby developing allergies later in life. After birth babies who are at risk should be exclusively breastfed for at least 6 months; delaying the introduction of dairy products, particularly cows' milk and egg protein, until later. But always obtain medical advice before embarking on a restricted diet.

ALCOHOL

Excess of alcohol is known to be dangerous to the fetus, especially in the first few weeks of life. No one knows exactly what constitutes a safe level – some doctors insist there is no such thing and advise all women to give up drinking altogether. Some couples decide to cut out all alcohol well before conception, just to be on the safe side. Many women do in fact find that they no longer want alcohol as soon as they become pregnant. Your partner can ask her doctor for a blood test to establish how well she metabolizes alcohol and this can provide you with a guideline. If your partner is a poor metabolizer, then she should try to give up drinking altogether, as the alcohol will cross the placenta in a form which is more harmful to the fetus. Alcohol is a drug, and during pregnancy should be regarded with caution. Sometimes it is not easy to change longstanding habits, so if you find that even with a shared effort it is impossible to stop drinking completely, then your partner should cut down to the absolute maximum of an occasional glass of wine.

DRUGS

If either of you is obliged to take any form of regular medication it is wise to check with a doctor well in advance of conception to be certain there will be no adverse effects on the baby.

Before trying to conceive couples should be warned about the possible danger that drugs might pose to the baby. A woman should not take any drug without a doctor's prescription and supervision; this includes those sold across the counter, such as aspirin or cold remedies and nasal sprays. Many people are surprised that substances like artificial sweeteners, food colourants and preservatives are listed as 'drugs'. But too little is known about their effect on the developing fetus to be sure they are completely harmless. As soon as there is a possibility of pregnancy, try to ensure that your partner takes extra care. Aerosol fly sprays are in common use in many households, but pregnant women should avoid inhaling them. Particular care should be taken during the second half of the woman's menstrual cycle, just in case conception has occurred. This is when the embryo is most vulnerable; well before the woman is even aware that she has missed her period. Remember, you can choose what you put into your body's system – baby can't!

'SOCIAL' DRUGS

Ideally if you are planning to have a baby you should, as a couple, cut down on smoking, or stop completely for nine months before hoping to conceive. Smoking is associated with low fertility in women but it may have an even more damaging effect on male fertility as sperm are more at risk. Although marijuana has become a socially acceptable drug to many people it too has an effect on reproduction. This drug interferes with normal sperm production which if united with the woman's ovum may result in an abnormal fetus.

Once your partner has conceived you should both consider the dangers of smoking to your unborn child. If your partner smokes nicotine will pass into her bloodstream and then to the baby's, whether she inhales or not. Nictotine is a potent drug; it seriously interferes with the baby's respiratory movements, and it diminishes the efficiency of the placenta, so that the baby receives less oxygen and other essential nutrients. Even if your partner does not smoke, if you continue she will still take in nicotine and tars in the cigarette smoke in the air around her.

ENVIRONMENTAL HAZARDS

Both of you should consider your work environment, especially if either of you has a history of exposure to radiation. As with drugs, no one can be certain what is an acceptably safe level of exposure. The most dangerous and vulnerable time for the baby is between two and six weeks after conception. It is then that the baby's organs and bodily structures are being formed. The kind of malformation and its severity will depend upon the precise stage of the baby's development. Exposure to radiation during the early weeks has been shown to affect the central nervous system and the brain. After the third month the risk is reduced considerably. There has been recent concern that visual display units might increase the risk of miscarriage, stillbirth and birth defects for the women who operate them. These machines do emit radiation, but at a level recognized as 'acceptable', and it has yet to be proved that they carry any real danger to the unborn child. However, there is another 'risk' factor attached to their use – the high level of stress they induce in some women who operate them. For the sake of avoiding even the slightest unnecessary risk at this time, it might be sensible for any woman who is planning to become pregnant to think about trying to change her occupation during the high risk period of her pregnancy. If that is impossible be sure to learn some form of relaxation and practise it regularly (see page 86).

STRESS AND RELAXATION

While you are assessing your personal lifestyle why not consider whether you or your partner are overstressed, and whether you both experience enough relaxation to maintain good health? Too much stress is one of the factors that may affect a couple's ability to conceive, so try to start well before the baby arrives to reduce your stress level and increase the time you spend relaxing. If you find it difficult to do this for yourself, consider how your 'addiction' may be affecting your partner. A woman wishing to conceive and carry a child needs to be physically fit; she must also feel relaxed and confident. Women who are overstressed for long periods of time produce hormones which are bad for themselves and their babies. To be able to 'let go' enough to find time to relax, a woman often needs the support of her partner. Try and practise some relaxation techniques together for at least fifteen minutes every day and preferably longer. The more resistance you have to relaxing, the more you probably need it.

EXERCISE

Reducing stress, increasing relaxation, lead naturally on to the next step in a good pregnancy health care programme – exercise. If you start an exercise programme more than three months before trying to conceive, then as a couple you can follow any sensible 'get fit' routine which attracts you – jogging, tennis, exercise classes or, best of all, swimming. Swimming can be continued right through pregnancy and is the safest form of exercise for pregnant women to take. In the water there is no risk of the muscular strain or skeletal jarring which is the hazard of land-based aerobic exercise. If your partner starts to take exercise later in pregnancy, swimming in this weightless environment is still the best way to improve or maintain physical fitness. Deep breathing, floating and stretching in water are also fun and good to do.

MEDICAL CHECKUP

When you are ready to start a family, you should both go to your GP and have a thorough medical checkup to make sure there are no physical problems which might adversely affect your future baby's well-being. The doctor will check that neither of you has any infections, nutritional deficiencies, or anatomical problems which might adversely affect conception, pregnancy or birth. You may also both request a blood test for Aids. He will check your partner's immunizations such as German measles and may test for Rhesus incompatibility. He will also establish whether she has any other medical conditions which need to be treated before the pregnancy begins, for example, thyroid deficiency, chlamydia, venereal disease, tuberculosis, or diabetes. If your partner has been taking the pill, some doctors will advise her to use another method of birth control for three months to allow her body to re-establish its normal hormonal rhythms before trying to conceive.

GENETIC COUNSELLING

If either of you thinks that a close relative suffers from any disorder which might be hereditary, you should seek genetic counselling before conception. Often fears of passing on a particular defect are groundless, or exaggerated. Some hospitals have genetic counsellors who can help you discover whether you are a carrier or not and assess the likelihood of your child inheriting the condition. Otherwise your GP should refer you to an appropriate clinic.

THE BEST AGE TO CONCEIVE

Men should have their babies before they are 45. Some studies suggest that if the father is over this age, the chances of stillbirth or congenital malformation are somewhat greater. However the age of the mother is still more important. Ideally a woman should have her babies between the ages of 18 and 40 years. Of course many healthy babies are born to women either side of these age limits. But over the age of 35 the risk of having a Down's syndrome (mongol) baby increases with each year. Any couple who would choose to abort if their baby were found to be suffering from Down's syndrome can ask for a special test – an amniocentesis, which will detect the condition (see page 57).

FAILURE TO CONCEIVE

Supposing conception does not happen within a few months? These days birth control is taught from primary school onwards, and the unspoken message is that conception is easy, in fact, automatic, unless carefully guarded against. The truth is rather different. The average time taken for a couple to conceive, once they have abandoned birth control, is 5.3 months, with a range of one to 18 months.

Even though your body is not directly involved you will probably feel the disappointment at failure to conceive as keenly as your partner. The fear of infertility has been shown to have a bigger impact on the man than on the woman. As every month brings a build up of hope, followed by acute feelings of disappointment at the onset of each period, you may very quickly begin to feel like a stud, not desired for yourself but only for what your body can provide. Both of you may begin to feel a sense of personal failure or blame each other for your lack of success, and the anxiety this generates can itself interfere with the natural process of conception.

INVESTIGATING FERTILITY

Infertility is much more common than is popularly believed and as many as one couple in six may suffer a delay in conceiving. If after one year of trying, your partner has not conceived, it is sensible for you both to consult your doctor. After preliminary enquiries into your sex-life – how often you have sex and whether you experience any problems which might impede conception – you might decide that your problems are more serious. Try contacting the National Association for the Childless (see Useful addresses, page 216) who can advise you on which of the clinics specializing in infertility would be most helpful. After your GP has referred you, more tests will have to be carried out to ensure that there is no physiological reason why conception cannot take place. Your partner will probably be asked to have hormone, blood and urine tests, keep menstrual and temperature charts and to undergo investigations of fallopian tubes, ovulation, even cervical mucus testing. And you will be asked for a sample of your semen so that it can be examined microscopically to determine the number, mobility and health of your sperm – a 'sperm count'. A low sperm count is the cause of infertility in about 30 per cent of couples.

It has been established that stress, marijuana, overwork, tiredness, poor diet, excess alcohol, cigarettes or being overweight can all affect your sperm count, and so too can anything that raises the temperature of your scrotum (for example, tight jeans and hot baths). If your sperm count is found to be marginally below the 'normal' level it is worth modifying your lifestyle to take account of these factors. A few days of abstinence from sex just before your partner ovulates may allow a sufficient build-up of sperm for conception to take place.

However, sometimes a man is upset by the very idea of sperm testing because he feels as if his masculinity is being tested, not just his sperm. He may feel inadequate by even the suggestion that infertility might be his 'problem'. The tension this creates (which of course will be very much worse if tests show that his sperm count is, in fact, low) may affect his capacity to make love. He may find it hard to get an erection, or lose it when he tries to penetrate.

A recently diagnosed bacteria, chlamydia, which is harmless to men, causing mild itchiness or burning in the urethra, can pose a serious threat to women who may be asymptomatic and therefore undiagnosed. Sexually transmitted, it is responsible for 40 per cent of reported cases of pelvic inflammatory disease which doctors believe to be a major cause of infertility in women. Diagnosed early chlamydia is easily treated with a short course of antibiotics; if it is ignored it can become very serious for the woman later on.

All this, together with the instructions you may receive to have sex to order, only on the right days, but be sure to *relax*, seems like a recipe for the breakdown of eroticism. One couple who had tried unsuccessfully to conceive for two years emphasized the need to keep a sense of humour. 'Well it was dreadful really, we got to dread the fertile days as sort of "duty sex" days. One morning I was in the shower and Gill shouted to me that we should try today as her temperature showed she was ovulating. I went towards the bed and cuddled up to give her a kiss when I found the thermometer was still in her mouth!' Wanting a baby and not being able to conceive one can be a heartrending experience for any couple. If you feel over-burdened by tension or unhappiness in this situation, consider seeking help from a sympathetic GP, a marriage guidance counsellor or a pregnancy advisory service where expert counselling and advice are always available.

Couples who have failed to conceive over a long period of time describe the anguish they have suffered. But when a couple have shared the disappointment and given each other loving support, they

also report feeling strengthened by the experience. Accepting infertility is hard, but once the reality is accepted, other options such as
artificial insemination (AID) or adopting a baby may seem entirely
appropriate. (See Further reading, page 213.)

Childlessness for a strongly paternal man can be a tragedy. When a
couple's inability to conceive is because of male infertility the man
will grieve just as acutely as any woman suffering the same fate. After
the medical tests and the humiliation of having your deepest fears
confirmed, the future stretches before you – empty. But as usual men
are far more likely to feel isolated, and it appears they often do not
receive appropriate comfort and support during the period of shock
and adaptation. Other people will offer consolation with well-meant
but painfully tactless remarks which leave the childless man feeling
resentful and frustrated.

Reactions will vary, but those couples who can share their pain
and disappointment will grow closer and feel strengthened rather
than weakened by this experience. No one can hurry the process
whereby a man and his partner come to accept that they will never
create a baby together – and of course some never do. However if a
couple feels mutually and creatively bonded, AID may eventually
become a viable alternative. Careful and honest talking together
about the feelings and fears that AID inspires has to be gone through
before both partners will feel ready to really accept that a child that
belongs to one belongs to both.

Chapter 3

Adjusting to pregnancy

MAKING THE DECISION

'About five years ago I really began to feel that there was more to life than just work and pleasure-seeking. At that time I didn't think Belinda and I were getting on well enough to have a baby, although I've always thought it was good to have children some time. I feel now we're trying, it will give one a definite purpose in life to have a baby.'

The decision to start a family is a momentous one. Becoming parents changes both parents irrevocably and marks a definite turning-point in a relationship. It means being willing to welcome change and commitment, not only to each other but also to a future life together with a child.

EXPERIENCING DOUBTS

You may be more likely than your partner to foresee the enormous upheaval that having a baby will entail, the restrictions on your freedom, changes in lifestyle, strain on your income – not to mention the disturbing sense of impending loss for which it is hard to imagine a baby as adequate compensation. Unless you are totally convinced of the essential, and very different, nature of your own role with your baby you may wonder how it will feel to have to share your partner, fear that you will be excluded, become 'second-best', while at the same time feel pressured into being continually strong and supportive.

It is quite normal to experience doubts about coping with the challenges of parenthood. There are real constraints sometimes masking deeper anxieties which you may feel are unworthy or inappropriate. It can be difficult to express these or to feel justified in so doing, especially if your partner is longing for a child. In 1974 an American study by Fein of thirty middle-class expectant couples found that all the men were generally positive about becoming a father, but all had moments of doubt, which one expressed nicely, 'Most of the time I can't wait. And some mornings I get up and say to myself, "Sure I can wait, I wish I could wait longer."' These men expressed four main areas of concern: labour and delivery, parenting, the amount of emotional and financial support they would give and receive and possible changes in the marriage and lifestyle.

The truth is that everyone has some worries about childbirth and becoming a parent, but because pregnancy is seen as a time of natural anxieties for a woman, your partner is far more likely than you are to find an appropriate venue to express her feelings and find reassurance. Put two pregnant women together in a room and they will probably share the most intimate details of their condition. But unless expectant fathers wear a lapel badge announcing their new status, how are they to get together to get support or information from each other?

PREPARATION FOR PARENTHOOD CLASSES

Antenatal classes are an excellent way of gathering information and sharing experiences. The aim of these couples groups is to cover every aspect of pregnancy, childbirth and becoming a parent – from both parents' point of view. Couples classes run by the National Childbirth Trust, where you both attend every class over eight weeks, are particularly useful for expectant fathers who may be finding it difficult to feel involved in the pregnancy or who have other doubts and worries. Classes vary in the number of sessions offered to the father so when you make enquiries early in the pregnancy make sure you are included. Research done in America by Fein showed that antenatal classes considerably lessen the father's anxieties about labour and delivery, although help and information about the realities of parenthood were often regarded as insufficient. Try and join an early pregnancy class, either in your local hospital, birth centre or branch of the NCT as this will help you feel more involved in the whole process of preparing for parenthood.

SHARING EXPERIENCES

Confirmation of pregnancy is an important event for every father. One man described his feelings. 'It would come in waves, I felt really breathless – like this is it, now I'm really going to be a father. Now they'll really have to listen to me. I realized that during the pregnancy I'd have to put off some things in my life until later, I have to take responsibility now.'

The news that you are a 'pregnant couple' may make you feel intensely elated, excited and proud of yourself and your partner. In some strange way you may feel that your potency and virility are proved, that you have done something special. A new phase in your life has begun and from now on you are to be entrusted with the care of another person – your child.

Expecting a baby makes you and your partner public property. Complete strangers, on hearing the news, will proceed to give you good advice or – worse – pour out stories which will make your blood run cold. But on the positive side, men who would not normally talk about their private lives suddenly begin to share their experience of pregnancy and childbirth. Women have always enjoyed this sharing of knowledge and feelings, but it is a relatively new experience for men.

Everyone needs time to adjust to big changes in their lives – getting pregnant is no exception. This is particularly true for the majority of couples who do not make a clear decision to have a child and for whom conception can be a real upheaval. Studies which have examined the role of parenting indicate that fathers adapt more quickly and positively to a planned baby than to a surprise or unwanted pregnancy. Adapting to father-hood is obviously more difficult for you than for your partner; you have neither the constant physical reminders nor the outside recognition to confirm your new status as a father.

FEELINGS OF EXCLUSION

As the expectant father you may be largely excluded from your partner's antenatal care, unless you take active steps to become involved. Your presence may be at best tolerated, at worst ignored, while another (usually male) specialist doctor will take over the care and medical responsibility for your wife and baby.

Because the challenges of becoming a father are less obvious, they receive little outside recognition. Like most men, you will probably prefer not to make a fuss but to take on the supportive role for your partner who can, at this time, be quite difficult to live with. She will certainly be suffering her own conflicting emotions about becoming a mother and need lots of reassurance and support from you. But neither she nor anyone else may be aware of *your* emotional needs – not many people will ring *you* up to ask specifically how you are. You can easily feel painfully excluded, too, from the new world, with its own predominantly female culture, into which your partner is drawn, and which will supply her with a much-needed support network from now on through the years of child rearing.

Lack of social recognition may be a special problem for those men who wish to break new ground in fathering and be more involved. 'Egalitarian' couples face more challenges adapting to pregnancy, unless they have outside support from friends or family, than couples who hold a more traditional view of marriage and family life, with clearly defined roles for each partner. For such couples there is less conflict, less self-assessment – everyone stays within the well-worn paths of accepted parenting practices.

Progressively during the nine months you will probably take on a supportive role in your relationship in response to your partner's need to be more dependent. You may feel the need to assert your own creativity too, by retreating into your work or taking up a new and demanding hobby. And many men feel a surge of ambition on behalf of their new family. There may also be a feeling of anticlimax, a realization that once the process is in motion the man has nothing to do for the next nine months but watch and admire. Men often experience conflicting emotional reactions, some of which are difficult to reconcile; for example, the wish to merge with the pregnancy, become a part of it, and at the same time a need to assert independence from both mother and baby. This was one man's reaction: 'The day after Ann told me the second baby was on the way, I went out and sold our Range-Rover and bought a two-seater! I felt, "this is my car", I really needed that car! We sorted it out in the end. I bought her a family car and kept mine for the two of us and me alone. Funny how things happen!' Unless you make a conscious decision to stay in close communication and to be actively involved, you can easily feel excluded and any misunderstandings or resentments which arise may be harder to overcome later on.

COPING WITH ANXIETIES

Fathers feel very protective towards their partner and the baby. Fears about childbirth may intensify towards the end of the pregnancy and worries about health and environmental factors loom large. Everyone has these fears, but men frequently hide them, as this father told me, 'I did worry about the baby a lot more than Susie did. I couldn't stop thinking about it, would it be deformed or not complete – I couldn't really handle the idea of my baby being deformed. But although I worried a lot I didn't talk about it to Susie until after the birth. She had been worried too, but we didn't want to bother each other so we kept it quiet.' It was a pity that this couple hid their anxieties – both might have found reassurance from each other by sharing these frightening and distressing fears. I was talking to a 'new' father recently who was remembering his feelings during his wife's pregnancy. 'I remember feeling anxious, quite often in a vague way. I worried about things like not knowing how to hold the baby properly and would it cry when *I* picked it up. I also worried about having to be home more and I felt annoyed at being forced to. What a joke! I find now he's here I rush home. I just can't wait to see him.'

LAYING THE FOUNDATIONS

Pregnancy can be seen as a crisis in a couple's life together. At some point the realization of parenthood, and the need to prepare in some way for the future, will compel you to start defining your role as parents. Here is where you can play an essential part. Just because you are not so physically burdened by the pregnancy, you have the extra energy required to establish a mutually caring, sharing relationship with your partner. Pregnancy is an excellent time to lay a secure foundation for your future family, where 'good' and 'bad' feelings can be acknowledged and freely discussed. A man who had enjoyed this aspect of pregnancy said, 'We used to take walks together – and just talk about the baby and what we felt about it. We were very close and Geraldine was very attentive to me, and I felt we were different, closer and more "open" in a way. Sometimes I didn't want the baby to come too soon because it might spoil all that!'

Pregnancy is a time when both parents are subjected to powerful emotional and physical influences. It is a time of feeling confident and buoyant and then suddenly inadequate and anxious.

Men who cannot find ways to express their anxieties or who feel that these conflicting feelings are unacceptable, either to themselves or to their partners, seem to react in several ways. They may become withdrawn or hostile to the pregnancy; or they feel competitive with it, or develop psychosomatic symptoms themselves, for example nausea, distended stomach, weight gain, backache, toothache, loss of concentration and fatigue. These physical symptoms are a common reaction to stress or anxiety during pregnancy and this phenomenon is called couvade, from the French word *couver*, to brood. Although most men acknowledge this to be a frequent reality, they seldom associate their 'symptoms' with the pregnancy until after the baby is born, perhaps fearing to attract ridicule rather than the empathy they clearly require.

The sexual relationship during pregnancy

Sex during pregnancy is like an English summer – unpredictable, demanding patience, but at times amazingly good. It is no good expecting your sexual 'sun' to shine with normal regularity during pregnancy; many things will change, including both parents' feelings about their sexuality. But most couples find that in the long term they benefit from the opportunity to experiment and enlarge their sexual activities that pregnancy provides. There is no need to feel that this is just another problem you have to worry about. Sex can always be fun, and as good for you and your partner during pregnancy as at any other time. If either of you do have problems, remember that they will only be temporary.

Most studies of pregnant couples show an overall reduction in sexual activity throughout pregnancy. Some data point to a temporary increase during mid-term, but a high proportion of men do report a steady decline in sexual activity throughout the last weeks.

There is still an assumption that men's sexuality is unaffected by emotional or physical upheavals, but it is an assumption that is often proved false during the childbearing year. The notion that as a man you are always ready for sex, no matter what is happening in the rest of your life, is not the experience of many of the expectant fathers I have talked to. In reality it is just as likely to be the man who experiences a temporary disruption in his enjoyment of intercourse. You and your partner will both find your sexual feelings vary from week to week, or even from day to day – that is the way it goes. Sex during pregnancy will be just as easy, or as difficult, as at any other 'crisis' point in your lives. Moving house, changing jobs, coping with a bereavement, will all produce echoes in your sexuality, so too will pregnancy. It may not be the easiest time, but when there is increased awareness, there will undoubtedly be some good side-effects.

Unless your partner became pregnant the first time you had intercourse, you will both have settled into some sort of sexual rhythm. You will know what turns each other on – and off. You will both have your favourite positions, places and times when love-making is special and satisfying. If you are sexually happily 'bonded', then pregnancy can only act as a positive confirmation of your feelings for each other. Even if you have intercourse less often, you will surely find other ways of staying close and enjoying each other.

CHANGING SEXUAL ATTITUDES

Nevertheless, pregnancy is bound to create some reassessment of your sexuality. Even if you do not feel very different, your partner definitely will. And even if you have long periods when the baby is less than real, when you think about making love it is a definite and, later on, a tangible presence – now there are three people involved. Some men feel this enhances their lovemaking and they relish the climax of intercourse as a fusion, an endorsement of their new family. This sentiment has an interesting similarity to the beliefs of fathers in a primitive society called the Arapesh which Margaret Mead studied. These fathers feel that part of their duty as good fathers is to have regular, purposeful sexual intercourse, 'directed toward making a particular child, towards feeding it and shaping it during the first weeks in the mother's womb. Here the father's task is almost equal to the mother's; the child is the product of the father's semen and the mother's menstrual blood combined in equal parts to start, to form a new human being.'

Unfortunately our so-called civilized society does not view the father's sexual contribution in such a positive light – rather the reverse. Sexual intercourse is often regarded by both partners as potentially dangerous. Rationally, you may know that sex is not harmful to the baby, and yet you and your partner may prefer a pause during the first few weeks – just in case.

But the baby is securely protected in the mother's womb, completely sealed in its own environment by the mucus plug in the cervix, which is like the cork in a bottle. The amniotic fluid in which the baby floats also protects it from outside shocks or bumps. There is no possibility of the penis displacing the plug or piercing the membrane to reach the baby. So normally there are no physiological reasons why you cannot enjoy your normal sexual activities throughout the pregnancy. So what happens to the average couple's sex life and why do most couples make love less often during a pregnancy?

The first three months
Most women go through a difficult time as their bodies make the huge adjustments to a normal pregnancy. Early pregnancy, with its exhaustion and nausea, can be rather like having flu for several weeks but being unable to take anything to make it better, and being expected to carry on as if nothing was wrong. Sex may be the last thing your partner feels like – perhaps a gentle back massage or a cuddle before sleeping, but not much more. All you can do is sympathize and be as caring as possible, and remember that after twelve weeks her system will probably settle down and she will feel dramatically better. However she may still not feel like intercourse and prefer other forms of lovemaking.

Of course, you may be lucky – some couples sail through the first weeks with no unpleasant symptoms to contend with. And some women find their libido actually increases when they are pregnant, perhaps through relief at not having to worry about getting pregnant, or the surge of satisfaction with their bodies that heightens sexual awareness. These couples find their sexual activity stays pretty constant throughout pregnancy and after the birth. However, this is far more likely to happen with the second or subsequent pregnancies when perhaps there is less anxiety over the whole process.

Mid-term pregnancy
By the time your partner is three months pregnant, she may be glowing with good health and optimism, with a new-found enjoyment of her body and a more relaxed attitude towards giving and receiving sexual satisfaction. There are physiological reasons for a woman's increased libido at this time. Her vaginal tissues have become 'ripe', or engorged with the extra blood flow to the pelvic

basin, so that she is in what amounts to a continual state of pleasant sexual arousal. She will reach orgasm more easily and more often (some women experience orgasm for the first time during pregnancy) and will feel more lubricated and juicy all the time. The pressure on her pelvic floor may make her want to masturbate more often, while intercourse becomes more important.

The last three months

These last months bring more challenges. The approaching labour and the reality of the baby are now undeniable. With this realization come natural anxieties for the future, which may again be expressed through a reluctance to make love. There will be physical difficulties too. The size of the baby may make some lovemaking positions uncomfortable or out of the question for your partner. She may no longer be able to lie flat on her back in the 'missionary' position, for example, without feeling faint or slightly dizzy, unless you pile pillows beneath her head and shoulders. Positions in which your partner is on all fours, or lying on her side so you can enter her from behind, reaching around to stimulate her nipples and clitoris, will be more comfortable and probably very exciting. If you try a side-by-side position, remember to put a cushion between your partner's legs to allow a smooth entry. Or you could try sitting on the edge of the bed with your feet on the floor while your partner sits astride you. The woman-on-top is another erotic favourite and has the advantage that your partner can control the depth and speed of penile thrust, while you have the added bonus that her breasts are close to your mouth. Remember that her breasts will be highly sensitive, so always check how she enjoys being touched.

ADJUSTING TO BODILY CHANGES

During the later months of pregnancy you will see the familiar body of the woman you know so intimately gradually becoming big-breasted, big-bellied and altogether different to touch and look at. Many expectant fathers find these changes amazing and exciting while others may be alarmed. You will naturally have feelings, and perhaps reservations, about them. Your partner may also be unhappy with her body, feeling awkward and 'fat', and sure that you cannot find her physically attractive. And of course, it is quite possible that you do not. If this is the case, better to acknowledge it to yourself and try to understand what it is that you find disturbing. Because your partner will probably sense your reservations, even if you are not explicit, try to reassure her lovingly of the temporary nature of the problem without making her feel upset about herself. You can always find some part of her body that is sexy and give this plenty of loving attention. Derogatory remarks about her body, even if you make them in fun, are risky and may make her withdraw physically and emotionally. She may be very unsure of herself and her attractiveness, and need you to appreciate her new feminine shape rather than tease her about it.

Luckily, these changes all happen gradually, and for every man who cannot enjoy his partner's ripe, rounded body there will be another who will find great beauty in the changing body and satisfaction in the swelling abdomen: their baby.

PHYSICAL PLEASURING

For many couples pregnancy can be a time of active sexual exploration, less exclusively centred on penis–vagina contact. Many couples develop a more or less set pattern in their lovemaking, so pregnancy can be an excellent opportunity to try out alternatives. You may be surprised and delighted at being 'obliged' to seek new ways to have intercourse, and give each other pleasure especially if one or both of you are enjoying sex more than before. On the other hand, you may not feel like trying anything new and simply feel frustrated that nothing stays the same. In this case it is essential for you to find a way to share your feelings with your partner and discover comforting ways to give and receive physical pleasure. Sex should always be fun. If you feel uneasy about trying new sexual activities, ask yourself why and, even better, discuss your feelings with your partner. Everyone has some reservations about some aspect of sex play; if you are hesitant about something, leave it for another time.

Oral sex
If you enjoy oral sex you will probably make this an increasingly important part of your lovemaking if intercourse becomes uncomfortable or tiring. If you are discovering the pleasures of oral sex for the first time, you will find it adds a new dimension to your intimacy which will last beyond the birth of your baby. The only drawback is that vaginal lubrication is more copious and has a stronger than

normal aroma and taste during pregnancy. If this makes you hesitate, the answer is for you both to have a bath or shower just before making love.

Masturbation
Men, it seems, tend to masturbate more at the beginning and end of pregnancy, while women say that they enjoy it more during the mid-term. Some people still feel that this pleasure is less satisfying than 'real' intercourse – probably a hangover from the old attitude that it was physically harmful and morally wrong. But once you overcome any uneasy feelings, you may discover the pleasure that mutual masturbation can bring. There is a special intimacy and trust in asking your partner to give you a climax this way. Far from being second best to intercourse, many couples appreciate the heightened give and take of this sexual contact, with each person allowing the other to understand the very essence of their sexuality in a way that straightforward intercourse need not do.

Body massage
One other easy, loving way to show tenderness and care, is to give each other a body massage. Touching a cherished person's naked body, utilizing the healing warmth that can flow through your hands, seeing your partner visibly relax and let go tensions and anxieties, can be intensely satisfying and erotic. Do not worry if you have never tried massage before. All it needs is patience and a willingness to learn what your partner likes. Always use some fragrant body oil or lotion to help your hands slide comfortably on her skin and remember that this is good practice for labour when massaging your partner will considerably lessen the pain of her contractions.

Loving body contact
It is probably unnecessary to remind you that kissing and love-talk are always needed in a loving relationship. It is a pity to forget the frivolous side of your loving – kissing and cuddling are still the best way to relax together, any time, any place. Even a brief holding in each other's arms can give just the warmth and security you need to face the rest of the day. Many men do not allow themselves the pleasure of being cuddled or stroked, except as a preliminary to intercourse. They can often be perplexed at their partner's need to have this erotic holding without necessarily 'going all the way'. Some men find they get too aroused and then feel frustrated if they do not

have the release of a climax. This is an area of sexuality where many couples fail to understand each other and feel exasperated at the apparent conflict in their individual needs. Try not to see this as a full stop, but as a chance to enlarge all your gentle powers of seduction to give her what she desires and be satisfied yourself.

SOME WOMEN 'GO OFF' SEX

The feelings we have about our bodies are usually reflected in lovemaking activities. Many pregnant women do not feel comfortable or happy about the dramatic changes that take place during pregnancy and a woman who does not like herself very much will feel less erotic. Often there are fears that the man will be 'turned off' by some aspect of the pregnancy which may further inhibit a woman's sexual appetite. And sometimes sex just becomes less important for a time – the physical demands of working and being pregnant are more than enough to cope with, there is no spare energy left over for lovemaking. For many women, but not all, this is a temporary lull, with a reappearance of interest in sex during the mid-term of pregnancy.

Some women feel that in becoming pregnant their bodies have become 'sacred'. These intensely maternal feelings seem to make erotic activities temporarily inappropriate, sometimes until well after the birth. (This feeling of awe is often shared by the expectant father who becomes gentler and more careful in his lovemaking; or even abstains from intercourse as a protective gesture towards mother and baby.) But however a woman feels about her body and however much or little sex she wants, cuddling and tender holding are always in demand.

When a couple both experience a lull in their need for intercourse there is usually no problem. But if a couple are sexually out of step it can be difficult and will gradually put a strain on the relationship. It is important to remember that every woman is different, and every pregnancy evokes a different response. 'Normal' sexual activity is whatever you both decide is right for you. But if your sex life seems to be diminished try to be patient and caring to each other. Talk it over and see if anything is upsetting either of you; do not withdraw, sulk, feel hurt or presume anything, and above all try and retain a sense of humour.

FEARS ABOUT SEX

Some couples do have problems in their sexual relationship during the childbearing year. If this happens, try to be clear about where the problem originates. Is it a psychological fear that makes one or other of you avoid sex, or is it a physical problem that makes you feel particularly vulnerable sexually?

BLEEDING IN PREGNANCY

It is extremely common for women to have slight bleeding in early pregnancy, usually around the time when they would menstruate if they were not pregnant. Normally your doctor will advise your partner to rest in bed for a few days if this happens. Most couples voluntarily stop having intercourse if the woman has experienced any bleeding, just in case. But there is no conclusive evidence to show that avoiding gentle intercourse in early pregnancy prevents miscarriage. Sometimes your partner may have slight spotting after intercourse if there has been very deep penetration, so that the penis brushes against the cervix and ruptures a few capillaries. This is not dangerous, but it is perhaps advisable not to use a position during pregnancy that makes for deep penetration.

INHIBITIONS ABOUT INTERCOURSE

While the most common anxiety among expectant fathers is that penile penetration might be dangerous to the baby, there are other fears which can inhibit a man's sexuality. Some men have told me they felt observed by the baby, or that its presence made sex unsuitable – 'not in front of the children'. One father laughingly told me, 'When Marilyn told me the baby's head was low in her pelvis, I felt sex wasn't on any more. I had this idea that if my penis was next to the baby he might bite it!' However funny your fears may sound, if they interrupt your capacity or willingness to make love they should never be ignored. Instead, bring them into the open and put them into perspective. By keeping in contact with each other and sensitive to each other's problems as they arise, neither of you will become isolated with your problems.

Some sexual difficulties reflect the fact that pregnancy and childbirth can so easily seem to become depersonalized and clinical. You may both feel that your partner has been taken over by medical restrictions and that her whole genital area has ceased to be erotic and become the public property of the hospital. In this medically charged atmosphere even contemplating sex may seem almost frivolous and irresponsible. You may even feel that it is somehow taboo to be sexually aroused by a pregnant woman, a mother. The message seems to be that not only does your partner now 'belong' to the doctors caring for her, but that it is not 'nice' either for her to feel sexy now she is a mother, or for you to desire her sexually.

WORRIES ABOUT ORGASM

Towards the end of pregnancy many couples fear that the woman's orgasm or the associated uterine contractions might trigger off labour prematurely. There is no evidence that this can happen, although later in pregnancy a strong orgasm can sometimes be followed by painful (though quite harmless) contractions (known as Braxton-Hicks contractions). However, some couples have found that intercourse helps to stimulate labour if they are past their due date. Sheila Kitzinger in her book *Women's Experience of Sex* gives detailed instructions if you want to try this effective and enjoyable method of encouraging nature to take its course.

EXPRESSING YOUR NEEDS

It is easy for a woman to become so self-absorbed during pregnancy that she forgets her partner's needs. If a man is loving and supportive, he probably sees his role as being undemanding and protective, and may feel almost selfish if he makes any demands.

In my antenatal classes I encourage the women to consider how their partners are coping, particularly if there has been a reduction of sex play. More often than not a woman will start talking about her man, but within two or three sentences she will go back to talking about herself again. This self-preoccupation is normal, but it can be uncomfortable for the man, who often feels neglected even if he does not complain. Perhaps it is no coincidence that many expectant fathers experience an increase in sexual fantasies, though very few actually follow them through.

If you are in this position, try to talk over your feelings with your partner. She may be quite unaware of what has happened. It is an important element in preparation for parenthood for you to learn how to nurture each other. To do this, both of you have to express your needs and not feel ashamed of making demands.

Helping an older child adjust

Most of us would agree that the arrival of a sibling can be one of the most influential events in a child's early years. In our family for some years, my eldest daughter would scream at me in the heat of any row, 'And anyway, the worst day in my whole life was the day Adam was born . . .'. A young child's worst fear is to lose the life-sustaining love of his parents. The arrival of a new baby creates a situation where this anxiety is aroused with fearful intensity. The natural capacity of first children to feel passionate love, hate, jealousy, anger or hurt can take some adults by surprise. Fortunately most young children have not yet learned the adult art of suppression, and they will let you know how they feel in no uncertain terms, either verbally if they are old enough, or non-verbally. However some do not, and parents should beware of complacency if their child is 'not jealous at all' – he is probably torturing the neighbour's cat instead!

But some children do cope easily and calmly so it is wiser not to anticipate a negative reaction – every child reacts in a different way. Judy Dunn and Carol Kendrick's recent research in England has shown that parents need not feel guilty or responsible if their child does react unhappily when the next baby arrives. It seems that some children became intensely jealous no matter how carefully and lovingly the parents had prepared everything. The personality of the child was the most influential factor. Some children, like some adults, simply find it harder not to feel threatened and insecure if they have to share their parents' time and affection. This does not mean that parents should not try to lessen what can be a painful time in a child's life. Sensible preparation during the pregnancy will always be bene-ficial, particularly if both parents are involved in demonstrating that more people in a family does not mean less love.

Gradually as the pregnancy advances your child will realize that something is going on. Reassurance is always helpful and if you are available you can explain in simple terms, using pictures or photo-graphs (see page 213), how the new baby got inside Mummy and, more important, how it will eventually get out. Even pre-verbal toddlers benefit from this kind of direct communication. They often understand much more than they can express themselves. All children have greater difficulty asking the right question, to get the answer they seek, than understanding the answer when it comes. Some parents worry that realistic pictures of a baby's birth might disturb a very young child. But this is not the case; on the contrary, if the child can begin to grasp the facts in a secure environment, it brings a soothing normality into what can otherwise be a source of problematic fantasy. (See Further reading, page 213 for suggestions.) A father told me about the confusion in his daughter's mind about how a baby is born. 'A few weeks before Justin was born Anna (3-year-old first child) started to be very difficult about using the loo. She'd been potty trained for quite some time, so we were a bit surprised. First she demanded her potty back, then she refused that too and got very constipated. She insisted on going with her mother every time – "What are you doing mummy?" We were getting quite concerned and then I wondered if Anna was worrying about how the baby was going to get out! I talked to her and tried to explain in her language about the birth. She didn't respond much, but I had been right. The constipation disappeared, but she stuck to the potty for a bit longer!'

GIVING REASSURANCE

Fathers can be invaluable in providing a continuing normality as the mother instinctively withdraws a little into her pregnancy. In one culture that Margaret Mead studied, the father actually takes the first child away and becomes exclusively responsible for his welfare until well after the next baby is born. Less dramatically, you will probably find your eldest turning to you more often for comfort and attention as if he intuitively realizes that his mother will not be able to respond in the same exclusive way. Fathers enjoy their new-found popularity when the chant of 'Mummy do it' changes to 'Want Daddy'! Mothers often worry that they may not be able to feel such intense love for the second child. The father is then the best person to reassure her that she will indeed be able to give equally to both children – that love nourishes love and never diminishes the capacity to give.

Many fathers find enjoyment in discovering their own links with the older child by taking up new games or hobbies together. One father told me of his pleasure when his small son moved closer to him towards the end of his wife's next pregnancy. 'He'd always been a bit of a "mummy's boy" really. I felt I didn't really know what he liked so much as Pam did. Then shortly before the baby was due I was putting up some shelves and Benjy came and watched me. We had a great time together, and now every night when I get home he rushes up to me and says "more boom-boom daddy", which means we have to get out the hammer and nails again!' This father found their special activity was sustained and enjoyed after the birth of the next baby, and he felt too that it helped to lessen the older child's jealousy of the baby. A child who feels special and cherished by his father is much less likely to be threatened by the demands the new baby makes upon the mother. A father's caring presence helps in the creation of a family with an abundance of love, in which everyone feels more able to share, no one feels in danger of being forgotten.

MAKING THE BABY SEEM REAL

If your next baby is to be born in hospital, it is a good idea to prepare your child for his mother's temporary absence. It will help if you all go to an antenatal check-up at the clinic. Hospitals tend to be associated with illness and accidents in the minds of even very small children. Being familiarized with the place where his mother will be, meeting the doctor or midwife who will help with the baby's birth will reassure the child and give him a point of reference later on. If he is allowed to hear the fetal heart and feel the baby move inside the mother's abdomen, this will make it more real. Talking about and to the baby – including it in every day events like listening to stories and music, or going swimming – helps the eldest child feel his sibling is already part of the family. Young children are often frustrated at the length of time it takes to 'grow' a baby. One family solved this problem by planting a seed in a flower pot and watching it grow. The parents then equated this with the time it took for their baby to develop inside the mother.

Including the eldest child in the practical preparations for the new baby will help him grasp that another person will soon join the family. Getting out the crib, preparing the baby's clothes, will stir up memories for everyone. Children are intensely interested in the tangible evidence of their own recent babyhood and development.

This is the time to tell the story of their birth (grandparents can be a great asset here) and early life with photos of what they looked like, if they are available.

It is essential, while you are making arrangements for the birth of your next baby to provide a familiar, caring and reassuring person to care for the older child (make sure your child agrees with your choice too). A close friend or a grandparent may be the natural person to ask, ideally someone who can come and be with the child in his own home so that his normal routine is uninterrupted. Try to be there yourself as much as possible and if your partner is to stay longer than twenty-four hours in the hospital, then you should begin your paternity leave (see page 168) before she comes home, to be with the older child. Check that the hospital of your choice encourages visits at convenient hours, so your eldest need not be separated from his mother for longer than necessary.

Finally, make sure that your child really understands what is prepared for him while the baby is being born and while his mother is away. This often needs a lot of repetition, as young children have a habit of 'tuning out' if something is emotionally charged, and missing the vital piece of information by so doing.

However much they are reassured, it is not surprising that during this time many children suddenly regress with dizzy rapidity. Sleep problems are a common way for a child to express fears that Mum or Dad may disappear if they are not kept in sight night and day. All this can be very wearing for a pregnant mother who is possibly feeling tired and anxious about shortly having to cope with not one, but *two* babies.

Once again, father can save the day (or the night). If you can physically embrace and emotionally 'hold' both exasperated mother and insecure child, they will quickly re-establish their trusting relationship. Young children are constantly testing themselves and their world; and their parents in particular. As the time of the new baby's birth approaches do not be surprised if your eldest shows some signs of distress. Try and understand how he is feeling, and rather than labelling his behaviour as 'good' or 'bad', give him continuous security from parents who can be 'tested' but who never fail to remain loving and present, no matter what.

Chapter 4

Practical preparations

Choosing the birth place

Early in pregnancy you will be given certain options about where your baby will be born. Where this is will also determine to a large extent what kind of experience the birth will be and with whom you will both share it. Before you commit yourselves you have to know what you both want and be prepared to ask questions. Nobody would buy a house or a car without doing some research, but sadly, when it comes to having a baby, many couples seem to become strangely absentminded and passive. 'My doctor gave me a letter for the nearest hospital and I just booked in there.' Or the often-heard excuse 'I didn't know I could ask for . . . a GP delivery, a birthing room, an early discharge' – the list is long and the ensuing frustration inevitable.

CHOICE MAY BE LIMITED

In fact, parental choice is very often limited, and will depend largely on where your home is. If you live in Holland, where 42 per cent of babies are born at home and only the 'high risk' mothers delivered in hospital, then you will have a choice. But in Sweden, where 100 per cent of births are in hospital, the only choice will be between hospitals and in some areas even that choice is not available. In the United Kingdom and some parts of America the official policy is for all babies to be born in hospital – though if you are very determined and fall within the 'low risks' category you may be able to arrange a home birth. But even within the hospital system there are various options you will want to consider. 'Low risk' mothers may be able to arrange for delivery by their own GP or by a community midwife in hospital, for example, so that they can be delivered by someone they know and yet have the security of hospital back-up. Special birthing rooms, with a relaxed, homelike atmosphere, are provided by some hospitals. And if all goes well, an early discharge six hours after the birth may be possible. In making your choice, the first step is to recognize how you both feel about childbirth, then gradually your personal needs will become clearer.

In many ways our society considers childbirth to be a fundamentally dangerous event, demanding hospital-based medical expertise to make it safe. On the other hand, some people insist that for the majority of women and their babies childbirth is essentially a normal function and should be a home-based event with medical support. In this case, the value of a routine hospital environment, regardless of individual preference, unless complications develop, becomes questionable.

Although when dealing with low-risk mothers there is no statistical evidence to prove that either home or hospital is safer, the attitude still persists that to want a home birth is a dangerous quirk, pursued by only a tiny minority. And as long as the message is that having a baby at home is hazardous, then sensible couples will obviously pick a hospital birth, 'just in case something goes wrong'.

When you are making the choice, decide first of all what, ideally, you would both like; respect your own feelings, and do not be put off by rules and conventions. Then discover what there is on offer in your locality, and be ready to be flexible and realistic about medical and safety precautions.

HOME BIRTH

These days having a baby at home is a rare opportunity. Even if your partner fulfils all the safety requirements – age, obstetric history, good general health, a normal pregnancy etc., it may still be difficult to arrange. As the father there are some definite advantages for you too, although like this man you may feel a little anxious in the beginning: 'Oh it was Jan's birth first off – I was definitely going to be there, wherever it was. We'd agreed all along we wanted a natural birth, and then it sort of came round to home being the only place where we could do as we wanted; we wanted to give the baby a bath like Leboyer. As to home or hospital, if it had been my choice I would have probably chosen hospital. I saw the risks of a home birth, but

Jan kept it very much as *her* decision, so I was with her if that's what she wanted.'

If your baby is born at home the medical team will already be familiar to you both and will come at your request. You are in your own environment, it's your house/flat and no one will treat you as a peripheral guest. You will have more responsibility, but you'll probably feel freer of outside constraints when it comes to taking an active part in the proceedings. You can arrange for other caring supporters to come and help you in the exhausting task of labour companion. This way you can be liberated to enjoy your own experience, because you have help; it's not all up to you.

Best of all you won't be sent home after the birth. Right from the start your contact with your baby is unbroken, you and your partner can be together, calmly getting on with the business of looking after each other and your baby. It's interesting to note that women who have their babies at home are far less likely to develop postnatal depression or have the 'baby blues', than those who have their babies in hospitals. There are many reasons why a home birth may not be possible, or may not be to your taste, but if all goes well what could be better, as this father described it to me: 'After Toby's birth, which was pretty amazing, really, I was "high" for three days . . . I remember one thing most vividly. It was after everyone had gone, the midwife and the doctor, it was still very early morning, just getting light and very quiet. Sian was sleeping as it had been a long labour. I had Toby all to myself. I took him, *my* baby in my arms and into the garden. I just walked round talking to him and telling him about the garden. Then I went upstairs and we all cuddled up in bed together. I felt we were the centre of the universe or something, you know?'

NEW BIRTH TRADITIONS

The move away from home birth has meant the evolution of a new set of birth traditions, the most dramatic being the accepted presence of the father in the labour room. Traditionally, women friends and relatives supported the labouring mother in her own home. Until the 1970s it was unusual for the man to be in attendance, and the few who did attend were reportedly at home births. However, since about 1970 most babies have been born in hospital and 85 per cent of their fathers have participated in some way during the births. In the

United States figures are slightly different but give the same overall picture.

This is at least partly because childbirth and child-rearing are no longer seen as exclusively the woman's responsibility. Women expect their partners to be with them giving support, especially during labour, rather than pacing the corridor outside. And because it is often hospital policy not to allow anyone but the father to act as labour companion, if a woman wants a known companion during her labour, the father has very little alternative but to be there. But what began as a rather vague, supportive role, has rapidly evolved into a more central and active participation, with father an essential member of the labour team.

It seems, too, that father's presence has measurable benefits. Studies confirm my own observations that when men supported their wives and assisted at the birth, the mothers reported less pain, and used less medication and felt that the emotional quality of their experience was enhanced. Babies who had immediate contact with their fathers seemed to benefit too, and have been shown to be particularly responsive to their fathers at three and six months.

THE IMPORTANCE OF A SATISFYING EXPERIENCE

This is all very encouraging, but sadly, it seems that medical staff seldom really appreciate fathers, or understand their unique contribution to the birth process. They may ignore them or eject them from the room when things go wrong. However, hospitals and their staff vary tremendously in their attitudes towards fathers. If you and your partner want to share the pregnancy and birth as much as possible it is essential that you find a medical team that respects and values the contribution you have to make. Discover as much as you can about the consultant and whether he sounds 'right' for you before your GP refers you, if necessary asking for an interview with him to find out more about his views. Try to visit the labour ward too before booking in, to get the feel of the place and the people (see Making a birth plan, page 69). The atmosphere is all important – it is the people who give even high technology a human face and will enhance your experience of the birth.

Make certain that the hospital you choose has a good special care unit for babies who are premature, small for dates or have other problems. Make certain too that if your baby is in special care you will have free access to him whenever you wish, to facilitate the 'bonding' that may need a special effort in these circumstances (see page 140).

What happens to a woman during her labour can strongly influence her future relationship with her baby, and the quality of the care and interest shown by the medical team and other supporters is a crucial factor in how she will feel about the experience. A long, difficult labour can be transformed into a wonderfully fulfilling experience by a sympathetic midwife or doctor, just as easily as a short 'trouble-free' labour can be ruined by someone insensitive. Those who share this experience with you will remain in your memory for ever, so it is important not only to know the place, but the people too.

THE LABOUR COMPANION

Ideally, during the antenatal period you and your partner should get to know the midwife or the doctor who will deliver her, make your wishes known and find out what your medical team's normal procedures are. It is important that you all know what to expect from each other before labour starts. It is a sad fact that in most hospitals it is impossible to know which midwife will attend you before you are actually in labour.

This arrangement means that as labour companion it will be up to you to form a relationship with 'your' midwife as quickly as possible. It is important to find out her preferences and attitudes because these will strongly influence the course of your partner's labour. It is also vital that your midwife know your partner's preferences – for example, what position she may want to give birth in and whether she does or does not wish to be offered drugs, and which ones, as this will inevitably make for a different approach.

As labour companion you become the bridge between the woman and her medical attendants, giving the necessary information and leaving your partner free to concentrate exclusively on herself as labour intensifies. This collaboration and communication between you and the midwife can undoubtedly be very fruitful. But it remains important to negotiate your preferences and get any specific requests written into your hospital notes, well before labour starts, to avoid conflict or misunderstandings on the day.

Gathering information

The medical profession is notorious for its jargon. It may seem sometimes as though doctors and nurses use mysterious initials or obtuse terminology to confuse the lay person. In truth the expressions you hear are nothing more than a shorthand means of communication between busy professionals. If you are planning to be an active member of the labour team, it will help enormously if you have a basic knowledge of obstetrics and a detailed understanding of the kind of birth your partner is hoping for. Always keep a flexible attitude, bearing in mind that childbirth cannot be controlled; never be afraid to ask questions or to appear foolish, it is essential that you really understand any procedure that is offered and its wider implications.

QUESTIONING PROCEDURES

During your partner's pregnancy and until well after the birth of your baby it is a good idea to be prepared to question any 'routine' medical procedure that is offered to you. Do not be pressured into anything unless you fully understand the short and long-term effect on both mother and baby. If necessary go to your local medical library and read up the latest research on the subject so that you and your partner can make up your minds from a position of strength. Parents are often in an extremely vulnerable position because of their intense concern for the welfare of their baby. Knowing the facts will lessen this anxiety, not increase it. These are some of the 'extras' that may be offered either during labour or in the routine clinical checks.

Ultrasound scan
A method of building up a picture of the contents of the uterus using high frequency sound waves. Research is inconclusive as to the long-term effect on the fetus, but one recent American study judges that 'ultrasound examination in pregnancy should only be performed for specific medical indications', and not done routinely or merely to provide an image of the fetus for the parents (International Childbirth Education Association). It is, however, necessary in order to pinpoint the position of the baby and placenta if an amniocentesis or fetoscopy is to be done.

Chorionic villus sampling

This is a new test at present only offered on a limited scale to women known to be at risk of having babies with inherited or genetic abnormalities, for example: Down's syndrome, thalassaemia and sickle cell anaemia, it can also determine the sex of the fetus. (Developmental defects such as spina bifida cannot be identified by CVS, therefore alpha-feto protein sampling done with a blood test, and amniocentesis will probably still be used to screen for this type of abnormality.) By passing a fine tube via the vagina through the cervix a sample of chorion, tissue which contains fetal cells, is removed. Ultrasound is used throughout the procedure to monitor the position of the fetus and placenta. CVS has the advantage of being an early and highly accurate test, usually performed between eight and eleven weeks of pregnancy but although it is a simple procedure it requires a highly skilled team to carry it out. If a termination should be necessary it can be performed at twelve weeks which is preferable to the mid-term date of an amniocentesis.

Amniocentesis

If a woman is 35 or older she may wish to have an amniocentesis to make sure that there is nothing wrong with the developing fetus. Sometimes it is the baby's father who presses for the test because he knows he would not be able to accept a handicapped child. The test is carried out by inserting a hollow needle into the uterus through the abdominal wall, to draw off a sample of the amniotic fluid surrounding the fetus. The text can detect certain fetal abnormalities such as spina bifida, Down's syndrome (mongolism), haemophilia, certain forms of muscular dystrophy and sex-linked hereditary diseases.

There is a 1.2 per cent risk that the procedure can cause the fetus to abort, so it is important that you are both in full agreement as to why you want the test done. You might also like to discuss beforehand with your GP or consultant the procedure for a late termination should it be required. If, as a couple, you would *not* choose to terminate the pregnancy if the baby was malformed, there is no point in having the test done.

Tests before induction

If the baby is more than two weeks overdue, tests to determine the condition of the placenta and the cervix should be carried out before the decision is made to induce labour. Some consultants favour testing the placenta by a blood test which measures the hormonal levels in the placenta and so determines if the baby is still being adequately nourished. Others prefer to use ultrasound scanning to look at the cervix to see whether it is 'ripe', i.e. ready to go into labour. Scans can also recognize post maturity in the placenta. Some consultants refer to the baby's condition before inducing labour. This would be done by twice weekly fetal monitoring, measuring fetal movement and checking the mother's weight loss – 80 per cent of women normally do lose weight towards the end of their pregnancy.

Induction means starting labour by artificial means. Your partner will have made sure that it is necessary and will have been checked to be certain her body and the baby are ready. Starting labour off may be done by protaglandin pessaries inserted next to the cervix, your partner will then start contracting within about eight hours. She will be able to move around freely, but contractions may feel rather more powerful than if labour had started spontaneously. The other method of induction is by a hormonal 'drip' (oxytocin) introduced into a vein in your partner's hand. In this case her membranes will probably be artificially ruptured too. Induced labours tend to be faster and its contractions stronger; be prepared with lots of encouragement, breathing and coping strategies right from the start. If your partner has an oxytocin drip ask for the dose to be increased very gradually – this gives her the chance to keep up with the contractions. Also request an extra long tube before the 'drip' is set up, to give her freedom of movement. It is very important that the woman feels she has retained some control, and does not become dominated and feel helpless because of the 'drip'.

Natural methods of induction
If you know your partner has to be induced it is always worth exploring natural methods first. Acupuncture works very well for some people, but a practitioner needs to see your partner to show her which pressure points do the trick. Homeopathic remedies are also helpful, but again you will need to see a qualified homeopath. Last, but not least, and for many couples by far the most enjoyable is lovemaking. See Sheila Kitzinger's book *Women's Experience of Sex* for the exact recipe.

Artificial rupture of the membranes
This may be suggested if contractions are weak and irregular or dilation of the cervix is slow. Once this has been done contractions

will get faster and stronger because the baby's head will press down more firmly on the cervix.

Accelerated labour
A hormonal drip (oxytocin) may be suggested to speed up a labour which has slowed down or stopped. Before accepting, suggest that your partner changes to a more upright position or has a relaxing warm bath or shower to get contractions going again. Often kissing and stimulating her nipples will encourage contractions. If this fails, ask for artificial rupture of the membranes. If a drip does prove necessary, always ask for it to be started slowly.

Internal vaginal examination
Every three or four hours an examination may be carried out to assess dilation of the cervix. Ask for this to be done in whatever position is most comfortable for your partner – and for it to be done less often to avoid disappointment if the cervix is dilating slowly. Ask, too, if your partner can feel her own cervix – this may encourage her.

Electronic monitoring
It is important that you find out what your hospital's policy is on fetal monitoring. Some consultants like to monitor the baby's heart at regular intervals at the beginning of labour and then continuously later on and during the second stage. This form of monitoring can give valuable and precise information about the baby's condition during labour. If there is any cause for concern, or if any drugs are given to the mother it is wise to accept for the well-being of the baby. However where there are no indications of anything being wrong, routine continuous monitoring can create problems for the labouring woman. Being confined to bed because of the monitor can slow the labour down and make the woman much more aware of the pain. Monitoring may be external early in labour, with a transducer strapped to the woman's abdomen, or internal, with an electrode introduced through the cervix and clipped to the baby's scalp later on and during second stage.

Early in labour try sitting on the bucket next to the monitor to avoid lying back on the bed which can be very uncomfortable during strong contractions. Or, if the belt is uncomfortable ask the midwife to let you hold the transducer on your partner's abdomen instead. Later in labour if your partner has internal monitoring, make sure that she has a long cable so she can still move freely about the room. During the periods of monitoring it is vital that you both try not to become too spellbound by the monitor with its flashing lights and pulsing sounds. However, if you are at all worried about what the monitor appears to be saying, do not hesitate to ask for another machine to check it – or better still ask the midwife to monitor the baby's heart using her fetal stethoscope.

Dextrose drip
This is a solution containing a form of sugar, introduced into a vein in the back of your partner's hand. If she is exhausted or dehydrated this can rapidly boost her energy. Always ask what is in the 'drip' – if oxytocin has been added to make a 'cocktail' your partner must be warned that her contractions will suddenly get stronger. Remind her to empty her bladder regularly every hour.

Blood test for fetal distress
If monitoring indicates fetal distress a blood sample may be taken from the baby's head during labour. Fetal distress produces changes in blood chemistry which will help to confirm whether a Caesarean section is necessary.

Caesarean section
Performed under either general or epidural anaesthesia. Sometimes you know in advance your baby will have to be born this way, sometimes an emergency Caesarean is decided upon during labour. Either way you and your partner should be able to remain together during the operation if you wish. Find out what your hospital's policy is with regard to Caesarean births (see page 125) and then discuss it with your midwife or doctor.

Forceps
These are used if the delivery has to be speeded up, or if the baby is in an unusual position, or very often when the mother has had an epidural. Forceps (or Ventouse) deliveries are becoming increasingly common, but if one is proposed, suggest first that your partner tries a different, more upright position, either squatting, kneeling or standing, to allow gravity to help the descent of the baby. Forceps are curved, metal blades like salad servers which form a protective 'cup' around the baby's head during use. A Ventouse extractor, which works by pulling the baby's head by suction, is sometimes used instead of forceps.

Vitamin K for the baby

Administered by injection or drops, this is given prophylactically soon after birth to boost the supply of vitamin K essential for blood clotting in the baby.

LATE TERMINATIONS

If you are planning to have an amniocentesis you have presumably decided that terminating the pregnancy is a possibility. Because hospital consultants vary in their provision for counselling couples who are considering a termination, find out what help and advice you can hope to receive before the test takes place. If the service does not seem adequate then be prepared to find outside help for yourselves. Try contacting SAFTA who can supply leaflets and telephone counselling (see Useful addresses, page 218). Try and discuss your feelings and find out what options are open to you if the fetus does have problems. Of course you may change your mind later on; some couples do decide to keep the pregnancy even if the baby is handicapped, but it is wise to be completely honest with each other about your feelings at every stage. Approximately one to two women in a hundred go on to have a termination after an amniocentesis.

Having decided to have an amniocentesis it is important that you go to the hospital with your partner when she has the test. Many women have reported feeling anxious and upset during the procedure – having their partners there to keep them calm and reassure them made all the difference.

Unfortunately amniocentesis can only be carried out at about 14 weeks after the last menstrual period and the results take between 2½ and 5 weeks to determine. This waiting period is often very difficult, many couples almost blank out the pregnancy until they have the results, just in case there is anything wrong with the baby. Find out when the results of the test will be available and make sure that you are together to receive them.

If the amniocentesis showed an abnormality you will both be invited to see your consultant, or senior registrar who will explain the extent of the handicap and answer any questions you may have. This interview may take place some days after receiving the news, but you may both still be in a state of shock. Because many parents find it hard to concentrate and understand what the consultant says, it is a good idea to write down all your questions and the doctor's answers so you can refer to them later when you are feeling calmer.

In many hospitals it is assumed that you will want the termination to take place as soon as possible; possibly within a couple of days. This may be the right decision for some couples but for others there may be a need for more time to plan and consider. It is absolutely vital that you take enough time to share your feelings and fully explore what options are open to you. When you are considering a termination, ask if your consultant or GP has a counsellor who you can talk to. In some hospitals this will be a midwife, or it might be a health visitor or social worker. Some National Childbirth Trust antenatal teachers are also trained counsellors, or else they can refer you to someone who can help you both get in touch with your feelings, particularly when considering a termination of a pregnancy where the baby is wanted and loved. Most hospitals will provide a genetic counsellor who will be able to tell you the exact nature and extent of your baby's handicap and advise you on future pregnancies. But if you are ambivalent about the termination you would probably benefit from talking to parents who have a child with a similar handicap as your own, to get an exact idea of what life would be like if you refuse the termination. If your hospital cannot arrange this, contact SAFTA who may be able to help you.

During the days when you are coming to terms with your situation you will find you are both liable to have emotional and possibly angry outbursts towards each other; it is quite normal to feel cheated, angry and helpless. How to break the sad news to grandparents, friends and colleagues will also weigh heavily upon you both. But experience has shown that those parents who are able to start the grieving process even before the actual termination are probably less likely to have difficulties adjusting to their loss later on.

Medical procedures

Make sure that you both know exactly what your hospital procedure is for the termination. In most cases you will not be given any choice as to the method of the termination, or where and with whom it is performed. Whether your partner is in a gynaecological ward or in a labour ward, for example, depends on the policy of the hospital. Many parents have found they received more experienced and sensitive understanding of their situation where the woman is delivered by midwives. If possible ask to see your consultant or a senior midwife and make a birth plan. This may seem inappropriate to you at first, but other couples have found it helped them to plan the birth, even when the outcome was a dead baby. For a healthy grieving process to take place it is very important that you and your partner feel comfortable with the plans for the birth and what happens afterwards.

Questions you might like to ask

Where will the labour take place, and who will be there with us? It is important for the man to be there to support the labouring woman, even more so because the outcome will be so unlike what was hoped for. Some couples have found that having a close friend or relative there was also a great comfort.

What pain relief is available? Some hospitals have the facilities for epidurals, while others do not. Because the labour will last between 10 and 15 hours it is vital that your partner has adequate pain relief.

What exactly will our baby look like – what will the physical manifestations of the handicap be? Many parents fear the baby will be a monster and are too frightened to look – often they are relieved to see that this is not so and find it helpful in the long term, although distressing at the time to look at their dead baby.

Can we look at and hold our baby after the delivery? If either of you want to see and hold your baby make sure the medical staff know this before labour starts. It is important, if she chooses, that the woman is not too heavily drugged to be able to fully appreciate what is happening to her; or that the medical staff are asked to preserve the baby for twelve hours while the decision is made. Research has shown that holding and having a photograph of the baby makes it a more real person to remember. This reality helps the resolution of the mourning process. If your partner does not want the photograph at once ask the hospital to keep it in their medical files in case she wants it at a later date.

How soon can the woman leave the hospital? Which ward your partner stays in, and how long she is in hospital will depend upon your consultant. There is no ideal solution and wherever she is your partner will need you to stay with her and support her.

Will the woman produce milk and can she have anything to stop this?
This is one of the most distressing features of losing a pregnancy –
having milk but no baby to feed. The breasts may become large,
swollen and painful, this will gradually disappear over four or five
days. Get your partner to rest, restrict fluids and take aspirin to ease
the discomfort; putting cold flannels on the breasts may help.

Will there be a post-mortem? A detailed post-mortem is a valuable
way of giving you information about your baby's condition, and it is
a good idea to request it even when it is not routine. You will have an
appointment to discuss the results with a senior member of the
hospital staff.

Can we arrange our own funeral, or does the hospital do it for us?
Legally there are no requirements to dispose of a baby delivered
before 26 weeks. These babies are normally incinerated after the
post-mortem examination unless the parents request otherwise. If
you do decide to have a funeral for your baby the hospital chaplain,
or administrator will advise you. Whether you have religious beliefs
or not, having a funeral has been found to help parents recover from
their loss. But arranging a funeral can be both distressing and
expensive – there is no death grant available; asking a relative or
friend to take the arrangements over for you may be a solution.
Having a memorial of some sort with the baby's name on it can also
be extremely comforting later on.

How long is it normal to grieve? The length of time it takes to
complete the mourning process varies according to each individual.
Gradually, after the initial shock wears off you may have good days,
but then suddenly feel overcome with sadness and loss once again.
No one can hurry the process – nor should they try. Patient caring,
and the ability to allow each other time to reach an understanding of
what happened is most helpful. Many people weep frequently for
weeks, others express their loss less openly. If either of you feel
overwhelmed by your grief try talking to a counsellor who will be
able to help you resolve your feelings. During the mourning period
take extra care of each other's physical and emotional needs; it is
unfortunately only too common for women to neglect their health
during this time. A regular massage and a good exercise class will
help to re-establish a feeling of well being after the trauma of the
pregnancy and the termination.

When should we try to conceive again? This varies according to the individual couple. Research does show that it is very important to finish mourning the dead baby before trying to conceive again; otherwise the new baby grows up in the shadow of its sibling. Once you have decided to start a new pregnancy get plenty of advice about preconceptual care and genetic counselling to enable you to feel fully confident.

GETTING TO KNOW YOUR HOSPITAL

Most babies are born in hospital, and every labour ward has its own attitudes, rules and culture, which will shape your experience. It is therefore important that you get to know your hospital and the people who work there. Try to go with your partner to as many of the antenatal visits as you can manage. Hospital staff need to be aware of you both, particularly if you are planning to be active during labour. But you too must appreciate and accommodate their feelings and the pressures under which they work. All this takes time, consideration and a willingness to listen on both sides. It is no good complaining after the birth that things were not as you wanted if you have not made the necessary preparations beforehand. These are some of the issues that you might want to discuss with the hospital staff beforehand, to see whether their attitudes are likely to conflict with your own:

Delivery of the baby

In many hospitals today the baby will be delivered straight on to your partner's abdomen as a matter of course. However, she might prefer the baby to be delivered on to the bed and then pick the baby up herself. You might like to help the midwife receive the baby and then hand him to your partner, and maybe also cut the umbilical cord if there are no problems. Discuss with your partner how she wants this important part of her labour to be organized, and find out what your midwife routinely does.

The position your partner adopts for the birth of the baby needs to be discussed with your midwife/doctor before labour starts. If your partner is planning to adopt a position other than the traditional one, i.e.: semi reclining, then it is vital that you negotiate this before labour starts with your medical team to be certain to have their full support. It is then wise to have a note made of your wishes to kneel or be on 'all fours' and attach this to your medical file.

Pain relief in labour

Because no woman can predict exactly what her labour will be like, or how she will react to it, neither you nor your partner should be disappointed if she feels at any stage that she needs artificial pain relief. Ask what drugs your hospital routinely uses and what effect, if any, they might have on the baby. You have the right to refuse, and if possible will want to avoid any drug which research shows to have adverse effects on your baby, for example pethidine (see below). Familiarize yourself with the forms of pain relief that are available so that you are aware of what could be offered to your partner, and what its effect will be.

Entonox. A mixture of 50 per cent oxygen and 50 per cent nitrous oxide − 'gas and air' − is inhaled and controlled only by the woman herself, taking slow deep breaths, through a mask over her nose and mouth. Entonox takes effect 30−40 seconds after inhalation, lasts approximately one minute and is completely safe for the baby − unfortunately not everyone finds it effective. You can help by handing the mask to your partner just before the contraction begins, and then after breathing the Entonox encouraging her to breathe lightly through the remainder of the contraction. Don't give up after one attempt, you sometimes need time to find the best way to use it.

TENS. This stands for transcutaneous electrical nerve stimulation and has been successfully used as a method of pain relief for many years by physiotherapists. Used in Sweden, it has also helped women cope with pain in labour for some time in a few hospitals in Britain. When contractions start the woman has four electrodes placed on her lower back, either side of the spine, and regulates the tiny electrical impulse herself during each contraction. TENS claims to reduce the pain of labour by stimulating the production of the body's own painkillers − endorphins − and by blocking pain messages. As a method of pain relief it is very helpful to many women in the first stage; however it does not take all the pain away and is reported to be less successful during the second stage. Those women who have found it positive all enjoyed having 'something to do' which gave them a feeling of being in control which is in itself helpful. Ask your hospital if they provide TENS; if not, it is possible to hire a machine yourself (see Useful addresses, page 216).

Acupuncture. This has also been used as a 'natural' method of pain relief, but you have to find your own practitioner and discuss how best to manage pain before labour starts.

Homeopathy. Yet another useful aid, and although there are not many practitioners who will go with you in labour, after consultation there are many remedies which you can use which can be helpful.

Epidural anaesthesia. A local anaesthetic introduced through a tiny plastic tube inserted into the space surrounding the spinal cord and left in place throughout labour, so that the anaesthetic can be topped up about every two hours. If your partner has an epidural she will be confined to bed with an oxytocin drip (see page 59) to accelerate contractions, her blood pressure will be taken every twenty minutes and she will have a catheter to empty her bladder. The baby's heartbeat will be continuously monitored (see page 59). If your partner wants to push the baby out herself the anaesthetic should be allowed to wear off before the end of the first stage, so it is wise to ask for a vaginal examination to assess the progress of dilatation before she has a 'top up'. If more anaesthetic is given too near the point of full dilatation she will probably be unable to push so effectively and forceps will often have to be used. Epidurals are useful if labour is very painful, or prolonged or because the baby is in an unusual position, and can well be used instead of general anaesthesia if a planned Caesarean section is needed.

Pethidine. Some hospitals no longer give pethidine routinely during labour because it crosses the placenta, and if given to the mother late in labour has been shown to have an adverse effect upon the baby at birth. Large doses (150mg) of pethidine given close to delivery can cause a combination of side-effects in the baby, including sleepiness, unresponsiveness and feeding difficulties. However, where an epidural is unavailable or does not work, it may be helpful to the labouring woman as an analgesic if given in a small dose (50mg) early in labour when it will reduce anxiety and tension, but will not block all the pain. This smaller dose given more than four hours before the birth will cause minimal side-effects upon the baby. A baby born suffering from any of the unpleasant effects of pethidine, such as breathing difficulties, will be given an antidote (naloxone) by an injection into the umbilical cord.

The mother, too, may experience unpleasant side-effects from pethidine such as nausea, vomiting, feelings of unreality and drowsiness even with a smaller dose. If your partner accepts pethidine when labour is well established your job is to rouse her because the drug will make her feel drowsy and encourage her to breathe her way through contractions as she has practised.

Episiotomy

An episiotomy is a surgical cut made to enlarge the opening of the vagina just before the baby's head is born. Having an episiotomy is what many women fear most about labour, particularly as its unpleasant after-effects have been shown to last, often interfering with a couple's enjoyment of lovemaking, sometimes long after the birth. Most hospitals do not do an episiotomy routinely, however it is wise to make absolutely sure that everyone knows you do not want it done unnecessarily. Before the labour go with your partner and discuss with your hospital midwife what are their criteria for doing an episiotomy so you are both prepared. Giving birth in an upright position, in a secure and unhurried environment, with a midwife you trust, is probably the best guarantee against having an unnecessary episiotomy.

Delivery of the placenta

This is normally speeded up by an injection of Syntometrine which is a chemical derivative of a hormone that the woman's body naturally produces after giving birth. Made up of two different forms of oxytocin, one fast-acting and the other slow, it is usually injected into the woman's thigh as the anterior shoulder of the baby is being delivered. It is given prophylactically to make the empty uterus contract down sharply, which for certain 'high risk' women, i.e. those with a previous history of post-partum haemorrhage or placenta praevia, lessens the risk of bleeding as the uterus contracts strongly to deliver the placenta quickly. If your partner has no contra-indications and the hospital gives a choice she may decide to allow her body to proceed naturally; she will produce the necessary hormones, particularly if she breast feeds or you kiss and cuddle after the birth. But she must be prepared for the delivery of the placenta to take up to 1½ hours. However she can help the natural process by squatting or sitting on a bucket or bedpan so that gravity assists the placenta to come out. It is also important to ask the midwife to allow the umbilical cord to stop pulsing before cutting it as this has been shown, where everything is normal, to be better for mother and child. Sometimes after the birth a woman loses blood from a small tear in the vagina which cannot be attended to until after the placenta has been delivered. If the waiting time is prolonged and she continues to bleed, the midwife or doctor will want to give syntocinon intravenously to stop this as quickly as possible.

Time alone with your baby
Discover whether you and your partner can have half an hour or more alone with your baby after the birth, to share your feelings and have time to get to know your baby in private. Find out how long you can stay with your family after the birth (try to stay until well after your partner is established with the baby in the ward), and the extent of visiting hours. It is important for you to be together as much as you can. Your partner will need you there, particularly if the birth has been a difficult one. And *you* need time to get to know your baby by handling him as much as possible.

Rooming-in means that your partner can have the baby with her all the time. If this is what she wants it is important to find out what hospital policy is about rooming-in. Breastfeeding is difficult to establish if the baby is removed to a nursery and only brought out at intervals. Rooming-in is essential from your point of view so that you can hold your baby and begin looking after him from day one.

Making a birth plan

Once you begin to have a clear idea of the choices available to you your personal preferences will emerge. You and your partner might each like to make a birth plan in the form of a list, starting from the beginning of labour through until the end of your partner's stay in hospital. These are suggestions to start you off: you may want to adapt them to your own particular circumstances, and you will probably find that your own ideas change as the pregnancy progresses. Try to keep an open mind and be as flexible as possible – remember that anything can happen and probably will!

EXPECTANT FATHER'S LIST

1   Would you like to find out what facilities the hospital provides for fathers, e.g.: fathers' rest room, food, drink etc.?
2   Would you like to meet one of the midwives or doctors who will look after your partner before labour starts, to discuss your personal preferences?
3   Would you like to be advised of any routinely used medication and its effect on mother and baby before labour starts. Ditto any other routine hospital procedure?
4   Do you want to stay with your partner all through labour?
5   Would you like to see the labour ward more than once?
6   During labour, if all goes well, would you like time alone with your partner?
7   Would you like to have a friend to give you both support during your partner's labour?
8   Would you like to be given information about the progress of your partner's labour?
9   Do you want to be able to help your partner move around freely during her labour?
10 If all goes normally would you like to be able to help the midwife deliver your baby?
11 In normal circumstances would you like to be offered the chance to cut the umbilical cord?
12 Would you like to have time alone with your family after the birth? How much time would seem appropriate?
13 If your baby has to leave the labour room for any reason would you like to go with him/her?
14 If your partner has to have an emergency Caesarean section would you like to stay with her to welcome your baby immediately?
15 Would you like to be sure that you could stay with your partner for as long as you both wished after the birth?
16 Is there any part of the labour that you would prefer not to participate in?

EXPECTANT MOTHER'S LIST

1   Would she like you to be with her all through her labour?
2   Would she like to be free to move around as much as she wants to?

3 Would she prefer not to be continuously monitored unless there is a medical reason and to have the choice between an internal or external monitor or the midwife to listen with a fetal stethoscope?

4 Would she like to meet the midwife or doctor who will care for her in labour so that she can discuss her wishes and make practical arrangements beforehand?

5 If she does not feel happy with the midwife assigned to her in labour, would she like to be able to ask for a different midwife to assist her?

6 Would she like to be able to choose whether she has a student doctor with her?

7 If her labour is normal, would she like to have periods when you are both left alone?

8 Would she prefer not to be offered any medication, but to request help if she needs it?

9 Would she like to be informed beforehand if any intervention becomes necessary, and given time to discuss it with you if possible?

10 Is she anxious *not* to have a routine episiotomy? If one is thought necessary, would she like to try a more upright position before the final decision is made? (see page 68).

11 If she is planning to stand, squat or kneel to deliver the baby, would she prefer to have a midwife who has previous experience of delivering women in 'alternative' positions?

12 Would she like to discuss whether she will accept Syntonetrine or not? (see page 68).

13 If stitching is necessary, would she prefer to choose who does it?

If, after reading these two lists there are words or procedures which are unclear, or unknown to you, please seek out the relevant information without delay, by reading or asking for an appointment with your midwife or doctor. (See Further reading, page 213.)

RUNNING INTO DIFFICULTIES

Once you have made your birth plan, the next step is to discuss your preferences with your hospital to find out what is possible. In a good antenatal clinic, the midwives will make themselves available to help you by answering your questions and reassuring you on any problems. If either of you is dissatisfied with the answers you receive, or feel that your needs are not catered for in the routine procedure of the hospital, then you might both ask to see your consultant. If you do not understand the answers he gives, or do not like what you hear, try asking again – still calmly – until you are entirely clear. If the weight of medical science is used against you, then politely request the reference of the research data so that you can look it up for yourself. Do not get aggressive or raise your voice, but stick to your question or request while reiterating your appreciation of the hospital's concern for yourselves and your baby. (If what you want is dangerous in any way, you will be the first to abandon the idea; nobody cares about a baby's safety more than the parents.)

BEING A MEDIATOR

Sometimes parents find a hospital refuses to meet their needs for reasons best known to itself. If this should happen your partner may find it too difficult or too upsetting to deal with the problem herself and fear a confrontation might jeopardize her or her baby's future treatment in the hospital. As the expectant father, you are the ideal person to step between the two sides and find a compromise to satisfy everyone.

When you approach the hospital, base your strategy on the assumption that the hospital is there to help you. If you can keep an open mind and remain flexible, what seems like a life and death situation during the pregnancy may suddenly evaporate in labour, as if by magic. Couples frequently focus on one particular problem or fear, and if you do not remain flexible it can take you over and become a peg on which to hang all your anxieties about giving birth and becoming a parent. Of course you should try and arrange what you want for your baby's birth, while being aware that some frustration is inevitable within present hospital systems. Also bear in mind that although labour is very important, it is still only a tiny fraction of the larger whole of becoming a parent.

If you reach a total deadlock, you can decide to opt out of the hospital system altogether and try for a home birth (see page 52) or, less drastically, you can try to find a more sympathetic consultant. Finally, you can consider changing hospitals, writing to your consultant to explain your reasons and sending a copy to the Board of Hospital Management and your GP if this is appropriate. Much better, though, is to avoid this upheaval by persuading your doctor or consultant to support you in organizing the birth to suit both you and the hospital. When labour starts there should be no loose ends or unsettled arguments; everyone should be free of conflict to be able to give their total attention and care to the woman in labour.

EMOTIONAL PREPARATION FOR THE EXPECTANT FATHER

For many men pregnancy is a moving bus which they only decide to catch at the last minute. The seemingly endless nine months of gestation enables a hesitant father to postpone conscious preparation or leave it to his partner. One father expressed his feelings like this. 'Pregnancy was happening to her, not to me. I wanted everything to be normal, the same as before. I don't like it when Phyl is ill, in fact she knows I'm no good at being sympathetic and all that. As for the baby, well, I couldn't think about me being a father. How can you know what it will be like until the baby's here? It only really hit me on the way to the hospital, when Phyl was already in labour, "This is it, in a few hours I'm going to be a father."'

For a man who has not troubled to prepare himself, this sudden confrontation with change can be powerfully disturbing. Possibly for the first time in his adult life someone else has the right to demand first place. The man who has not participated very much in the pregnancy and birth, or done any of his own emotional 'homework', runs the risk of finding these demands overwhelming.

Research by Fein in the United States in the 1970s showed that men adapted better to pregnancy and found the transition to fatherhood easier to negotiate if they had had the opportunity to examine their own feelings, share their own concerns and involve themselves in the process of pregnancy and childbirth.

The sifting and talking about your feelings that is an essential undertaking for all expectant couples, is one that many men find a difficult and bewildering part of their preparation for parenthood. Communication has rarely been thought of as an important life-skill for men. But several recent studies confirm my own experience in antenatal teaching that, given the opportunity, expectant fathers welcome the chance to express themselves. However, vague encouragement to discover your feelings may make you feel uneasy or reluctant. So what I suggest is that you concentrate on some reasonably specific questions to set the ball rolling and then continue the process with your partner at your own pace.

Coping with pain

To some extent we all fear the unknown and an interesting and highly revealing exercise for expectant fathers is to discover their visual images of a woman in labour. Try to imagine this scene, the woman's position, attitude; the kind of sounds she is making. When I ask couples to do this exercise in an antenatal class it helps them to realize what they are bringing with them into the labour room as their learned perception of childbirth. Sadly the most frequent image is of a woman alone lying down in hospital and crying out in pain.

These preconceptions of childbirth need to be set against reality, or they will influence your whole approach to the birth and your capacity to enjoy what really does happen. If you believe, for example, that childbirth is painful, bloody, undignified and dangerous, however often you are told of the psychological and physiological benefits for mother and baby of a drug-free, active birth, you will find it hard to stick to your new approach when labour gets difficult, or to contemplate the birth of your baby with anything less than apprehension. And if you believe women lie down in labour, when you see your partner climbing into bed, it will not be your automatic response to help her up and encourage her to move around. (See practical suggestions for positions for labour and birth in the next chapter.)

FEELINGS ABOUT PAIN

First consider *your* attitude to pain. Your ideas about coping with pain can be an influential factor, not only for your partner but for the medical team as well. Everyone knows that pain is magnified by fear; diminished by not fighting it, and made bearable by the supportive presence of someone in whom one feels confidence. The pain of childbirth is mysterious, individual women feel it in varying intensity and even in different parts of their body. It is rhythmic, coming in waves of increasing strength, rising to a peak of intensity then falling away again. It is self regulating; given the right circumstances, the woman's body will itself produce natural pain killers (endorphins) which can even induce in her a state of euphoria. It is temporary; between each contraction the woman feels quite normal, and minutes after a long and difficult labour, the baby safe in her arms, many a woman will talk of the next time quite calmly! You meanwhile, may still be reeling, exhausted, and incapable of imagining ever going through all that again.

Fear is contagious. If you are frightened by the sights and sounds of your partner's instinctive reactions to her body's demands, then your fear will inhibit her. Many women are anxious that if they 'let go' during labour, the man will be shocked or deeply upset. And because childbirth is so powerful, the woman fears she will be unable to support or comfort the man who may be overwhelmed by the experience. It is very hard to see someone you love in pain; especially if they become touchingly dependent, and plead with you to stop it in some way. You may feel you have to 'do' something – anything, to take the pain away. This father expressed it so well when he said, 'During this period Jo started pushing because of pressure on her rectum. The midwife said not to and taught her how to breathe lightly. I explained she couldn't help it – couldn't stop. It got worse, and Jo was saying "I can't do it" and "I don't want any more, I want to go home, Peter." I agreed and said, "Yes, go home soon." I started to cry and had a huge lump in my throat, particularly when Jo talked to me directly by name. I was very emotional – lots of tissues!'

KEEPING CALM

If you can keep calm and unafraid it reassures the medical staff who will look to you to interpret how the woman is coping. 'Ah yes,' you say reassuringly to an enquiring midwife who has watched your partner crawl round the room, rocking her pelvis and moaning like a storm, 'we've practised it all at home!' Medical staff often resort to drugs, not because the woman needs, or requests that kind of 'support', but rather because of their own training, and distrust of the woman's capacity to cope naturally with pain compels them to suppress what they assume is intolerable. In any other circumstance pain is a danger signal – in labour it is more like the herald, sounding the alarm from the battlements, at the approach of a very important person!

WHAT A LABOUR COMPANION CAN DO TO REDUCE PAIN
DURING LABOUR

Dealing with pain is one of the biggest challenges facing a couple hoping to avoid medication during labour. Naturally, as labour companion you will want to be as helpful as possible so I suggest we consider some practical methods of giving support which will significantly reduce the pain experienced by the labouring woman. Try to have an open mind about pain in childbirth. Some fortunate women do not experience intolerable pain – on the contrary they find it exciting, elating and satisfying. And there is no way of predicting how a woman will experience childbirth until she is having the baby.

Depending upon the relationship, the emphasis the man puts upon being companion or protector will vary from couple to couple according to the circumstances. During labour a woman needs companionship on a continual basis with the knowledge that she can ask for protection if and when she feels the need. Most men feel confident about feeling protective towards their partners – they frequently feel very unconfident about what taking on that role might mean during labour in a hospital setting. The feared confrontation of 'experts, who must know best' is often cited by men as a reason for not wanting to question hospital policy before or during labour. But however much you may feel daunted by the prospect it is very important to find the confidence to protect your partner should the need arise.

Pain is diminished by feeling trust in those people around who are offering support. We have all had the experience of feeling vulnerable and powerless, with a longing for someone strong to recognize our feelings and voice our needs if we cannot. During labour it is essential for the woman to feel that she can rely upon you to listen, to join with her in accepting her needs – whatever they might be. Then, and this may be the difficult part for many, to speak up for her to those around when she may not be in a position to do so herself. A labour companion may have to be assertive on behalf of the woman – it is essential that she can rely upon this support. If you can gain her confidence and trust this will inevitably reduce the stress and the pain associated with childbirth.

One thing is certain. Your calm, supportive presence will reduce the pain by as much as 30 per cent. But to be calm you must know what the normal process of birth entails; there will be differences between a home or hospital birth. You should also know what to expect if problems arise. The place of birth should be familiar to you and the medical team who will assist you and your partner should also be known to you. Fortified by knowledge and familiar with the general aims your partner has for her labour you can now look at your very particular role.

In practical terms this means being a willing, patient caregiver: fetching iced water, or ice chips to suck between contractions; arranging and frequently re-arranging furniture, pillows, covers etc. as the woman gets hot or cold and needs to change her position to relieve the pain; quietly observing the woman, and then trying to anticipate her needs, e.g.: if her shoulders look tight and tense then getting a hot-water bottle, or a flannel wrung out in hot or cold water to put on her shoulders, or doing some gentle massage to relieve the ache. Massage reduces tension and pain and is another useful skill for you to have (see Further reading, page 213).

It is important that you know the positions that are most helpful to reduce pain and facilitate the progress of labour. During the first stage the woman should not lie on her back but rather be upright, spine tilted slightly forward, legs apart. But because every woman is different it is vital that you know which positions your partner favours to help her move around during labour. When contractions get painful, often a change of position and/or place will bring relief. And whenever the going gets tough suggest a bath or a shower: this is both distracting and soothing.

At the second stage, when your partner begins to feel the urge to 'push' it is vital that you know how to support her then, and during the actual birth of your baby. (See labour positions, pages 97–99.)

Verbal encouragement and reassurance is another way of reducing pain. By expressing confidence in your partner's strength to cope with her body's demands, and offering yourself as a source of energy for her to draw upon you will enable her to cope better. Tell her frequently that she is doing well, that you care for her, that her baby will soon be born.... You will know what to say and how to say it so that your partner feels cherished and yet free to explore her own strengths. By your confidence and willingness to let the natural process take its own course, your belief in her strength to cope with her body's demands will enable her to draw on your energy and so replenish her own.

If the pain is too much and your partner is becoming exhausted and overwrought by the experience, then outside help should be offered to her. Naturally, before labour starts you will have discussed which methods of pain relief are available. Your role is never to prevent your partner's access to pain relief if and when she asks for it. If she decides, for example, to accept an epidural then your role should be supportive, not disappointed or critical. Listen carefully to what your partner tells you she is feeling. Encourage her to seek relief when she needs it and try to discourage her from the attitude which drives her to feel that 'success' equals no medication, and 'failure' equals having an epidural or other medication.

Sometimes when your partner has decided to have an epidural there is an unavoidable delay, perhaps for up to half an hour before the anaesthetist arrives. This can be very distressing for you both – the woman because she feels at the end of her tether with pain and exhaustion, and you because you long to be able to do something, anything to make the pain stop. In spite of your own anguish it is vitally important that you remain calm and optimistic. Try to encourage your partner, try massage, or firm holding, ask for the Entonox (gas and air) and help your partner change her position which might ease her distress. While you are thinking about possible delays, bear in mind that epidurals do not always work for every woman. Occasionally the pain is not eliminated, or perhaps only on one side of the woman's body. This too can be very distressing, particularly if at the back of her mind the woman was relying on an epidural for complete pain relief. That is why it is essential to have alternative ways to deal with pain available to you – breathing and relaxation methods, TENS, pethidine etc.

Make no mistake about it, being a labour companion is hard work, you will almost certainly be physically exhausted and emotionally drained by some aspects of the labour. One of the hardest things for many fathers is the sight of their partners in great pain. Frequently there is not very much you, or anyone else can do to stop it completely, without the risk of problematic side effects. But however much you may feel helpless or impotent to help your partner, please remember that the pain would be much worse if you were not there. As it is, many women have reported that even when their labours were far from what had been planned and ended up very hi-tech, their partner's presence turned a medical procedure into a moving and satisfyingly human event.

FEELING SQUEAMISH

If pain is the first great fear men have concerning childbirth, the second – for many men – is the sight of blood. Your baby may be blood-smeared at birth, and the delivery of the placenta will bring more blood with it, but this is absolutely normal. The blood on the baby comes from an abrasion or tear to the mother and it always looks copious because it is mixed with amniotic fluid. Involved with the worries about seeing blood are the more intense and often unspoken anxieties about seeing the baby emerge from their woman's genitals. That area of a woman's body is normally associated with lovemaking. Many men fear that seeing the birth might have a negative effect upon their sex life – that they will be so revolted or frightened that they will become impotent or reluctant to make love for fear of damaging their partner. Although these fears are quite common many men never voice their feelings. But honesty is the best policy – you know yourself best and you should not feel ashamed of your fears or obliged to look at something you are reluctant about. If you prefer not to watch the baby emerging from your partner's body there is no need. Instead put your face close to your partner's, and hold her in your arms during the delivery. Most men, even those who are squeamish, find they can cope because the excitement of the birth carries them over their anxieties. Fathers most often report that in any case the reality of birth is not as horrifying as they had feared but rather an intensely moving, though dramatic event.

After the birth a woman frequently has a few perineal stitches. It might be because of a small tear inside the birth canal, or perhaps from an episiotomy (a cut made by the doctor to enlarge the opening of the vagina). It is worth discussing whether stitches are essential as some women prefer to allow a small tear to heal by itself. If your partner has a forceps delivery with an episiotomy she will probably require stitches.

Some men have found the sight of their partner's perineum being stitched disturbing and even traumatic. One father described it as 'quite awful, like the aftermath of a car crash'. It is quite unnecessary for you to look at this procedure, and is possibly better if you avoid it. Sit down at the head end beside your partner and hold your baby until it is all over. Alternatively you could leave the room. Of course your partner will not be in any pain and will probably be talking excitedly throughout.

CLARIFYING YOUR FEELINGS

Because having a baby is so full of unknown possibilities it is a good idea to explore those aspects which *are* under your control – the kind of support you feel able to give. It is important to talk about this with your partner too: you may each have quite different ideas about the role you expect the other to take. Finding your ideas match, or accepting a mis-match and discussing a compromise, is all part of preparation for parenthood and will help you avoid misunderstandings and disappointments. As a starting point you might both find it helpful to make a specific list of your thoughts and feelings as a father-to-be, for example:

> As a labour companion, I want to care for you, look after all your needs, be actively involved in every stage.
> I want you to rely on me – I'll deal with the practical arrangements, especially the midwife or doctor.
> I want to feel we share everything as much as possible. I want to know what you feel about everything.
> I can't do more than be with you when you're in labour. I want you to make the decisions about the birth – it's your birth.
> I can't promise to stay all through the labour with you. I will come back as soon as the baby is born. I'll help you find a replacement supporter.
> I want to be free to enjoy my own experience of labour. I would prefer to have another person with us from whom you can get support as well as me.

Similarly, a future mother's list might include some of these thoughts:

> When I am in labour I want you to remember suitable positions for me to take up during contractions, in case I forget.
> I want you to be strong, I will need to lean on you if things start getting difficult and I feel like giving up.
> I want you to protect me from anyone who might disrupt my confidence, or make me anxious.
> I don't want you to interfere – just be there and leave it all to me.
> I want you to help me plan my labour, but if I change my mind I also want you to support me and not make me feel guilty.
> I want you to look after me, be 'mother' to me and comfort me. Get me drinks, massage my back, tell me I'm great!
> I don't know if I want you to be with me all the time. I may want to be alone with the midwife when I'm actually giving birth.

Once you have both clarified your thoughts find time to discuss your feelings together. It is very important that you both go into labour feeling as secure as possible. The woman in labour needs to be able to rely upon her companions to help her in whatever way she may need. But you may discover that you have certain reservations about the depth or scope of the support you feel happy to provide. If this causes any difficulties then you might both like to consider finding a third person to fill the gap. Check with your hospital that a third person will be allowed into the labour room and choose someone who you both feel comfortable with.

You may find that this sifting and talking about your feelings which is an essential undertaking for all expectant fathers is both difficult and bewildering. But it is only by thinking about yourself, deciding, with your partner, what you want out of the experience of childbirth, that you will allow the full emotional experience to affect you. You don't have to be Superman, just aim to be more truly yourself.

Preparing to breastfeed

When I am working with couples in antenatal classes and the topic of breastfeeding is mentioned, most men react positively. Everyone knows that breast milk is the best for the baby. It not only provides the essential antibodies which protect the baby from catching infections, but it is nutritionally ideally balanced for human babies. Cows' milk is ideal for baby cows and although it can be fed to humans too it is not without drawbacks. For example, bones develop differently if a baby is fed cows' milk. And then all babies benefit and enjoy the comfort and security that sensitive and joyful breastfeeding provides.

Fathers see it as the natural way to feed a baby. But they feel, too, that the decision to breastfeed must be the woman's — that there is not much that they personally can contribute, although once the baby is there they quickly realize it is not quite that simple.

During her pregnancy every woman thinks about how she will feed her baby. Her thoughts and fantasies will most strongly reflect her deepest feelings about her own body. Whether she was breastfed herself, whether most of her friends breastfeed, if she plans to return to work and when, will all influence her decision. But overall it has been shown that it is *your* attitude — your fantasies and feelings, e.g. whether you feel able to share her breasts with the baby and not feel excluded — that will be the single most influential factor in helping her make the decision and then to carry it out.

This father's feelings would have made a positive contribution to the mother and baby's experience of breastfeeding. 'It was very special for me to be with Viv and Suki while she was being fed. Specially in the night when we'd all be in bed together and I was close to them. All those little noises of sucking and breathing. I felt very proud of Viv. Her breasts seem so big and how it all worked seemed so amazing. I felt like putting my arms around them both, very protective. At times I wished I could have that special contact with Suki. I told myself it would come, later, not quite the same though. When she cried I did feel frustrated – even angry sometimes, all she wanted was the breast – I was useless.'

MALE CONCERNS ABOUT BREASTFEEDING

Every expectant father has some concerns about how breastfeeding might affect his relationship with his partner. After all, from one day to the next you will have to share your partner with another very demanding person – your baby. In fact some men have told me that 'share' was the wrong word, to them it felt more like a total take-over, they felt abandoned. If you feel like this it is important to be open and discuss it with your partner, who may be quite unaware of your sadness and feelings of being excluded. Then the best way to accommodate your discomfort is to recognize the temporary nature of the situation and take positive action by getting involved right away in the daily care of your baby. Even if your partner is breastfeeding there are still lots of ways you can develop your special relationship with your baby; after all, eating is only part of his day. Some couples want the father to share the feeding too, which can be done if the mother expresses milk (see Further reading, page 213) so that the father can give a bottle feed. Or your contribution can be changing the nappy and settling the baby down after a feed. Rocking, singing and just holding the baby relaxing together build up your special relationship and relieve your partner of having the whole responsibility.

Even those men who are in favour of breastfeeding have concerns about its possible effects on the woman's body. It may be reassuring for you both to know that it is not breastfeeding that changes the shape of a woman's breasts, but pregnancy. In fact, breastfeeding helps a woman's body get back to normal after giving birth, and may even help her lose excess weight. Meanwhile, offering to look after the baby while your partner goes to a good exercise class is a more positive way of helping her recover her figure than making jokes or teasing her about something which is not under her control for the time being.

Some expectant fathers understand that breastfeeding is good for the baby but are not sure how they will react until the baby has been born. Not everyone finds they enjoy it. 'Well frankly it was not too good. It gradually dawned on me that I didn't like it too much. I found I'd go into another room when Anne was feeding Tom. I began to get irritated with all the time it took. One day when he was about six weeks old I said something like, "Isn't it time that baby was put on a bottle, he's had his share?" Anne's face, well she looked amazed. I suppose I hadn't said very much before that, it just burst out, all of a sudden!'

It can happen that over a period of time a father becomes really disturbed and unhappy about his partner breastfeeding. This may be a painful and difficult problem to resolve, especially if the woman is enjoying breastfeeding her baby. But if talking about the problem fails to find a compromise solution then remember there are alternative ways to feed the baby. Combining breast feeds with bottle feeding may relieve the situation, but each couple has to make the decision best suited to themselves. In the end it is more important for a baby to have parents who are united and happy than to be breastfed. Sometimes a man will have been shocked by seeing a mother openly feeding her baby in public and know this is not something he wants his partner to do. It is perfectly reasonable to discuss this and work out a solution together. Breastfeeding can be very discreet; apart from the odd 'slurping' noise from the baby it is possible to feed in public without anyone seeing anything.

DEMAND FEEDING

Fathers are often worried that demand feeding – feeding the baby when she wants food and not according to the clock – will lead to the baby becoming 'spoiled'. This usually indicates a more generalized worry that the baby may take over and totally dominate the parents's lives. But a baby under three months *is* very demanding and at that stage in her development it is perfectly normal. Feeding a baby on demand is the only sensible way to feed; routines are a long-term aim and not a short-term expectation.

Those babies who are comforted and fed when *they* ask for it will soon settle into a secure understanding that you can be relied upon to respond and to be there when needed. This lays the foundations for a secure, unspoiled child who will carry this confidence into adult life. Withholding a feed until an appointed hour will produce a miserable and fretful baby who may be too upset and tired to feed and be harder to live with in the long run.

A FATHER'S ROLE IN BREASTFEEDING

Even if your partner is generally enthusiastic about breastfeeding she too may have some reservations. She may worry that she will not be successful, or feel protective about her body – particularly her breasts – and wonder if you will continue to find her sexually attractive if she breastfeeds. You may find it natural to give your partner the support she needs to enjoy breastfeeding or you may have to make a conscious effort to overcome your own reservations before you can do this. But if you can it will inevitably bring you closer and benefit your relationship in the long run. This father told me his thoughts: 'I saw Cathy's enjoyment of breastfeeding as hers – it was all happening to her, her body and the baby in their special world in a way. It seemed to be intense and obviously giving pleasure to them both. I did feel outside the "magic circle", any man will if he gets close to it, I think. But I know she needed me to share her pleasure and I got some enjoyment from that.'

HELPING YOUR PARTNER PREPARE TO BREASTFEED

If you and your partner both want her to breastfeed your baby, you can help her prepare during pregnancy. A woman's experiences of breastfeeding are inextricably entwined with her sexual self image. The hormonal changes and the emotional responses which naturally occur during childbirth, breastfeeding and lovemaking are all inter-related. If you caress and enjoy your partner's breasts during lovemaking this will increase her positive self image. It will help her, too, if you can express your encouragement and confidence in her capacity to breastfeed. Some women worry that they lack 'maternal' feeling – other people's babies just do not 'turn them on'. Usually after giving birth they are pleasantly surprised by the gradual swell of motherliness which comes in response to their own baby. If your partner needs reassurance that she is capable of motherly feelings, it may be a positive contribution if you can help her recognize that she probably *has* experienced them though in an entirely different context. In essence they are the same as the warm loving glow that many women feel after good lovemaking. If she enjoys holding you, enfolding and caressing your body, expressing her great tenderness, she will go on to feel the same emotions towards her baby. Most couples relish this aspect of their sexual relationship without connecting these same feelings with motherliness. And indeed, some couples may worry about the blurred edges of these overlapping experiences and try to compartmentalize them into what 'should' and 'should not' be in the sexual department. But if you can reassure each other that there is nothing bad or shameful about any spontaneous expression of this whole range of feelings, then you will both feel able to relax and enjoy whatever happens, in whatever context.

You can help prepare your partner's breasts for breastfeeding, too, by gently sucking the nipples. This is not only sexually exciting but it also prepares your partner for when the baby will suck usually with much greater determination. Try rolling each nipple gently between your thumb and first finger to help your partner get used to being touched and to ensure the nipple stands up erectly so the baby will be able to 'latch' on satisfactorily. Women are usually told to massage their breasts and to prepare their nipples in this way themselves – but it is much more fun if you do it together!

Chapter 5

Exercise and relaxation

A woman who wishes to avoid pain relieving drugs in labour has to find alternative ways to deal with the problem of pain, stress and fatigue. With your support she can build an attitude of self reliance to enable her to cope with labour in her own way. However it is important for you both to remember that nothing will absolutely guarantee that she will succeed – childbirth is always unpredictable and the need to remain flexible and open to medication if necessary will always remain.

What follows is not an exercise programme – rather some positions you and your partner can try together which will heighten awareness of the body's own mechanism to breathe, and relax while coping with unusual sensations which may be painful. By gradually increasing the time she maintains each stretch position she will learn to release into it and breathe calmly through it – just as she will to cope with contractions during labour. With practice she will find it possible to relax tension areas of her body (shoulders, mouth, pelvic floor) while holding the stretch. These exercises also improve circulation and pelvic floor awareness; learning to relax and breathe 'open' these muscles prepares her for the second stage of labour, giving her the confidence to allow her body to open up for the birth of the baby.

If you are planning to support your partner through her labour, then you should find time on a regular basis to help her practise these exercises. They will help establish mutual trust and give you valuable insight into how she likes to move, breathe and relax. Together you can discuss which positions could be comfortably adapted for use during labour. And if you intend to support your partner in a semi-squatting, kneeling or standing position during the delivery you may need to strengthen your legs and back. Most men, even if they are physically strong and fit, carry unnecessary tension in their bodies. Working as a couple on simple stretching exercises is an excellent way to undo some of this tension and also gives you the opportunity to begin thinking and planning for the approaching birth.

Because one of the purposes of these exercises is to enable you both to tune into your body's signals, I suggest you always begin with a short 5-minute session of relaxation. This allows you time to clear your mind of other concerns and focus your concentration. Then when you have finished the exercises repeat the relaxation routine giving yourselves at least 15 minutes.

Relaxation practice for the couple

Most people find it easier to relax if they hear a comforting voice giving them instructions. If you can practise regularly with your partner you will quickly adapt and personalize these suggestions according to your own taste. Take it in turns, always speak very slowly and not too loudly. Make sure you feel calm and pause for a few seconds between instructions as suggested here. If your partner lies on the floor always give her plenty of cushions to support her head and shoulders. Initially, a warm, quiet room is helpful, later when you become more skilled you should both be able to relax your body and disconnect your mind from surrounding noise and irritations whenever and wherever you feel the need. Because there are different approaches to relaxation, I suggest you try out as many as possible to find the one you prefer and then adapt it to your personal lifestyle (see Further reading, page 213). The following is one example.

RELAX YOUR BODY

Lie down as shown and begin by adjusting your body. Close your eyes and count very slowly down from 10 to 1 while listening to my words. Then as you take several slow, deep breaths, lower your chin slightly, roll your head from side to side, allowing it to stop where it feels comfortably supported . . . Ease your shoulders down away from your ears. . . . Push your elbows away from your body a little . . . Turn your palms to face the ceiling, or rest your hands lightly on your lower abdomen. . . . Feel the length of your spine – and your pelvis settling down on to the support . . . When you are ready, slide your feet together along the floor until your thighs are supported on the cushion . . . Now allow your feet to roll outwards and feel the length of your body is completely supported. (When you are skilled at relaxation these adjustments will only take a few seconds. While you are learning always give yourself plenty of time and really be aware of how each part of your body feels as it starts to relax.)

RELAX YOUR MIND

Most people can quickly learn how to begin the process of relaxing their muscles – learning how to concentrate in order to quiet their buzzing thoughts, which is the only way to achieve complete relaxation, is much harder. Following on from the instructions above, try this:

'Gently close your eyes . . . lower your chin and allow your lips to part slightly as if you were about to smile . . . feel your tongue low in your mouth behind the bottom teeth . . . become aware of your breathing . . . now make a sighing noise as you breathe *out* – slowly – completely empty yourself of air – then allow the *in* breath to take care of itself . . . allow your awareness to sink inwards . . . now repeat the word *calm* in your head every time you breathe *out* . . . don't bother to give it any meaning – just as a sound in your head, like a distant bell . . . and with every breath that you sigh out, your body and mind will become more and more *calm* . . . after a while just allow the sound *calm* to fade away . . . now go into the deepest and most relaxed state you have ever experienced . . .'.

Allow your partner to rest without disturbance for as long as you had agreed before starting. Lie down and relax yourself, or sit quietly. When it is time to continue, ask her to take a few, deep breaths to energize herself, stretch and open her eyes and feel fit and well. . . . She should then bend her knees, roll on her side and sit up. This may be a good time to exchange any thoughts or feelings that surfaced while you were both relaxing.

Many methods like this can be helpful during childbirth if you or your partner needs to calm down. Also, and most importantly, when labour starts every woman has to develop the capacity to withdraw into herself and concentrate exclusively upon her body's signals. Try setting aside a short time every day or several times a week to help each other to practise these new skills. As an expectant father you too have stresses to cope with now and later when you are 'in labour' with your partner. Then it is essential that you can remain calm and allow the process to take its own course without feeling compelled to interfere.

First stretch exercise to release tension

This stretch prepares the woman's body for labour as it loosens the hips and groin and stretches the inner thigh muscles. If you find it difficult to keep your spine straight try sitting against a wall for support. Either rest your hands on your ankles or as shown. Remember to lengthen your spine up, relax your shoulders down and open your chest to facilitate your breathing.

When you are both ready, sit down in position No. 1. You may find this 'opening up' stretch quite difficult because of tightness in the upper, inside thighs. If you dislike this sensation at first try not to resist by tensing up in other parts of your body. However painful it is initially try not to reject the experience, rather try and observe your reactions and learn from them. You will find if you can persevere, that in time you will feel more positive, particularly if you can learn to relax into the stretch – rather than fighting it. In the beginning only stay in each stretch position for a short time. Try not to be impatient, but gradually aim to hold it for one and a half minutes which is the time of a good contraction.

When your partner tries a position, encourage her to focus on the sensations in her body, suggest she breathes freely, responding to her body's signals, just as she will do when her contractions begin. Remind her to relax her mouth and to check that there is no tension creeping in anywhere else in her body. It may help if you massage up the length of her spine, or just rest one hand on her back, lower pelvis and the other on her forehead. Observe her breathing and notice if she holds her breath or puffs out too hard – in fact become aware of any variation in her normal breathing. Leave her free to experiment and discover her own rhythms and preferences – your role is that of an observer and a supporter, you should not interfere unless she asks you to. Always take it in turns to try out these positions. It is important that you learn through direct experience what your partner is trying to achieve. Your response is pertinent and can often provide insight into a particular problem of posture or breathing.

In the beginning when you are working together you can take it in turns to read these instructions out loud. Always pause between sentences to give her time to respond to each new sensation. Never force yourself or your partner into a position – aim to develop a finely tuned respect for your body and what it is 'saying' to you and remember that every day feels different.

Instructions to increase body awareness

'Close your eyes if it helps you concentrate better. Focus your attention on the pelvic area, including your baby of course! Rest your hands lightly on your abdomen, just above the pubic bone. Allow your breath to flow gently *out* from that point – now as your body fills with air, without forcing, or straining, appreciate the sensation, now continue to breathe freely without strain. As the stretch builds up put your concentration into relaxing your mouth, pelvic floor and those muscles where you feel the stretch most intensely. Release towards the stretch, don't bounce, or force your inner thigh muscles down – rather try and relax from your pelvic floor outwards. Remember there is a sympathetic relationship between the area round your mouth and your pelvic floor – notably the vagina. Try to soften your lips, and as the stretch continues to intensify it may help your concentration if you breathe more rhythmically and try to visualize those muscles that are stretching. For example, see the muscular folds of the pelvic floor like a field of ripe corn, swaying gently in the breeze – softly parting, relaxing as you breathe them open.' Images have to be appropriate to the individual, always try and find your own because they will be much more powerful.

If your partner finds visualization easy it can be used as a powerful aid to help her cope positively with pain during labour. But this technique has to be practised over a period of time to be really effective (see Visualization, page 104).

Move away from the wall and support yourself with your arms if necessary. Your partner kneels in front as shown with his hands supporting your knees. Try relaxing your legs apart, allowing them to drop into the supporting hands. Do not bounce, or force your legs – wait patiently, breathe calmly and feel yourself opening up.

Next take it in turns to try this idea. One of you sit in position No. 1 again, perhaps with the support of a wall or with hands behind on the floor. The helper kneels in front and gently supports your knees in their hands. Now try again to breathe rhythmically and relax from the pelvic floor outwards and allow your knees to sink into the support of the hands. You will need another two minutes or more to experience this pleasant feeling of letting go. Always think of the out breath as a releasing breath, but never force your breathing – allow your body to regulate the pace and flow quite spontaneously and naturally. This is of course true for labour as in any other situation, the body just takes over if we can allow it to do so.

SECOND STRETCH POSITION

Kneel down, your knees wide apart and your toes pointing towards each other about six inches apart. Settle your pelvis down between your feet onto the floor. Slowly lean forward, and keeping your spine straight slide your hands, arms straight, along the floor until your forehead rests on the floor. Try and keep your back straight and your pelvis touching your feet. As you loosen up this will become easier. (When the baby gets bigger fold your arms one on top of the other and rest your head on them.)

Always do this when you are warm and and relaxed. This position (see above) will give you the same opening-up feelings as No. 1 but you have the added weight of your body pressing you down. Many men find it very difficult to hold for more than a few seconds at first, but you can gradually increase the time. *You* can also experiment by holding your breath to see the difference it makes to your perception of pain. (Your partner should never do this, as holding her breath is not good for maintaining the essential oxygen supply to the baby.) As the pain of the stretch begins to build up hold your breath, go on holding it until you have to breathe again. Notice how the pain felt worse during that time and now when you breathe calmly, towards the stretch, releasing rather than fighting the pain becomes less intense – even bearable. When you start to relax into this position, ask your partner to massage the length of your spine with smooth firm strokes. Do the same for her in this position.

This position is good for the woman to practise too, but she must breathe and release her pelvic floor all the time. (When the baby gets bigger she may prefer to do it in a sitting position and stretch her hands up the wall instead of along the floor.) With practice, this stretch becomes almost comfortable as you learn to relax into it. Start gradually and then hold it for a little longer each time, until you can do so for at least two minutes. Check every time you do this that you have no tension in your neck and shoulders.

On the next pages are some further ideas for exercises to do together or for you to do to strengthen back and leg muscles, which are particularly called into use as a labour companion.

Labour positions

A woman in labour will probably want to try many different positions before she finds one that is 'right' for her, but it is a good idea to try some out beforehand, so that you will know preferences, what she is trying to achieve and what you can do to help.

ALL FOURS

'All Fours' is not difficult or uncomfortable, but because it is a good position for labour – in the first stage if your partner has any backache or in the second stage to give birth – it is a good idea to try it. Some women feel instinctively happy on all fours and know immediately that is a position they will use in labour, either on the bed or the floor. Others have reservations which can be overcome if they think it through. Get your partner to kneel down with her knees hip-width apart. She then leans forward on to all fours (arms shoulder-width apart) making sure knees and hands are in a straight line. Never make sudden jerky movements. Say things like: 'Now gently sway backwards and forwards and keeping your back level shift your weight around in a circle, too . . . Rock your pelvis, slowly from side to side, and in a circle and imagine how it will feel to do this when you are in labour . . . Relax your pelvic floor, allow your breathing to flow naturally and enjoy the feeling of looseness and openness in this position.'

Afterwards, if either of you felt uncomfortable or inhibited, discuss these feelings and try to discover why, and if anything could help.

This position stretches the groin and inside thighs but it also strengthens the muscles at the front of the thighs. Sit down, move your legs an equal distance apart until you feel a stretch on the inside thighs. Keep your knees facing directly up, and flex your feet, pushing away with the heels until you feel the top of your thighs tightening and the back of your legs stretching. Your partner does the same facing you. If one person is looser than the other, do not force your legs apart, put your feet inside near the ankles, or wherever it feels comfortable. Lengthen your spine upwards from the point of contact on the floor, relax your shoulders down and hold each other's hands. Breathe rhythmically and calmly throughout, do not hold this position too long in the beginning if your muscles are very tight. If it is easy take turns to move forward from the hip, keeping your spine straight all the time as it is important never to press down on the uterus.

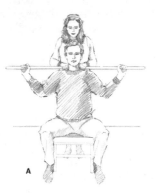

A

B

This exercise strengthens the shoulders, upper back and arms. Sit down as shown with your feet flat on the floor. Rest the broom handle, or pole on your shoulders as shown. When your partner lifts and lowers the pole exert a counter pressure to work your muscles. Work smoothly, not too fast and never jerk. Both people must keep a straight back, pelvis tucked under and breathe freely throughout. Breathe out with the effort and in with the release.

This exercise stretches the spine and works the waist muscles. Sitting with your feet flat on the floor and the pole resting on your shoulders, hold the pole as shown. Slowly twist round as far as you can to the right, and then move in the opposite direction to the left. Keep your pelvis still, only move from the waist and above. Breathe freely all the time.

A   B

This is a good exercise for the man to strengthen his legs and back. Stand with your feet hip width apart, spine lifted, shoulders relaxed, arms stretched out in front at shoulder height. Now slowly bend your knees until you feel your thigh muscles working, allowing your spine to move forward. Hold briefly and then rise up again. Repeat until you feel well worked. Breathe out with the effort, in with the release.

Squatting with your feet flat on the ground is an exercise not a birth position – then you would always stay on your toes. (See page 100 if you want to try squatting during labour.) This exercise will strengthen your thighs and feet, stretch your Achilles tendons, calves, inner thigh muscles and pelvic floor muscles. Squat down on your toes, facing your partner with your feet hip width apart, hold on to each other's elbows and slowly allow your weight to tilt backwards until you have your feet flat on the floor. Try and keep your spine lengthened, shoulders relaxed and chest open throughout. Breathe freely and calmly, notice where you feel the stretch. When you are pregnant if you practise a little every day it will get easier. Hold this position until you feel well worked, do not hold it if you feel the baby is uncomfortable, or if you feel the blood circulation is restricted in your legs. If you have varicose veins check with your doctor before practising this exercise.

Practise moving from all fours to kneeling, to a supported semi-squat (on the toes) all of which can be done either on a bed or on the floor (see diagrams). In each position encourage your partner to spend a few minutes practising for labour; relax her jaw and open her mouth; breathe gently and lightly and then to open up the pelvic floor with the sighing out breath, and if she would like, visualize her baby's head slowly moving down, through her body, gently passing through the layers of soft, relaxed muscle. You can help your partner by reassuring and encouraging her now and most importantly during labour, by assisting her into the positions and giving her the confidence to 'let go' and give birth gently and in her own way.

SOME ALTERNATIVE LABOUR POSITIONS

The first two positions shown are for trying during the first stage of labour, the third can also be used for the birth itself.

Breathing awareness

Breathing is a natural function – unless there is conscious, or unconscious, interference it automatically adjusts itself to the body's needs. However there are circumstances, and childbirth is one, when it is helpful to know how to use breathing, linked with concentrated relaxation, as a positive aid.

'BREATHING' FOR LABOUR

Conscious breathing patterns are seen to be used in labour among several cultures. Rhythmic rocking of the body, with conscious breathing; or chanting where the breath becomes incorporated into the sounds the woman makes are all instinctual responses during labour. We tend to be a silent, tight-lipped society where voicing strong emotion is frowned upon except on a football pitch! But in childbirth a woman is compelled to surrender her well-brought-up *persona* to allow her body free expression – this means her breathing too. What happens when she does 'let go' may be disturbing or even shocking for those people unprepared for the undeniable passion of childbirth. Many women make sounds more reminiscent of a bed of love than a bed of pain. One expert postulates that there is a universal cry common to all women, which they make just before the birth. Certainly there is often a need to cry out, but what may sound like a scream of intense pain or anguish, is more frequently an exquisite release for the woman herself. If a woman is breathing, relaxing, and confidently responding to her body's messages she will cope better with her labour; the essential oxygen supply is maintained and her energy will not fade so quickly. When she can withdraw into herself her body begins to produce its own painkillers, called endorphins, which can even induce a state of euphoria.

When contractions start, what can you do to help your partner? Many couples worry about 'the breathing' for childbirth, but in a secure, loving environment there is an intuitive process which comes into action for every woman whether or not she has ever thought about breathing techniques. Spontaneously a woman's breath starts deep and rises to a lighter, faster rate as the contraction builds up its intensity. Sheila Kitzinger suggests we think of the waves of the sea to evoke the rhythmic rise and fall of contractions. Imagine you are swimming in the sea, trying to keep your head above the crest of the waves which get larger and larger, and closer together as time goes by. Naturally your breathing becomes faster and more vigorous as you swim hard, rising up with the swell of the wave, trying to keep on top, and then just as spontaneously the breath deepens as you float down the far side, ready for the next one. It is interesting that when practising stretching with visualization, women often report spontaneously choosing waves as an image to concentrate on.

Breathing and relaxing through contractions can be exhilarating and intensely satisfying. If you can endorse your partner's trust in herself to breathe, move freely without fear or tension interrupting the natural flow, then her body – her breathing – will function instinctively without difficulty.

Learning complicated, controlled breathing patterns to use during labour is not helpful for everyone. Inevitably when labour gets difficult your partner will draw upon her own natural breathing rhythms. Because of this it is far better to help her build up her own awareness and self confidence right from the start.

Stand facing each other, as shown. Then gently encourage her to rock her pelvis; to release any tension in her mouth, jaw and of course her pelvic floor as she breathes rhythmically with you.

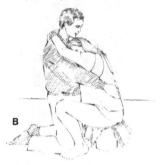

The woman in labour sits down on a bucket (normal way up) with a towel spread over the brim. She opens her legs, feet flat on the floor and the man kneels down in front of her as shown. The man can reach round to massage her shoulders, or lower spine. (Try sitting on the bucket to be monitored during labour, it is much more comfortable.) When you go for a walk during labour, take your bucket with you to sit on, or be sick into if the need arises! And from time to time swap over; the man sits on the bucket, the woman kneels down, leaning forward to rest her arms on the man's knees and rocks her pelvis.

C

The man sits down on a chair, puts his knees apart and the woman squats down on her toes, supporting herself. The man can also massage her neck and shoulders if necessary.

D

This position can be done either on the floor or on the bed. The man kneels down and then sits back on his heels – with a cushion under his pelvis if necessary. (If this position is very painful for the man, practise it a little every day – without the cushion, to stretch out tight thigh muscles.) Then the woman squats down on her toes and lets her pelvis rest on his legs. He can reach round and hold her legs or knees, whichever feels comfortable, to support her.

E

Try kneeling or squatting on a bed, on your toes supported on either side for part of first or second stage. If the woman is pushing for more than 20 minutes in the semi-reclining position and the baby does not move down try an upright position.

TO FACILITATE SPONTANEOUS BREATHING DURING CHILDBIRTH

When labour starts many women feel they need support to remember everything they have planned. As a labour companion you can help by reassuring your partner of your confidence and trust in her innate capacity to cope with childbirth. Encourage her to breathe rhythmically and never to hold her breath during contractions. Try not to criticize or interfere with what she is doing, but if you sense fear or tension building up, try breathing with her – sighing gently with the out breath.

ANXIETY AND HYPERVENTILATION

We have all experienced anxiety and stress interfering with our breathing. Our chest tightens up, breathing becomes rapid and shallow, we may break out into a sweat, or feel shivery. During childbirth there is a risk that tension, or excitement can make a woman huff the breath out too hard. This uneven, tense breathing where the out breath becomes harshly accentuated can cause hyperventilation. This means an oxygen/carbon dioxide imbalance in the blood which is potentially dangerous if it continues too long. If during labour you become aware that your partner is beginning to sound anxious, or is gasping for air then take action at once. She should cup her two hands over her mouth so that she will inhale carbon dioxide and restore the balance. Try and reassure her, calm her down and get her to breathe more slowly and freely. Balance the in and the out breath, so that neither is longer than the other. Concentrate on depth of breathing rather than rate, and encourage her to lift and expand her ribcage outwards with the flow of air. Everything will return to normal quickly, but if you are in any doubt ask for the midwife's help. The physical signs of hyperventilation are tingling in the fingers, or numbness around the mouth. But hopefully you can prevent that happening by listening carefully to your partner's breathing.

BREATHING AND DISTRACTION TECHNIQUES FOR PAIN CONTROL

If this is your first baby it is worth learning as much about breathing, meditation and relaxation as possible. Childbirth is an unknown quantity and your partner may benefit from a particular approach, however unlikely it may have seemed before the birth. When your partner finds something appealing it will be important for you to learn about it too; she may need reminding once labour starts. There is nothing magical about breathing in labour, it is rather a question of learning to trust an instinctual process and then allowing it to proceed without interference. Some people find learning specific techniques helps them to do this by giving them a sense of purpose which also enhances their self confidence. Then during labour they adapt these learned techniques to suit their own needs.

Having decided how you intend to approach pain in labour try practising during your stretch exercise sessions. Then feel free to adapt everything to suit your own ideas. The suggestion is that each couple prepare a series of check-points which will be used when contractions become painful. The aim of this list is: to occupy the conscious mind by providing specific focal points for intense and exclusive concentration. By superimposing this positive information when the pain is at its most intense you are attempting to interfere with, and interrupt, the pain signals to the brain, thus diminishing their negative effect. The pain remains the same, but by flooding the conscious brain with positive activity you feel it less, while you liberate the unconscious body processes to take over and function with maximum efficiency.

When the pain begins to gather strength your partner can try this sequence – focus her concentration exclusively on herself, refusing to allow outside stimuli to impinge upon her in any way • Next visualize how she ideally wants to be, including posture, facial expression, overall demeanour, and then hold that image firmly • Now she should scan and modify body signals: are her shoulders raised, tense? O.K. drop them down • Are her hands tight or clenched? O.K. Stretch and relax them, and so on, checking round her whole body • Progressing on from that body scan – what about her breathing? Only interfere if necessary by sighing on the next OUT breath and then concentrate on expanding and lifting the ribcage, breathing freely • Finally, try repeating your own pre-selected song or mantra as a focal point for your concentration. (Choose something with a strong rhythm and positive associations and chant it together. Some women also find it helpful to tap the rhythm with their fingers at the same time.) Or try visualization • During each contraction

get your partner to visualize her cervix slowly opening up •
Both of you should put all your energy and concentration into
that image – you can help the process in this way.

You may use all, or some of these items, probably adapting them
to your own needs as labour progresses. If you decide to work on
these ideas as a method of dealing with pain in labour it is vital that
you spend time together regularly during the pregnancy preferably
during exercise sessions, working out your plans and building up
your confidence. In this way you will be able to give your partner all
the support and positive stimulation she will need when labour
becomes demanding – possibly testing you both to the limit.

Visualization

When labour becomes difficult try using visualization like this, at the
beginning of each contraction encourage your partner to visualize
her cervix gradually opening up. It is not vital to have an anatomic-
ally correct image of the cervix – suggest she find her own which will
be just as effective, if not more so. Anything which opens smoothly,
for example, the bud of a large, soft petalled flower, slowly opening
in the sunshine, or the shutter in a camera which opens when the
photograph is taken.

When the second stage is under way and the baby begins to
descend through the pelvis, suggest that your partner visualizes her
baby – seeing her pelvic floor muscles gently opening up to allow her
baby to be born.

RESTRUCTURING INNER IMAGES

If you have both become reasonably confident in your abilities to
relax your body and focus your concentration you might like to try
this exercise. The concentration here is a relaxed/alert state – a
'widening of awareness with an alert responsiveness to changes'.
And the purpose of this particular relaxation is to use visualization
linked to positive affirmation in order to improve your inner perception of childbirth. This will strengthen positive attitudes and help
you to cope with childbirth joyfully and creatively – liberated from
any past negative influences. Of course positive affirmation is not a

new idea, nor is visualization – both techniques have been extensively and effectively used in such different spheres as sport and health care.

. . . 'YOU ARE WHAT YOU IMAGINE YOURSELF TO BE.'

We all carry around a powerful store of acquired internal images and responses. These perceptions of what certain life situations are like may be hazy or clear; a force to be reckoned with they are only modified by real-life experience or conscious effort. Childbirth is a particularly potent and emotive event to which we have all attached ideas, fantasies and prejudices – often negative ones. For most of us, these are inherited from parents, or absorbed from TV, films and books. When parenthood becomes a reality these ingrained ideas can often prove to be severely restrictive. Couples who embrace new methods and attitudes to childbirth may experience conflict on a very deep level between their newly acquired understanding and that which they had already accepted as 'best' and 'normal'.

Consider this idea; 'childbirth is dangerous and painful'. If we believe that statement and close our eyes we will conjure up an image of a woman, probably alone, certainly lying down, screaming in pain and fear. If, on the other hand we have seen pictures, or better, assisted a woman who has laboured upright, cheerful and powerfully in contact with her own feelings and needs, then our inner vision of labour will be entirely different. Those new positive inner images will powerfully support our intellect in finding similar coping strategies when we ourselves give birth, or when we are supporting someone else in labour.

There is another dimension which cannot be ignored; inside us all there is a critical, and potentially self destructive 'voice' which negatively interferes with our perception and hence our capacity to act satisfactorily. This running commentary – it might be visual or auditory, which flows freely, needs to be brought into conscious awareness, recognized and accepted as part of ourselves, then modified where necessary using positive affirmation. These three steps form an integral part of this exercise.

Part one
This exercise should be done by everyone who will support the woman during her labour, and the woman herself! Allow plenty of

undisturbed time when you are both feeling calm and receptive – this may mean in bed last thing at night, or before the daily rush starts in the morning. In fact the pleasant, open feelings associated with waking or falling asleep are good times for the right side of the brain to become more active. Most of the time we function with our left brain – the logical, verbal and analytical part, but during this exercise I would like you to become more aware of the right hemisphere which gives us the intuitive, integrative and visual side of ourselves.

Read these instructions slowly and quietly with the pauses as suggested. Be aware of the person's breathing and try saying the word 'Now' during their out breath, this will facilitate their sinking into a deeply relaxed state.

Sit comfortably, making sure your whole body is supported, or lie down with pillows under your head, shoulders and thighs if necessary. Gently close your eyes, breathe deeply and freely while you slowly count down from 10 to 1 . . . (Allow the person to breathe at least five breaths, observe when the out breath comes and then speak.) Now . . . starting with your toes work up through your body, putting your attention in each part in turn, allowing it to relax and let go any tension . . . Now . . . feel all tension dissolving and flowing away . . . Now . . . I wonder if you can see . . . feel . . . sense yourself in labour . . . can you see where you are? . . . smell the particular smell of the place . . . can you feel what you are standing on? . . . what can your hands touch? . . . what sounds can you hear? . . . what kind of light is there through the window? . . . Now . . . as contractions get stronger can you see . . . feel . . . hear yourself? . . . Is there someone with you . . . or more than one person perhaps? . . . what are they doing? . . . and I wonder if you can see what position you are in? . . . Perhaps you are hungry, I wonder if you can taste a delicious snack? . . . Now . . . I wonder if you can see yourself going to the hospital? (If you are having a home birth adapt the words to suit your circumstances.) . . . Now . . . If you have arrived at the hospital, I wonder if you feel different? . . . what kind of room are you in . . . I wonder if you can smell anything? . . . what can you touch? . . . I wonder if there is anyone with you? . . . Now . . . as the contractions get stronger, rhythmic and closer together . . . what do you feel . . . what sounds can you hear? . . . I wonder what position you can see yourself in now . . .?

Continue asking questions taking yourselves through the whole story of labour, until the baby is born or as far as you feel is appropriate. Always use the phrase, 'I wonder if . . .' never be specific, this gives the person complete freedom to find their own images and sensations. If you do not have time to go all through labour in one session, decide how far to go and then round it off gently, always affirming the present state of the pregnancy: 'We have finished for today so I'd like you to take your time to bring yourself back to the present . . . and feel . . . see . . . sense yourself as x months pregnant again. (Then in a louder and normal voice continue.) And when you're ready . . . take a few deep energizing breaths . . . and in your own time open your eyes and feel fit and well.'

If you do visualize right through to the birth and see the baby, always remember to put the baby back inside the mother, asking her to feel quite comfortable and confidently pregnant again, perhaps massaging her abdomen a little before coming out of the relaxation in the way already suggested.

Part Two

Now is the time to discuss the images and sensations that surfaced during the relaxation. Try not to be embarrassed or critical about anything that came into your mind – increased awareness is the aim. It is very important for both partners to recognize and then accept their own feelings – whatever they are, before moving on to the next step.

While you are sharing the experience you might like to note down any gaps in your stories and then pool resources to find ways to fill them in. Look at pages 94–101 for ideas about positions for labour, find time to re-visit the hospital labour ward together and so on. Any questions you have need to be answered in depth, while anxieties need to be understood to be resolved. Negative reactions are also an important indicator and need to be explored objectively – try not to feel threatened if hostile or unhappy feelings come to the surface; self acceptance is an essential part of this process.

Part Three

This is the dynamic use of relaxation to integrate new visions into your existing inner landscape. I suggest each person writes their own positive affirmations to be added to the relaxation story of labour which will be read to them by their partner later on. (You could also make a tape recording and play it back in the car or while you are in the bath! Repetition will be helpful.) Tell the same story of labour, but this time not using the format of 'I wonder if you can see . . .' but rather, 'contractions are getting stronger – I can see X standing up, leaning on my shoulder while I massage her shoulders', and so on. These images, composed by each individual, and linked to the spoken affirmation, are a powerful method of endorsing a new approach and establishing self confidence.

Sharing stress

As a couple you may have already shared an experience of intense stress or pain, and know how you both react. If you have confronted and dealt with these problems, working together as a team, you can take that confidence with you into labour. But if you have never had to test that part of your relationship before, you might like to try an experience which will increase your understanding of each other.

The first experiment is related to trust. A woman in labour enters into a state of extreme vulnerability. She has to be able to trust you, as her partner; her medical back-up; and perhaps most vitally she has to trust herself. Many women find this gradual drift into dependence hard to do, their intellects stay on guard, preventing them from letting go. You, on the other hand, have to trust your partner's innate strength and encourage her to use it to the full, while at the same time accepting her periodic need to be totally dependent on you.

Each of you in turn sits comfortably in a chair, eyes closed, as relaxed as possible. Your partner, with as little verbal instruction as possible, helps you to stand up, and then gently and silently guides you around the room, or out into the garden. After a short walk your partner then brings you back, and helps you to sit down again. Then you reverse roles. Afterwards, discuss how you felt; whether you enjoyed being cared for and dependent, and how you could help each other achieve a greater degree of trust.

Secondly it will be helpful if you and your partner discuss instinctive reactions to stress. Some of us, when faced with either an emotional or physical problem 'dissociate' ourselves from it and by ignoring it hope it will disappear. Others face the problem, 'associate' with it, accepting the discomfort and anxiety and work through it as far as possible. Finding out how you and your partner react can be a helpful guide to the kind of help you will need to provide in labour. If your partner tends to 'dissociate', she will probably use techniques for coping with contractions which reflect that pattern. She may feel comfortable with a more structured breathing pattern, or use singing or counting as distraction techniques. Alternatively, if she 'associates' to stress, her method will be to concentrate as fully as possible on the pain, and cope by 'going towards' it. (In fact a woman who has prepared herself with exercise and body awareness will probably develop a capacity to use either approach.)

As a labour companion it is helpful for you to be aware of your instinctive reactions too. You may be called upon to 'harmonize' with your partner and be ready to help her shift from one method to the other. For example, early in labour it may be appropriate for her to 'dissociate' concentrating on distraction techniques. But as the intensity of contractions builds up, this will gradually become impossible – the rhythms of childbirth demand total commitment and the only solution is to 'associate' completely. She has to go with the driving force that flows through her body with each uterine contraction, and not struggle against it. To make this shift your partner will need courage and a calm, supportive environment: your understanding and appreciation will be invaluable.

Chapter 6

Birth

Having a baby in a hospital setting can be complicated, often involving the use of medical high technology to help the natural process of labour. However, in the end birth is an intimate human event which centres on the first meeting between a man, a woman and their baby. Whether you have a drug-free natural birth, or use every existing medical aid, the fact that you are together to welcome your baby is really what matters. Your touch, smell, and the sound of your voice are what the baby needs and will respond to the moment he is born.

During the nine months of pregnancy, every expectant father wonders what labour will be like, how he will cope, and what he will feel when he finally meets his child. Whatever self doubts or misgivings you may have experienced during this time, once labour starts these fears become less significant. Gradually the uterine contractions establish their rhythm and you are swept up in the process of giving birth. A few men have told me of their gradual realization, once labour started, that their participation was inevitable and their presence invaluable. This man told me: 'I had wondered what I'd do, you know, be there or not? When it actually started I was run off my feet and it was only much later, when we'd already been in the hospital a couple of hours that I suddenly remembered, "Hang on, I wasn't sure that I was going to be here!" Actually it was never an issue once labour started. Paula could never have managed without me, she really needed me and I felt good about that. I don't know how a woman could manage alone, not really.'

Traditionally in our society fathers have not been active participants during labour. Only in the last ten years has it become hospital policy to 'allow' fathers into the labour room. In many, but certainly not all hospitals, the father's role still remains ill-defined. But having talked to many hundreds of women who have given birth supported by their partners the message is clear. The man, simply by being there, provides an essential and intensely humanizing link with the family. The father keeps the glow of intimacy alive in a situation which, for the woman, may feel alien and public. The man also fulfils another fundamental need for the woman – a familiar person who can be an emotional 'lighthouse' for her during labour. She can take her bearings from him at any time because he is a constant presence when midwives and doctors have to come and go. His strength and care provide her with a light from which she can find her own way through the experience of giving birth.

THE IMPORTANCE OF KNOWING

When a man has not received adequate antenatal information and preparation it is easy for him to feel anxious and unsure of himself in the unknown, and often alien environment of a hospital birth. Couples who plan to share the labour as fully as possible must realize how vital it is for the man to prepare himself for what is, after all, his experience of birth too. Reading, thinking and talking about all aspects of childbirth, attending both hospital and National Childbirth Trust antenatal classes are essential, for every couple planning to share their birth experience. It is only after such thoughtful preparation that a couple can hope to gain the necessary insight to understand each other's very different roles, and accept the unpredictability of the natural process.

To enable you to feel confident and to be fully supportive to your partner it is essential that you are completely familiar with the normal process of childbirth. Attending antenatal classes and hospital visits, reading books, asking questions, discussing labour with your partner are all part of the process of preparing for parenthood – not just for childbirth. I propose we look at the basic process, and then at what you, as principal labour supporter, can do to help the progress of labour and birth, whether at home, or in a hospital setting.

Labour is divided into three parts. The first stage is often the most difficult, painful and long; it could last anywhere between three or twenty-three hours. Most babies are head down, deep in the pelvis when uterine contractions start, become established into a rhythm and gradually accomplish the task of dilating the cervix. Most women experience pain during this stage, but how intense it is, where they feel it, and how it manifests itself will be very individual. The woman, with support from those around her, can only help the process by relaxing and concentrating on remaining calm while accepting that her uterus will do its work. Every time your partner has a contraction her cervix dilates a bit more, gradually stretching until it is open enough to accommodate the diameter of the baby's head. Dilatation is measured in centimetres and the goal is reached at around 10cm. However it is worth remembering that dilatation gets progressively faster, so that from 6 to 10cm will go faster than from 0 to 5.

The second stage begins when the cervix is fully dilated and the baby can move down the birth canal and ends with the birth of the baby. Uterine contractions continue, but now they are slowly pressing the baby down through the vagina towards the outside world. Some women find this the most exciting and fulfilling part of their labour; now at last they feel in tune with their bodies as everything harmonizes in the process of giving birth. But for others, particularly if they feel unsupported, this can be a frightening and painful time when they feel taken over, confused, helpless and out of control. As with each stage of labour there are no rules; every woman, every labour is different and has its own challenges, excitement and triumphs.

The third stage of labour is the delivery of the placenta. This is completely pain-free and often the woman will be almost unaware of it taking place because she will be cuddling her baby.

It is essential that you understand the normal process of each stage of labour and that you find out about any choices which may be open to you. Having thought about your preferences – if everything is normal – and discussed your wishes with your medical team, you can then relax, secure in the knowledge that everyone is clear about your objectives. Finally, having acknowledged your feelings and preferences please tell yourselves that although you may feel the need to try and control childbirth, that it is really unnecessary and you can, if you wish, choose to be flexible and open to whatever comes.

CREATING AN ATMOSPHERE

Dr Michel Odent, who worked for many years in a French hospital, revolutionized how the women in his care gave birth. His sensitivity towards the woman included the environment in which her labour took place. Dr Odent believes that a room where a woman gives birth should feel like place where she could also make love. His labour rooms have dim lights, warm colours on the walls, lots of cushions on a raised area (no high, narrow hospital beds unless requested!), and semi darkness to enable the woman to withdraw into herself and tune into her body's messages. Nearby there is a pool of warm water in which to relax, but most important there is a minimum of interference with a maximum of caring support.

Even if you cannot find the ideal place of birth, remember that your presence can go a long way towards creating your own island of intimacy and calm. You are the familiar and constant figure, the one person she can trust to stay with her and accept her as she is. Amidst the alien atmosphere generated by hospital high technology you keep the woman firmly in touch with her roots which are in the real world outside.

IT IS YOUR LABOUR TOO

Make no mistake, a labour companion works hard. It is physically demanding and emotionally exhausting to give your complete attention, possibly over a number of hours, to a woman in labour. She will draw upon those around her, sucking your energy as voraciously as she does that delicious cool ice cube you hand her between contractions. Far from having nothing to do, as many men fear before labour, you will find that, for example, during a twelve-hour labour you have hardly had time to go to the lavatory or eat a sandwich!

A man who is working with his partner – holding her head, massaging her back through every contraction, is in labour too. Of course your body is not being taken over by waves of uterine contractions, but by giving your calm attention to your partner you are a powerful and positive influence on her labour. Your loving presence ensures the support every labouring woman requires to discover her own strengths and cope in her own way with childbirth. How you give practical aid depends upon individual taste and on the kind of labour your partner has. But if you have a clear idea before labour starts about positions and relaxation techniques (see pages 89–109) to help the process, then you will both improvise according to how the labour develops.

LABOURING AT HOME

The beginning of labour, while you are still at home, can have a delightful, even party-like atmosphere. You can be undisturbed and can create your own feeling of intimacy. Candles, soft music, a specially perfumed bath and delicious snacks all contribute to the feeling that this is the beginning of a special event. Encourage your partner to rest as much as she can – try not to get too excited, remember labour may go on for many more hours and she will need all her energy to cope.

As the contractions last longer and become more demanding you will notice that your partner has to concentrate exclusively on the sensations she feels. If contractions suddenly become more intense she may need you to remind her how to relax and breathe rhythmically to cope with the pain. And at some point the decision has to be made to go to the hospital. Unless your partner's membranes have ruptured, or either of you feels anxious there is no need to rush into hospital too soon. Ring the hospital and discuss it with the midwife, but normally you can stay at home until contractions are coming regularly and are strong enough to require total concentration from the woman. Most hospitals recommend you go in when contractions have been coming regularly every five/ten minutes, each one lasting approximately one minute, for at least an hour. Of course if you are anxious about anything go to hospital immediately, or ring for advice. And however you travel, the safest and most comfortable way for your partner is on all fours in the back of the car, looking out of the back window.

A father's role during first stage of labour

During the first stage your role as labour companion is clear. You will give physical and emotional support when and where necessary. No woman can happily give birth alone – it is an experience where the physical process demands outside reassurance and involvement. Here are some guidelines from which you can evolve your own ideas.

- Be calm. If you feel yourself getting tense, do some slow breathing and consciously relax your muscles wherever necessary. If you can, call on another helper to stay with your partner (a medical student or midwife will always be available, or you may prefer a personal friend) while you take a break. A short walk will relieve the tension and refresh you.

• Observe your partner carefully and try to anticipate her needs. Encourage her to save her energy by relaxing completely between contractions. Make sure she can curl up and doze if she feels like it.

• Reduce verbal communication to the minimum. A woman in strong labour cannot and should not be expected to communicate with words but rather be allowed to withdraw into herself. You can facilitate this essential process by dimming the lights, making sure of a secluded, calm environment and speaking quietly and sparingly yourself. Make sure that everyone who comes into the room respects this need for quiet concentration. This is not the time for mindless 'chat', or for swapping stories, as this is a distraction and dilutes your partner's concentration. On a practical level you may have to interpret the odd word, or non-verbal signal which means, 'more ice', 'massage back', 'too hot/cold', 'change position' and so on.

There is another aspect of being a labour companion which many men find difficult. The patience and willingness to observe sensitively without interfering during labour can be one of the hardest things for a man to do and understand, particularly if the woman is in pain. The first stage often feels very long, especially once you are in hospital. Not so for the woman, who naturally loses all concept of passing hours and enters her own timeless zone of childbirth. This father remembered his fatigue during the first stage of labour: 'We got to hospital about 11 p.m. and then time really seemed to drag. Mind you I was very busy, but it was just endless, one contraction after another. I longed for something to happen. Every contraction Chris sat on the bucket. I had to press down hard against her lower back. She leant her head against me and in between I gave her ice chips to suck or mopped her face with a cold cloth. This went on for hours. At one point I lay down on the floor to rest while Chris was in the loo. She came back and snapped at me, "Well if you can't be bothered to help me, bugger off!" We both laughed and it helped to break the tension.'

ROUTINE HOSPITAL PROCEDURES

After the initial admission procedures which the hospital will have warned you about, if everything is normal, you will find you are left alone during the first stage. The midwife and doctor will come and visit you, but if you and your partner are coping happily she will not interfere. Of course if you want help there is always someone available.

All hospitals have routine procedures which you will have to deal with during labour. About every three hours the midwife may wish to give your partner an internal vaginal examination to assess the progress of the dilatation of the cervix. (Usually the baby's heartbeat is monitored at the same time. See page 59.) In many ways it is wise to keep these examinations to a minimum because if progress is slow then everyone gets despondent and suddenly feels their fatigue more acutely. So always be ready with lots of morale-boosting encouragement if the cervix has not dilated as much as you had all hoped. Look for ways to help your partner feel how well she is doing, and try not to look ahead, just take each contraction as it comes. If lying on her back is uncomfortable for your partner, ask the midwife to give the vaginal examination in an alternative position, such as half kneeling, or lying on her side.

Many hospitals want to monitor the fetal heartbeat at intervals during labour (see page 59). This is usually done every three to four hours for 20-minute periods. Ask the midwife to put the external monitor on your partner in a position which is comfortable – kneeling and leaning forward on to a pile of cushions, or sitting on a bucket next to the monitor rather than lying back. Another good alternative is to ask the midwife if you can hold the monitor in position on your partner's abdomen rather than having it fixed on by a belt. While your partner is linked to the monitor, try not to allow the presence of the machine with its lights and pulsing sound to interfere with her concentration. Sometimes machines are not 100 per cent efficient. If you are concerned always request another one, or better still ask the midwife to listen to the fetal heart herself.

Whatever position your partner finds comfortable during labour remember to encourage her to move about regularly during the first stage. Either during, or between contractions, in whatever position is comfortable, she should rock her pelvis in any direction she wishes. If she can visualize the baby, head deep down in the pelvis searching for the way out, she may intuitively feel the need to swing or rock her hips to help this process. Going for a walk is also helpful, not only to aid dilatation but also to give you both a change of scenery.

HELPING HER RELAX

Tension and fear can be a problem during labour. It is helpful if you frequently reassure your partner and create a calm environment around her. Be aware if her mood is changing and she is becoming anxious so that you can try to avoid the negative chain reaction that fear and tension always create. It is impossible to remain totally relaxed during strong contractions. Usually other parts of the body 'join in'. You can help by checking for sympathetic tension in your partner's body. Pay particular attention to her mouth, jaw, neck and upper shoulders. Help her to relax and doze if possible between contractions. Try gentle massage, or just by resting your hand on the area which is tense remind her to let go completely during the pause.

Encourage her to make as much noise as she wants to. Holding in sounds can mean that she is holding in tension – encourage her to roar like a lion if she wants to! Sometimes sighing loudly yourself will get her started, but usually if she feels secure sounds which facilitate labour will happen spontaneously.

As the labour becomes more intense you may find your role becomes that of interpreter between your partner and the medical staff. Obviously it is vitally important to know what your partner is aiming to do, but at the same time to remain flexible in case she changes her mind or circumstances make something impossible to achieve. This father's description is typical of a couple who worked well together during the labour. 'When we got to the labour room things became more difficult, although I never felt out of place. Periodically a nurse would come and ask "Do you want something?" Then she would list all the drugs available! She was a great distraction for us both because Sally was really concentrating on her breathing during contractions. I finally asked for some tea just to get rid of her. In between contractions Sally was very still, I was quiet and tried to really concentrate with her. Sometimes I breathed with her and sometimes I just held her strongly in my arms with her head pressing into my shoulder. I felt a special closeness with her during labour. I felt that the pain wasn't too awful, I felt that Sally was very strong. I would say to the midwife, "No, no she's fine, we're all right." After, Sally told me she was really glad I had been so sure, it gave her courage to go on.'

DISCOMFORT AND PAIN IN LABOUR

Your partner may feel sick or feel nauseous at any time during her labour. Although this is unpleasant, it is often a welcome relief and seems to help the labour along. Your partner may have an attack of shaking at some point before or even after the baby is born. Keep her warm, try giving her honey, or sips of grape juice, do some firm massage of the shaking muscles and hold her in your arms giving her lots of reassurance.

Backache is another common and often painfully distressing problem for many women during the late first stage of labour. The pain feels nagging and persecuting, gradually destroying a woman's self confidence. If it continues too long it will probably be relieved most successfully by having an epidural (see page 67). When backache starts to be a problem try firm massage, or a hot water bottle, or a cold flannel, or firm pressure from your hand on the painful area. Suggest a change to a more upright position and get your partner to sway her hips, or get into the 'all fours' position which will take the pressure of the descending baby off her spine.

If there is any need to slow the labour down – or your partner is told she must not 'push' because her cervix is unevenly dilated, then the position to try is on hands and knees with her head lower than her pelvis.

Fatigue, fear and loss of confidence can also pose problems for a woman trying to have her baby without using drugs. You can help by getting the midwife to add her encouragement and support in your partner's capacity to carry on. This support from the hospital staff, with their practical suggestions to help the woman who is trying to avoid taking drugs, is essential when you and your partner may feel at the end of your tether.

Make sure that you have explored before labour starts as many different methods of pain relief which do not affect the normal progress of contractions, in case your partner needs some help (see page 66).

If your partner needs medical help to cope with the pain, i.e., pethidine or an epidural, always make sure she is fully consulted and understands all the pros and cons before it is administered. When a woman feels she has reached her decision freely, without pressure, it will not cause difficulties and will not make her feel disappointed or let down, even if it means a completely different kind of labour than the one she had envisaged. There is absolutely no need for anyone to suffer more pain than they feel able to cope with. Everyone is free to choose, no one should feel pressured to be anything other than true to themselves – only the woman herself can judge when the pain is unbearable. Once having made a decision to take medication think positively and begin to plan for the next phase of labour.

The second stage

Contractions change their character when the second, 'expulsive' stage of labour begins. The cervix is completely drawn up and there is now nothing to prevent the baby moving down the birth canal. There is more of a pause between contractions, which will now last for about one and a half minutes. While the contraction lasts your partner will feel three or more urges to 'bear down', or push. These urges come and go in waves of sensation, when they reach a peak your partner will automatically hold her breath and bear down for about four or five seconds each time. In between she breathes normally and waits for the next rush of sensation to build up. It is helpful if you remind your partner to relax her mouth and jaw while visualizing the pelvic floor muscles slowly relaxing open. She might like to talk out loud to the baby, or tell herself to relax and 'open up' while she is pushing. Your partner may be in this second stage for an hour or longer. As long as neither she nor the baby are getting too tired there is no reason to hurry what is for many women the most satisfying part of the whole experience.

THE FATHER'S FEELINGS AT BIRTH

I have often been told that the first stage of labour feels endless for the father – particularly for a first baby. In contrast the second stage seems to go by in a flash. Once the midwife decides, by doing a vaginal examination, that your partner's cervix is fully dilated she will stay with you continuously. If you are in a teaching hospital you may be asked if medical students can come in for the delivery. If this influx of strangers makes you or your partner feel uneasy then you can politely refuse.

The changes that this second stage brings can sometimes be disturbing for the father. If you have been actively supporting your partner during the long hours of the first stage you will have felt an essential part of the proceedings. But now suddenly you may feel relegated to the second division when your partner fixes her entire attention on the doctor or midwife who is to deliver the baby. Men have told me of their surprise at the feelings of impotence, hurt or hostility which swept over them – while all the time recognizing the inevitability of what was happening.

During the time when you are coping with these developments your partner is going through a transformation. The first stage of labour is forgotten – now she is giving birth, creating life in front of our eyes. Some men have told me they felt out of touch with the woman which caused another rush of conflicting emotions ranging from awesome pride to intense anxiety. Luckily for the majority of fathers the inexorable thrust of labour takes over and they find themselves swept up in the excitement and thrill of the final minutes before their baby appears.

It is important that you keep close to your partner and re-establish contact. If you have planned to support her in an upright position, or can hold her in your arms for the birth of your child then you will feel closely involved.

FINDING THE RIGHT POSITION FOR A GENTLE BIRTH

Your partner is now entering the final part of her labour; she is about to give up her pregnant state and 'lose' her baby to the outside world. In one moment she will experience an ending and a beginning. A woman who has waited many months to see her baby should not be hurried though these final minutes; like a climax in lovemaking she needs time to savour to the full every aspect of her experience.

This is the time when you and your partner have to cooperate willingly and trustingly with your midwife or doctor. You should have made your wishes and hopes clear and know what your midwife plans to do. Remember that with a first baby many women have to learn how to push. Your partner may need to try several different positions before she finds the one that suits her best. If after twenty minutes or so the baby is not moving steadily down the birth canal you should suggest a more upright position, for example, kneeling, supported squatting or sitting on the bucket. If there is a birthing chair available now is the time to try it. In all these upright positions the urge to bear down is more compelling, and less strenuous for the woman. The pelvis is free to open completely and the pelvic floor muscles can relax to facilitate the baby's gentle descent through the birth canal.

Throughout the opening phase of the second stage it is very helpful if you reassure your partner repeatedly. It is important that she feels relaxed and self-confident so that she can settle into the natural rhythm of her body. No one should make the woman feel rushed. Remind your partner to relax her jaw and mouth, breathe freely and only to bear down when the urge to do so becomes irresistible. It is a waste of energy and often painful to push against tight pelvic floor muscles. The burning sensation that some women feel when they are told to push will stop if she is unhurried and consciously relaxes her pelvic floor. Talk quietly and lovingly to your partner; ask her to focus her concentration, not on forcing or straining, but rather on letting go – opening up, or giving way to the baby as it moves through her body. Encourage her to direct all her energy flow downwards towards the baby. Try visualization (see page 104) or suggest your partner touches the baby's head as it begins to emerge.

GOING WITH THE SENSATIONS

Although your partner may seem to be oblivious to her surroundings it is important to maintain the atmosphere of calm, quiet concentration. There is no need to speed up the natural process – in fact the evidence shows that forcing a woman to push, overriding her spontaneous impulses, is painful for her and may cause difficulties for the baby. Where there are no complications, an unhurried delivery is going to benefit both mother and baby.

As the baby moves down the birth canal and the urge to open up becomes stronger, like rising to the peak of an orgasm, the need to go with these sensations is unforced and even intensely pleasurable. If you are holding your partner in your arms you may find you begin to whisper your own words of love and encouragement to her. If you are both well supported by the medical team you will feel a strong sense of working together which is very satisfying. As the baby's head slowly comes into view, looking a bit crumpled, wet and dark the midwife will be in close contact with your partner. The midwife will want the baby's head to come out very slowly to avoid a tear, so she may tell your partner to stop pushing and slowly 'pant' or 'breathe' the baby's head out. The delivery of the head is the hardest part; usually after the next contraction the rest of the body slithers out, wet and amazingly large. There at last is your baby being lifted into your partner's arms – or being handed to you to give her.

Everyone's experience of birth is different and if your partner has to have a forceps delivery or a Caesarean birth you may feel dazed and shocked afterwards. Usually the relief at seeing your baby safe and well more then compensates for any disappointment about the style of the birth. Whatever happens try and allow your emotions to come to the surface and accept them – there is no 'right' or 'wrong' way to feel. This is how one father remembered his birth experience. 'For me the best moment of the labour was the five minutes before and then the moment of birth. Pat wanted to squat and so I asked the student midwife to stand on one side, I was on the other. I was surprised how tightly Pat held on to me – she was really strong. She gripped my arm and shoulder, actually it was quite painful but I didn't mind that. She had quite a hard time pushing, she never really had that strong urge you read about, not until just before the end when the head came out. There was some blood as the baby came out, but I didn't mind as no one seemed worried! The baby was put straight onto Pat's tummy and I had this incredible urge to touch, hold, cuddle – both of them really. I just wanted to be physically close. It was all so sudden, our child lying there and I had to touch her all over. I did count her fingers and toes before I looked to see if it was a boy or a girl. I talked to her, she was beautiful really . . . I said things like "you're OK now, now you're here everything will be all right." She looked me straight in the eye, as though she knew me already, knew all about me. I did feel very moved, I had tears in my eyes. Yes it was all amazing really, I was very pleased with everyone and everything, like I'd won the Olympic marathon!'

Aftermath

After the nine months of pregnancy and then the long, hard work of labour, the last few moments before your baby finally emerges, and the first minutes after the birth happen incredibly fast. One minute you feel disbelief that the process will ever end; then suddenly there is your baby before your eyes.

LOOKING AT YOUR BABY

Even after attending antenatal classes many fathers have told me of their shock and dismay when they first saw their baby. A newborn infant may be a strange colour, perhaps greenish-greyish blue until breathing is established and then the colour changes to pink. She may have a creamy white substance sticking to her body called vernix. This is to protect her skin while she is in the watery environment of the uterus; it will wash off. She may be streaked with blood – this will be maternal blood, probably from a small tear as the baby emerged. A newborn baby is a little damp, but not slimy, and has a wonderful smell. Her head may appear odd, perhaps with the skull looking squashed and the face a bit crumpled from being squeezed down the tight fitting birth canal. This is all perfectly normal; a baby's skull is not hard and is designed to alter shape to facilitate the descent down the birth canal. However, many fathers have reported a moment of panic when they wonder if there is 'something wrong' because their baby's head looks so strange. Not all newborn infants have such a crumpled look, and even if yours does, remember her head will gradually change shape over the next few hours, and within a few days she will look perfectly normal. Finally, please do not worry if your baby is quiet at birth – not all babies cry when they are born, in fact if they have had a gentle birth there is no reason for them to do so. A baby who has a pleasant, gentle welcome into her mother's or father's arms may only wimper a little. And no baby will be held upside down and smacked to start her breathing; a baby who does not breathe spontaneously will have her nose and throat cleared of mucus and then be given oxygen. It is interesting to note that in most cases the mother is totally unaware of her baby's appearance being unusual – fathers are much more likely to be disturbed and need to remember that at birth babies do not look like the 'ideal' baby of a TV advert.

WHAT HAPPENS AFTER THE BIRTH?

Routines vary slightly, so it is a good idea to find out exactly what your hospital's procedures are after the birth.

The baby

By looking at your baby at birth the midwife can assess her Apgar score which is an indication of the baby's well being. This initial test of heart rate, breathing, skin colour, reflex responses and movements gives the baby a score out of ten – most babies score between 7 and 10. It is followed shortly afterwards by a second observation when usually the score will have increased. This test will probably be done without you noticing anything, but later on when you have thoroughly cuddled your baby the midwife will want to weigh and measure her. This usually takes place in the delivery room – you should not be separated from your baby unless there is a problem. Even though you may find the temperature in the delivery room unbearably hot, your newborn infant must be dressed and warmly wrapped to avoid getting chilled. After that she should remain with her mother all the time and your partner may well want to try breastfeeding if she has not already done so.

The mother

After the birth of the baby, the delivery of the placenta is the next important event. The midwife will thoroughly examine it to make sure it is complete; it is a complication if any fragments are left behind inside the uterus. Only then can your partner be examined by the midwife or doctor for any tears or grazes to her perineum and surrounding areas. An episiotomy will have to be stitched, but a small tear may be better left to heal alone. When the mother is comfortable and has been washed and put into a clean nightdress she and the baby will be taken to the postnatal ward. By this time you and your partner will probably be thirsty and starving hungry so be prepared to have a picnic, whatever the time of day or night, either in the delivery room, or later in the postnatal ward. Unfortunately around this time you will have to leave. From now until you take your family home you will be a visitor and subject to hospital rules. You will probably be exhausted yourself and relieved to be able to go home and have a long sleep and spread the good news. But make sure before you leave that your partner is happy and comfortable – she may feel very lonely in the school dormitory atmosphere of the hospital ward.

Caesarean birth

These days Caesarean birth is considered a relatively safe operation, used not only as a last resort but wherever there is any reason to suppose that a normal delivery might be dangerous for mother or baby. However, the realization that birth is a family event, even when it involves surgery, has inspired some hospitals to allow the father to be present in the operating theatre, so that the delivery can be as fulfilling and as 'normal' an experience as possible for the couple.

Often a couple know in advance that a Caesarean delivery is inevitable, because of the position of baby or perhaps because the placenta is partially blocking the birth canal (placenta praevia) or the mother has some medical condition, like high blood pressure, that would make labour or vaginal delivery dangerous for her or the baby. Sometimes, though, an emergency Caesarean is the only way to avoid trauma to the mother or save the baby's life. If you have already been told to expect a Caesarean you should ask for an appointment to talk it over with your consultant. And even if you have not, it is advisable to make sure you know what is involved and prepare for the eventuality. The effect of an unforeseen Caesarean can be devastating for the couple who have carefully prepared for a natural birth.

GATHERING INFORMATION

When you are expecting a baby it is important that you find out as much as possible about your hospital's normal policies regarding all aspects of labour and post-natal care. Expectant parents need information to be able to make informed choices. It is perfectly normal to ask questions of the professionals who will care for you; they are there to help you and will be only too pleased to supply information, and try to accommodate your preferences – once you know what they are (see Chapter 4).

Caesarean rates vary slightly from hospital to hospital, according to individual consultants' policies. If you have more than one hospital to choose from it might be interesting to compare the figures for Caesarean sections during the last couple of years. There are excellent medical and life-saving reasons for performing this operation, but everyone needs reassurance that medical intervention will be carefully controlled.

When you talk to your consultant or midwife here are a few questions you might like to ask.

1   What is the Caesarean rate in your hospital?
2   How will the doctor test fetal maturity before making a date for the delivery? (With an elective section it is important to make sure that the baby has reached full maturity.)
3   If a Caesarean section is planned can labour be allowed to start spontaneously and continue for a while? (It is thought to be better for the baby to have experience of labour – even if only for a time.)
4   What type of incision will be used – vertical or horizontal? (The latter is thought to be safer if it is hoped that future births will be vaginal.)
5   Is it possible to chose between an epidural or a GA (general anaesthetic)? (If your partner can have an epidural Caesarean she will be fully awake to greet the baby.)
6   If your partner is expecting twins, will she automatically have a Caesarean section?
7   Are you allowed to stay with your partner all the time? (It is important for you to hold your baby as soon as possible.) If you are kept outside the operating theatre – or wish to remain outside – will someone bring you the baby immediately after the birth?
8   What method of 'stitching' will be used to close the incision? (Ask the pros and cons of different methods if there is a choice.)
9   If the baby is healthy can he stay in the recovery room with you and your partner? (It is important for you all to get to know each other.)
10   If your partner has a GA how quickly will she 'come round', and can you and the baby wait by her bedside so that she can greet the baby immediately? (It is very important that a woman sees and holds her baby as soon as possible after the birth. If the baby is ill and in special care try and have a polaroid photo by her bed when she wakes up.)
11   If your baby is ill can you go to the special care baby unit with him? (This is essential because then you can bring back information to your partner who will be unable to move for a few hours.)
12   If the baby has to stay more than a few days in the SCBU are older children allowed to visit him there? (It is important that

older children see their new sibling, but they need to be prepared for how the baby will look.)

13 Can you stay an unlimited time with your partner in the hospital ward to help care for the baby? (Your partner will not be able to lift the baby for a day or so after the operation and will need extra help.)

14 What kind of pain relief will be offered to your partner after the operation? (It is important to know if the drugs have any effect on the breast milk if you plan to breastfeed.)

15 If necessary can your partner have help and access to a pump to express milk for the baby? (If not you could hire one through the local branch of the NCT.)

16 How long will your partner have to stay in hospital after a Caesarean birth and what kind of help will she neeed after coming home? (Be prepared to be at home to help a lot more than after a vaginal birth.)

17 Finally, can you be put in touch with other couples who have recently had a Caesarean birth to discuss the experience? (If this is not possible, try through the NCT; talking to other parents can be very reassuring.)

SENSE OF LOSS

Emotional healing after a Caesarean birth can be slower than physical recovery. You may feel anger, shock and a sense of loss that you were denied the natural birth you had both longed and planned for. By talking about the labour with the medical team which performed the operation you can build up a precise picture of what happened. Then sharing your feelings with your partner means you will discover a shared emotional experience which can draw you closer together and soothe any disappointment. But whatever the regrets there is also the obvious sense of relief, the immense joy at having your child and beginning your new life as a family.

RECOVERY AFTER A CAESAREAN BIRTH

For the first two days after the birth your partner may be weak, in considerable pain, and unable to lift the baby to comfort or feed him. Unfortunately she will not have much time to rest, as the baby has to be cared for from day one. This is where you can take over a large part of the baby care if you can be there. Some men think that while their partner is in hospital they will not be needed, but usually every woman wants her partner there to give moral support, if nothing more.

Try and stay all the time with your family, at least for the first four days after the birth. You can change and hold the baby, help your partner find comfortable positions to breastfeed and then settle the baby afterwards. Breastfeeding a baby after a Caesarean birth takes a little more time to establish and a certain amount of persistence. You, better than anyone else, can encourage your partner to persevere with her feeding relationship with the baby.

On a practical level you can speed your partner on the road to physical recovery by encouraging her to do her postnatal exercises each day. Gentle massage, perhaps a foot massage – anywhere but on the abdomen – can also help her to relax and feel happier about her body.

HOW TO HELP YOUR BABY

Contrary to some parents' expectations, a Caesarean birth can be difficult for the baby. It poses more of a risk than a vaginal birth and is more likely to cause complications, particularly respiratory disorders after the birth. Pediatricians who are always present have noticed that at birth these babies tend to be more lethargic, cry less and have decreased reactivity than those born vaginally.

The extent of the complications and what kind of labour preceded the Caesarean section will strongly influence the baby's experience of birth. A baby who was in labour for a long time, developed fetal distress and was finally saved from death will have had a very different birth from one who was delivered suddenly, with no prior warning, because he was in a transverse position. Some people believe that it is better for mother and child to have some experience of labour even if a Caesarean is inevitable. It appears that it is the sudden shock which is disturbing for the baby.

Experts think that some of these postnatal complications may be related to the lack of cutaneous stimulation which a vaginal birth normally provides. But you and your partner can partly compensate for this after the birth. Try holding your baby in your arms as much as possible. Several times a day stroke and caress him – skin to skin contact is best but always make sure the baby does not get cold. Talk and sing to him and while he breastfeeds allow him plenty of time to enjoy this exquisite comfort and essential stimulation. Premature and Caesarean birth babies benefit from sleeping on a lambskin which not only gives them extra warmth but also provides a gentle massage as well. But while parents should never expect complications it is undeniably better to be aware in case your baby does need extra attention. Babies who cry persistently or who demand to suck for extended periods after a Caesarean birth may benefit from a specially gentle treatment given by a cranial osteopath (see Useful addresses, page 216).

GOING HOME

When your partner is allowed home, which may be anything between four and seven days after the operation, your role will continue to be vital. It takes at least six weeks to recover and maybe longer if there have been complications. Your partner will tire easily and should take a nap every day to speed her physical recovery. Ordinary household chores are often too much to cope with, especially if you have other children who need care and attention. Lifting heavy objects is not allowed, and your partner will need help with shopping and moving the baby in the carry cot. If you are aiming to provide this level of care single-handed you will find you get pretty exhausted yourself! Try and enlist the help of friends or relatives, but make sure they can give you the support you need without interfering. Older generations, or couples with a more traditional lifestyle, may give out a sense of disapproval at a time when you may be feeling too vulnerable to cope with that kind of distraction.

In some ways a Caesarean can be an unforeseen benefit for a father who really wishes to share in the care of his baby. By being 'chucked in at the deep end' you will get over a number of practical and psychological hurdles very quickly. You will simply not have time to concentrate on those fears of not being an adequate caregiver that many new fathers experience after a 'normal' delivery.

PLANNING FUTURE PREGNANCIES

There are certain limitations to the kind of birth that you can sensibly plan once your partner has had a Caesarean birth. She would never be eligible for a home birth, for example. But it is worth asking your doctor if there are any reasons why your partner should not try for a vaginal birth next time. Even if your partner is allowed to go into spontaneous labour next time she will probably have to go into hospital as soon as labour starts. She will have to be continuously under medical care, with a high degree of monitoring because of the slight risk that the uterus will rupture during labour.

Even if a woman is told she can have a natural birth after a Caesarean she may well feel vulnerable. Her body has shown itself 'unreliable' and it is important for her to have a sympathetic doctor who will help her to regain her self-confidence. She will need your reassurance that she will never be a 'failure' in your eyes. After all, as with any birth, your baby is the triumph, how he was born is secondary to the fact that he is here in your family.

Chart I – When labour starts

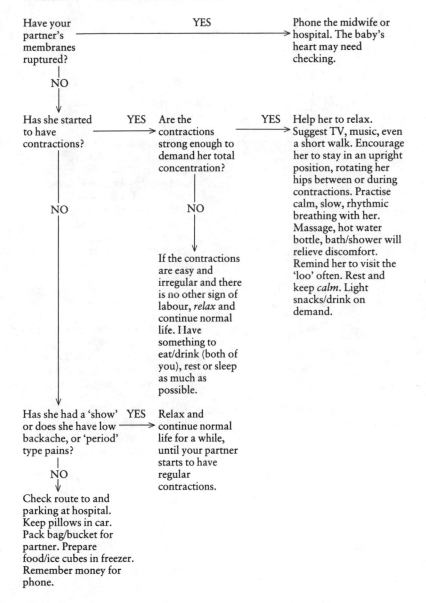

Have your partner's membranes ruptured?

YES → Phone the midwife or hospital. The baby's heart may need checking.

NO ↓

Has she started to have contractions?

YES → Are the contractions strong enough to demand her total concentration?

YES → Help her to relax. Suggest TV, music, even a short walk. Encourage her to stay in an upright position, rotating her hips between or during contractions. Practise calm, slow, rhythmic breathing with her. Massage, hot water bottle, bath/shower will relieve discomfort. Remind her to visit the 'loo' often. Rest and keep *calm*. Light snacks/drink on demand.

NO ↓ (Has she started to have contractions?)

NO ↓ (Are the contractions strong enough)

If the contractions are easy and irregular and there is no other sign of labour, *relax* and continue normal life. Have something to eat/drink (both of you), rest or sleep as much as possible.

Has she had a 'show' or does she have low backache, or 'period' type pains?

YES → Relax and continue normal life for a while, until your partner starts to have regular contractions.

NO ↓

Check route to and parking at hospital. Keep pillows in car. Pack bag/bucket for partner. Prepare food/ice cubes in freezer. Remember money for phone.

Chart 2 – Established labour

Are contractions very
strong and frequent ————YES→ See Chart 3
(lasting a minute and
coming every two
minutes)?

Have you met your midwife ——NO → It's a good idea to make contact
yet?   with her and discuss your aims.

Does progress seem ————————YES→ Encouragement, privacy
discouragingly slow?   and *quiet* is needed. Give
                                your partner 'Walkman'
                                head-phones with soothing music,
                                dim lights. Try nipple stimulation
                                – lots of kissing/cuddling. Go for a
                                walk or have a bath or shower.
                                Both try visualizing the cervix
                                opening up with every
                                contraction.

Have the staff suggested ———— YES→ Get your partner into an upright
electronic fetal monitoring?   comfortable position before
                                   monitor is attached – sit on the
                                   bucket, kneel leaning forward on
                                   to beanbag. Or ask to hold the
                                   external monitor yourself to
                                   enable her to be able to change
                                   positions more easily.

Does she have pain in her——— YES→ Heat or cold on her lower back
lower back?   may help, or massage. Try her
                                 standing, leaning forward and
                                 rocking her hips, or on 'all fours'.

Is she finding contractions ———YES→ Suggest she try the gas and air
painful/alarmingly strong?   machine. Breathe deeply between,
                                    or at start of each contraction.
                                    Reassure, don't anticipate; every
                                    contraction is an achievement.
                                    Try breathing through each
                                    contraction together – eye to eye
                                    contact – sing or count.

Chart 3 – Strong labour

Does your partner feel she ——— YES → Ask for the gas and air. Suggest
needs some pain relief? she breathes deeply at the start of
each contraction, or as it fades
away. Reassure – tell her she's
doing well, soon be there! Remind
her to relax tension areas. Try
another bath/shower?

Is she beginning to feel tired, ——— YES → Try to deal with tiredness with
frustrated – she's had enough firm encouragement. Keep very
and wants to go home? calm yourself. If you need a break
ask midwife to sit with your
partner, go for a short walk. Give
her ice cubes to suck, sips of water
to drink. Observe changes of mood
– this is a good sign of progress.
Is she too hot/cold? Accept
expressions of dependency.

Is your partner very tired, ——— YES → Hold her close, reassure her all is
does she feel overwhelmed well. Ask midwife for support too.
by pain? Delay internal exams; they may
lower her morale still further if
progress seems slow. Sponge her
down, look for distraction.
Encourage her to make a noise to
release tension and feelings.

Has your partner 'stuck' at ——— YES → Give her confidence. Make sure
some point, e.g. 4 or 5 cm she has privacy. Try the
dilatation? bathroom. Keep people away –
peace and quiet. Try
kissing/nipple stimulation/
cuddling. Be *calm and patient.*

Strong Labour – *continued over*

Strong Labour – *continued*

Does your partner want an ———— YES➤ If you have tried all the methods
epidural?   of support already suggested and
                                              your partner is exhausted/in too
                                              much pain ask the midwife to give
                                              your partner an internal exam to
                                              see how dilated she is. If 6cm or
                                              more, try to continue a bit longer
                                              – she may soon reach second
                                              stage. If after discussion the
                                              epidural seems appropriate, then
                                              accept it and start planning for the
                                              next stage.

Does she feel a premature ———— YES ➤ Get your partner into the
urge to push, before the   knee-chest position (all fours,
midwife says she is fully   with head lower than pelvis) –
dilated?   breathe the gas and air. Nearly
                                             there! Try breathing two short in
                                             and out breaths followed by a
              NO   sighing out breath. Repeat this
                                             rhythm while pain is at the peak.
                                             'Huff, Huff, Sigh'.

Is the urge to push building ———— YES➤ See Chart 4.
up, is her cervix fully
dilated?

Chart 4 – The birth

Has your partner been pushing for 20 mins or more without much progress? **YES** → Is this because the contractions have grown weaker, or her urge to push has died down?

YES ↓

a) Relax – accept a pause. Reassure your partner – everything will be OK. Now is the time to ask the midwife if you want to cut the umbilical cord after the birth.

b) Suggest that she changes position, try supported squatting on her toes, kneeling, standing.

c) Perhaps your partner is too tense or frightened to 'open up'? Get her into an upright position. Encourage her to listen to her body's signals, *relax* her jaw and mouth and only push when she feels the urge. Get her to visualize her energy flowing downwards, towards the baby.

d) She may like massage on thighs or back of her neck. Hold her in your arms, stay close with lots of quiet encouragement.

Chart 4 – The birth – *continued over*

Chart 4 – The birth – *continued*

Is the top of the ——— YES→ She may like you to hold
baby's head in   a mirror so that she can
sight?   catch this first glimpse
                              of the baby, or feel the
                              head with her fingers to
      NO   reassure her that she can
                              'open up'.

Is the baby's head ——— YES→ Remind her to pant
about to 'crown'?   slowly – mouth open –
                              sing/shout so that the
                              baby's head can be
      NO   delivered slowly and
                              gently. Listen to the
                              midwife's advice.

Is the delivery over? — YES→ Has your partner ——— YES→ The delivery of the
                              accepted Syntometrine   placenta will
                              to speed up the delivery   follow shortly.
                              of the placenta?   Have a look at this
                                                            amazing organ
                                                            which has
                                                            supported your
                              NO   baby through the
                                                            pregnancy.

                              She should squat over a
                              bucket/bedpan to aid
                              the descent of the
                              placenta. Breastfeed the
                              baby soon which
                              stimulates the body to
                              produce the necessary
                              hormones to deliver the
                              placenta naturally.

Has there been a ——— YES→ Make sure your partner
long delay (more   is offered more gas and
than 30 mins)   air or local anaesthetic
between the birth   before stitching. Her
and any necessary   perineum will be numb
stitching?   for a while after the
                              birth, but feeling will
                              soon return. Also make
                              sure whoever does the
                              stitching is experienced
                              in the art!

USEFUL THINGS TO TAKE WITH YOU DURING LABOUR

Your partner will have been given a list from the hospital or antenatal class so check with her that you are not duplicating anything. You will be working hard as a supporter so make sure that your clothes are comfortable. Hospital wards are kept extremely warm so always wear something cool and loose.

An ordinary round, household, plastic bucket, plus a towel to put over the brim. During contractions your partner sits on it, right side up (see page 99).

Two small cushions if your partner wants to kneel on the floor.

Woolly socks and a warm shawl to wrap your partner in if she gets cold or shaky.

Ice cubes in a wide-topped thermos flask. Make some plain and some from grape juice or from another non-acidic fruit. You and your partner will enjoy sucking on these between contractions.

Food for you to eat during labour. Nuts and raisins, fruit and chocolate. Keep away from strong smelling/flavoured food as this may make your partner feel nauseous when you eat.

Food and drink for your partner after the birth – she may be ravenous and the hospital kitchens may not be open.

Oil for massage.

A fine water spray to refresh and cool your partner down.

Small natural sponge to keep in iced water for your partner to suck on between contractions.

Soft face flannel.

Small change to make phone calls.

'Walkman' cassette player with headphones, plus favourite tapes to calm and soothe your partner during labour.

Camera and film to take pictures of the baby after the birth.

A good book to read in case your partner has an epidural and the labour is prolonged.

If you still have room, a change of shoes to ease your aching feet.

If your partner is going to use a TENS machine, take some spare batteries with you in case they run out at 3 a.m.

It may seem as if you need a truck to transport everything to the hospital, but it is always better to have too much than too little!

THINGS TO DO DURING LABOUR

Before labour:
Pillows in car, pack bag, phone numbers, hospital tour

In the beginning:
Know the signs of labour: diarrhoea, 'period' pains, 'show', rupture of membranes (ROM), easy contractions
Time contractions. If nothing much, stop until something changes
Eat and drink sensibly

2nd Babies: Phone midwife/hospital when in labour or ROM

1st Babies: Phone midwife/hospital when ROM or when contractions so strong they need total concentration and 'breathing' to cope

Comfort measures: relaxation, massage, walk/sit, bath or shower

Movement: Begin slow chest breathing when can't walk or talk through contractions. Pass the time with TV, music, going for a short walk, talking with friends

During the accelerated phase:
Contractions 45–60 seconds long every 5 minutes, coming for at least an hour (less for 2nd babies)
Ring and then go to hospital; settle in
First vaginal exam/monitoring baby, stay in upright position
Watch for disappointment if dilatation not so far on – give support
Adjust breathing patterns to light, mouth centred
Walk, sit, lean forward, change position often, *have a bath*
Sip iced water between contractions or suck ice cubes, sponge face
Back massage, try cold or heat. Look for signs of 'transition'

During transition:
Irregular contractions, sickness, low backache, shaking
Lots of *encouragement*, eyes open, position upright, 'huff, huff, sigh' breathing
Take contractions one at a time – you're almost there . . .

During the second stage:
May have a rest period without urge to push

Mobilize energy, bear down when urge becomes strong
If no progress after 20 minutes, *change position* to squat or stand on
all fours
Use imagery, mirror, think of your baby, touch the baby's head if
possible
Massage thighs, back of the neck, relax mouth and jaw
Relax as baby's head crowns – ease the baby out, pant slowly SING!
BIRTH!

During the third stage:
If necessary squat over a bedpan or bucket for the delivery of the
placenta
Hold baby with skin-to-skin contact – breastfeed if wanted
Father hold baby, supervise weighing etc.

Chapter 7

Special problems

Premature and 'small for dates' babies

As the pregnancy draws to an end your baby will seem very real. You will have built up a picture of what he looks like, and he will have taken on certain characteristics to match the physical image. If your baby is born prematurely you and your partner may not feel emotionally 'ready' for the birth. You may be practically unprepared too, with no baby clothes or an unfinished room. Labour may seem more frightening because of fears that the baby is coming too soon for its own good. And once the baby is born the reality may confirm these fears. This baby does not look like *your* baby. Premature babies sometimes look more like scrawny little animals than the chubby baby you have imagined. If the baby is taken away immediately after the birth to the special care baby unit your partner will feel even more distressed, shocked and disorientated.

SPECIAL PROBLEMS OF PREMATURITY

About 6 per cent of all babies weigh less than 5½lb (2500g) at birth, either because they are pre-term (premature) or are 'small for dates'. 'Small for dates' babies have spent the full 40 weeks in the womb but were still born weighing under 5½lb, perhaps because they have been undernourished by the placenta during the last few weeks of pregnancy. Multiple pregnancies and twins may have to be delivered early, but not all of these babies will be underweight or at risk. Some of these fragile babies will spend time in the special care baby unit immediately after birth and a few, because they have severe difficulties in breathing and feeding, will be cared for in a neonatal intensive care unit.

BREATHING AND FEEDING PROBLEMS

One in ten premature babies are born before their lungs are sufficiently developed for them to breathe normally. Babies of diabetic mothers and babies born by Caesarean section often have breathing problems too. Oxygen is given in a variety of ways to help these babies breathe, and some may be put into a miniature iron lung or mechanical ventilator to take over completely the work of breathing. Sucking is also a problem for these tiny infants, who may have to be fed intravenously, or through a tube passed through the nostril and into the stomach. Mothers are encouraged to express their own milk for their baby because it contains vital antibodies. When the baby grows strong enough to be put to the breast your partner will need encouragement and practical support from you as she will have to spend long hours patiently coaxing the baby to suck.

JAUNDICE

Perhaps half of all newborn babies develop mild jaundice, which is not harmful, a few days after birth. Jaundice is caused by an excess of red blood cells in the baby's body which the liver is initially unable to cope with. But for premature or small for dates babies, jaundice can be more severe and is treated with phototherapy (light treatment). A protective mask is placed over the baby's eyes during treatment, but is usually taken off when you visit the baby or when he is being fed, to enable you to have eye contact.

A FATHER'S ROLE

If your baby has to be taken into special care, your role becomes crucial. Any separation at birth is very distressing for the mother and her baby. The longer it lasts the more difficult it can be to repair the feeling of strangeness between them, of not belonging, or wondering if this is really the right baby. But luckily you can go with your baby, talk to the pediatrician and then carry detailed news back to your partner. Many units today will give you a photograph of your baby to show the mother, and if they do not you should take one yourself. Research both here and in America has shown that this is very helpful and provides a useful link between mother and baby until they can be together again.

Because you have seen the baby you can reassure your partner and help her face the reality of the situation. A mother who has 'lost' her baby to the special care unit will feel very emotionally vulnerable. She may feel inadequate and jealous of the nurses who are skilfully caring for her baby; even guilty because she feels responsible for her baby's suffering. All this may seem irrational to you, but it is helpful if you can accept these kinds of feelings without censure, and allow your partner to express her thoughts freely. Remember that she is faced continually with other mothers and their babies in happy partnership, while she is alone. Her arms are literally empty.

STAYING CLOSE

Ask for your partner to be moved into a single room so you can stay with her as much as possible for the first few days after the birth. It will help you both and enable you to stay close during this difficult period if you have time and privacy to share your feelings without restraint. Ask the pediatrician to visit your partner while you are there to discuss your baby's condition and progress. If your baby is seriously ill you may find that some doctors and nurses have difficulty telling you the truth about her condition. They often feel distressed themselves, so make sure you get all the information you require to feel reassured about the true situation by asking direct questions.

It is very important that you fully realize how vital your visits to the special care unit are for your baby, both before and after your partner can visit him. Research has shown that premature or ill babies thrive better and have fewer disturbances when their mother or father are with them. Impress upon nursing staff your wish to care for your baby as much as possible right from the start. At first this may mean simply touching, or stroking an arm or a leg while talking to the baby, but eventually you can learn to do nearly everything for your baby if you want to. Two American doctors who specialize in promoting the attachment between parents and babies who have problems have found a method of 'sending messages' to the baby most successful. It is important to have eye contact, which means asking to remove eye pads if they are being used, or waiting patiently for your baby to wake up. If you cannot hold your baby in your arms, get on the same level so he can see you. Follow the baby's expression and respond to him. All babies enjoy and need this kind of dialogue and it has been found that it is particularly helpful for those born prematurely.

FATHERS HAVE FEELINGS TOO

However calmly and capably you respond to these obvious problems your emotions are undeniably present throughout, even if you do not have a chance to 'let go'. Many men report that they had fantasies of wishing to flee at some point. They feel intense anger, and helplessness that the situation is beyond their control. Coping with the practical problems helps to soothe these feelings and fathers find they become more than normally forceful and challenging of authority to get what they know is right for their family. Fathers also seem to grasp the long term problems more fully, and will often begin making practical preparations for the family's future needs while the mother is still shocked and primarily concerned with the immediate welfare of the baby.

CONFLICT BETWEEN WORK AND FAMILY

Even if it means difficulties at work, or braving the disapproval of some hospital staff it is essential that you stay with your family. All fathers who wish to be fully involved are faced with a conflict of needs at the birth of their baby. Problems such as premature birth, Caesarean section, or, worst of all the illness, or death of a baby, only serve to highlight this conflict. But your presence is the most vital contribution to your family's well-being now, and as a basis for your future life together. What other people think is their affair – ask your partner what she really wants and follow your feelings about what is right for you, even if it seems difficult or unusual for others to accept.

PREPARING TO GO HOME

As soon as the baby is well enough it is a good idea to request some time alone with him in a side ward, or somewhere else suitable. You and your partner will find it very helpful to have had at least twenty-four hours of complete responsibility for your baby before leaving the security of the hospital. Before you go home make sure that you know who you can contact if you need help, day or night. The first few weeks, or even months at home can be a very trying and difficult time and leave you both feeling depressed and depleted. You may find it helpful to contact a support group of other couples who have passed through similar experiences. (See Useful addresses page 216.)

The death of a child

Most babies are born healthy. For those unfortunate couples who lose theirs the experience is all the more distressing because it is rare. The devastation and loss that the death of a loved and wanted person – whether it be a fetus of only a few weeks or a full-term baby – cannot be evaluated objectively by an outsider. For some couples an early miscarriage (or spontaneous abortion) can be just as heartbreaking as the death of a live baby, with the same depth of grief and requiring the same depth of mourning.

MISCARRIAGE

Unfortunately some doctors seem to dismiss an early miscarriage as 'nature's way' of getting rid of a defective fetus; they offer comfort in the idea that there is plenty of time to try again. But the mother and father have lost part of themselves, their hopes and aspirations for the future are dashed in a profoundly affecting way.

Because it is often assumed that a miscarriage is not so upsetting for the father, whose body is not directly involved, his feelings are often overlooked. Naturally the father wishes to be supportive and helpful to his partner, but this does not mean that he should ignore his own emotional reaction to losing his child. Too often after a miscarriage a woman finds herself isolated in sadness and depression which her partner seems unable to understand. His inability to physically experience the loss himself may make him impatient with what seems like an exaggerated reaction from the mother.

Each couple has to find their own way to mourn their loss. Sometimes a father will have to postpone expression of his feelings until later, particularly if the mother is grieving and in need of support. A couple who can share their disappointment, anger and guilt will often find relief in recognizing each other's distress and so feel less alone with their pain. Some men do find it difficult to let their partners talk repeatedly about what happened and how they feel about it – it is like running through a painful film for the umpteenth time. But for many people it is just this repetition which provides its own healing power. Mourning the loss of a loved person cannot be hurried, it has to find its place in the wider context of everyday life to have some meaning, and so be accepted. This acceptance brings with it a feeling of personal growth which in the end gives even the experience of loss some value.

STILL BIRTH

If a miscarriage is a sad and devastating loss, how much more painful is the death of a baby. Approximately 11 per 1000 boys and 8 per 1000 girl babies die just before, during or after the birth. No one can comfort you for the death of your child, all anyone can do is to support your efforts to understand your loss.

Sometimes a woman is aware that all is not well with her baby. But sometimes the baby's death is sudden, and a terrible shock. If your baby has died *in utero* your partner will probably be offered an induced labour. However some doctors prefer labour to start spontaneously, even when the baby is dead. Your partner may be distressed if she is forced to carry on her daily life knowing that the baby is dead inside her, and if so, you can request an induction. If your partner is to be induced, make sure you are with her all the time and ask your doctor to explain exactly what will happen before labour starts.

COPING WITH GRIEF

Always ask for the truth from your medical team. You will regret having been 'protected' later on. It will help, too, if you have a photograph of your baby to keep. It has been shown that the parents' mourning process is facilitated if they have a private time with their baby, to hold, touch, admire and love him before the body is taken away. Even if your partner rejects this idea initially, she may change her mind later on. Insist that the hospital staff do nothing with the body without your express permission.

The hospital will help you make arrangements for your baby's funeral, perhaps after there has been a post-mortem. Even if you are not religious, it is strongly advised that you do have some sort of ceremony to bury your child, and a burial place which later on will help you to know that the baby really did exist.

DEALING WITH THE OUTSIDE WORLD

Friends and relatives will vary enormously in their ability to be patient, loving and not try to hurry you through your grief. Our culture lacks rituals for coping with death and the mourning couple are often left feeling isolated and unsupported. You may have to reassure others that it is all right to talk about your baby, even comforting to do so.

Usually it is the mother who feels most desolate after a stillbirth and you may find it demanding and exhausting to give her the loving and patient support she needs over a number of months. Of course if you, too, can share your feelings it will be a healing experience for you both. Inevitably your relationship as a couple will be affected by your loss; either drawing you closer or pushing you further apart. Your sex life will probably reflect what is happening between you outside the bedroom. It is quite common for couples to 'go off' sex after a stillbirth. Depression and mourning are exhausting to live through and many women feel a deep distrust of their bodies for a while. Sex may also bring back memories which are just too painful to contemplate for the time being. But other couples find close sexual contact very important for them at this time; their lovemaking feels like a retreat, where they can feel safe and close when the outside world is just too difficult and painful.

PLANNING THE NEXT PREGNANCY

Once you have experienced the death of a baby at whatever stage of its development, you and your partner may feel the need to plan the next pregnancy with extra care. Organizations do exist to counsel couples who have had a miscarriage, and some hospitals also offer this service (see Preconceptual care, page 23). Some doctors suggest waiting only three menstrual cycles before trying to conceive again. If either of you feels this does not allow enough time to finish mourning it is wise to follow your instincts and give yourselves some more time.

The baby that has died cannot be replaced, or forgotten by having a new baby. Make sure you and your partner have accepted this loss before trying to conceive another child. Otherwise there is a danger that the new baby will carry the burden of being a replacement and not be loved and accepted totally for himself.

A baby with a handicap

The first thing all parents say after the birth of their baby is, 'Is it all right?' If the baby has a congenital malformation the blow is crushing. The feeling is that a less than perfect baby means less than perfect parents. Doctors and midwives are also 'faulty', everyone feels guilty and angry at fate and themselves.

It has been estimated that approximately two in every hundred births in the United States will have a congenital malformation. Hospitals vary in their policy of informing parents. Some prefer to tell the father and leave him to break the news to his wife – others do the reverse. Research has shown that it is easier for parents to adapt to their blow if they are seen together, in private. Inevitably the parents are in shock and will only absorb a limited amount of information at this first interview. Couples should be allowed to stay together and the father's role becomes highlighted right from the start, particularly if the baby is ill and has to be cared for in the Intensive Care or Special Care Baby Unit (see Premature babies, page 140).

PARENTS' REACTIONS

Normal parental reactions to the news that their baby has a congenital malformation have been seen to follow quite a predictable sequence. The first reaction is shock, with feelings of disequilibrium and helplessness, numbness and an urge to run away. This is followed by disbelief, and then overwhelming sadness and anger, sometimes with violent feelings against the baby or oneself. Gradually, after a few weeks or months, parents reach a stage of equilibrium, feel more in control and begin to trust in their ability to care for the child. But a few people never quite come to terms with what has happened to them.

The final stage is one of reorganization, adaptation and acceptance of reality. How successfully a couple achieves this seems to depend on their capacity to sustain each other and stay close during the initial catastrophe of the early weeks. Some couples grow closer and feel stronger, whereas others will fall apart with the inevitable stress that a handicapped baby presents.

Research suggests that fathers in this situation try to cope with the external and practical difficulties of the situation while the mother is often more overwhelmed by the internal adjustments necessary to accept and care for her baby. If you find yourself in this situation here are some guidelines which may be helpful to you and your partner.

Stay with your partner as much as you possibly can – day and night for the first few days at least. Find out the truth about your baby's disability and try and get the doctor to talk to you and your partner together several times to answer your questions. You may find it hard to absorb all the information you need, never feel worried if you have to ask the same question again. Do try and share your feelings with your partner as this will help her, too. If you can set the lead for your partner, your acceptance of the baby will help her. If the baby is in the SCBU, start visiting as soon as you can and even if your partner is unwell, or seems reluctant to see her baby, gently encourage her to try and visit him, too, even if it is only for a short time. If she cannot visit him, take several photographs for her to have. If you realize that the baby's condition is worsening, do not hide it from your partner; rather make sure she sees and holds the baby as much as possible.

If there are times you cannot be with your partner arrange for sensitive friends or relatives to take your place. Most special care units encourage grandparents, close relatives and siblings to visit the baby. Find out about local support groups and contact them to talk to now, or after you leave the hospital. Sometimes talking to other couples can help to allay your worst fears for the future.

Many fathers experience a strong desire to flee the situation and leave it to their partners to cope with. But this obviously is damaging for the whole family. It polarizes the couple and puts an unfair burden upon the woman, often making her withdrawn, depressed and overprotective about the child. Most men seem to cope better if they have a special role to play, rather than a vague 'helping' one. Fathers tend to be good at practical teaching situations with their handicapped child, and you may find that you get much more involved later on when the child is ready to start learning skills. This father said of his deaf child, 'I did some research and found there was a whole programme I could follow with Jeff. I found it fascinating and very satisfying. When he does something new I feel so proud, he's done it because *I* helped him, I don't take anything for granted now, that's for sure.'

Chapter 8

Caring for each other in the postnatal period

The phase following the birth of your baby will be overflowing with excitement, practical concerns and emotional adjustment. The feeling of being 'high' and 'over the moon' lasts for several days. For some fathers returning home alone after the birth from hospital is a sad and painful separation, while for others it is a welcome chance to take stock of their feelings and prepare for the next step. But whatever your internal mood there are the unavoidable practicalities to be taken care of. You may have the urge to tell the world about your recent experience and telephone everyone, or you may prefer quiet and solitude to digest the events of the last few days. Because most men are obliged to work while their partners are in hospital, those five or seven days will pass incredibly fast. Working, finishing preparations for the baby's homecoming, rushing to the hospital with food and extra clothes, while beginning to take the first steps towards getting acquainted with your baby – it is a full programme.

Each time you see your family in the early days your sense of wonder and pleasure will be renewed. Your partner quickly becomes an expert on baby care – feeding, holding, changing and settling the baby. If the birth went well she will be radiant and bubbling over with pride and achievement. But it is very important that you keep up your active role and make it clear to the midwives that you too want to be shown how to change a nappy and bath your baby etc. As a couple this may be the first separation you have had for some time. Visiting your own family in hospital is a strange experience, and you may feel awkward and displaced in the intensely female world of the postnatal ward of which your partner is now very much a part. Add to this the continuous stream of relatives and friends who will arrive from all points of the globe and it is no wonder that many couples decide to leave hospital before their time is up, just to get some privacy. Most men do not really feel they can begin to get close to their babies until the family is reunited at home.

COMING HOME

Many fathers have an idealized, even romantic picture of what life is going to be like with mother and baby in their care at last. The majority are totally unprepared for the holocaust of the first few weeks of living with a newborn baby. In a recent English survey 72 per cent of fathers took between two and seven days away from their work to be with their wives and babies when they came out of hospital (see Brian Jackson's *Fatherhood*). These men made themselves available as primary supporters and it seems the majority did not know what had hit them! Their dream of a 'holiday' with the added bonus of a new baby was quickly shattered by the reality of the baby's constant, imperative, demanding presence. Before the baby's birth it seems improbable that it can take two competent adults all their time to look after one tiny infant, but it does. Coming to terms with this 'new world' is unlike anything you have ever experienced before: it is no wonder that couples vary in the time it takes them to do so.

Many babies behave well while they are still in hospital. Perhaps, like everyone else, they sense the atmosphere of authority, and just bide their time! They often sleep regularly, seem to cry less and are generally 'good'. Often the first or second night home feels like a disaster. The baby may be awake non-stop and seems to cry and need feeding all the time. Two anxious parents hover, cuddle, change, feed, rock, wind and finally despair. Sleep becomes a thing of the past. This father vividly remembered the first night his son came home. 'He seemed to need feeding all the time. In the end we went to bed and Tina fed him next to me. I dozed a bit. Then the crying began again and then silence as he was fed. Next time I woke it was dark and he was screaming *again* . . . .'.

Babies have no idea of time. Parents struggle to maintain normality but as one day merges into another, days and nights become blurred. If you are sharing the care of the baby, running the household and maybe even trying to keep an eye on your work as well, you will find yourself nearly as exhausted as the breastfeeding mother. As this father told me, 'I was like a zombie, I got to the point where I was convinced the baby was an agent of the KGB trained in sleep deprivation! I was awake the minute she cried, even before her mother sometimes, and I knew what her cries meant too, sometimes it was "come and get me I'm hungry", at others it was just "come and get me!" If it was the latter I would stagger up and walk her about and Alice didn't even have to wake up!'

FINDING TIME TO BE TOGETHER

Finding time to be together is difficult for any couple, particularly if both parents work. Children of all ages devour their parents' time with singleminded determination. And although loving parents find this perfectly normal and an enjoyable aspect of their lives, it is important to stay in contact as a couple. Some couples who are sharing the parenting roles find they have more time together, because of the father's deeper involvement, while others have found the reverse. The women in one study (see Russell) were more unhappy than the men about the continual rush from one demand to the next. They complained of never having enough time just to enjoy their families and partners. Finding time to be alone – and alone as a couple – is important for all parents. It is too easy for time to fly past without finding any opportunity to relax together. It is hoped, though, that you will not get to the point of one couple, who found that writing dinner appointments in each other's diaries was the only way to be sure of meeting!

EMOTIONAL VULNERABILITY

If you decide to share work and baby care you may encounter disapproval or hostility at work, or from family and friends. You may feel you have to work harder than your colleagues to make up for any time taken to be with the baby away from work. And probably there will be times of hardship and frustration when commitment to your child demands real sacrifices. Couples who are both attempting to reconcile their parenting and working roles will see these as natural challenges to living a different lifestyle, and be able to give each other support to cope with outside criticism. What is harder to deal with is hostility or resentment from your partner. We all have our vulnerable spots – shared parenting will often highlight just those we might otherwise choose to hide. For example, it is very important not to feel competitive with each other or displaced by your partner's success in or out of the family. At times your baby may show a preference for one or other of you in certain circumstances. It is vitally important that neither of you feels less important or in any way diminished. It will help to share any feelings of hurt or rejection, however foolish they may sound. Your partner may feel rather vulnerable if you do everything too efficiently. You may feel hurt if the baby rejects your efforts to give comfort and only wants his mother. As usual, acknowledging your feelings will make you both more comfortable even in circumstances which may be temporarily difficult.

Postnatal feelings

In these early weeks you are the best person to take on the outside world to free your partner to continue her barely separated communication with her baby. You may feel intensely involved and satisfied with this strong, holding role. On the other hand you may feel slightly abandoned, bewildered by the 'loss' of your partner to her all-absorbing link with her baby and overwhelmed by the dependency of both mother and baby. One father who felt great satisfaction told me, 'I felt I was the hunter-gatherer and I loved it. Clare left it all to me, and I took great delight in it – a sort of basic delight. At first with the baby I felt a bit awkward, but not too much. I did pick him up in the hospital and cuddle him. I got closer when they came home. Then I changed nappies and carried him on my shoulder. But I did feel like an outsider in a way, in *their* relationship. I still thought of them as one person really.' However you feel about your role at this time it is likely that you will gradually have a sense of disappointment, even depression, as you come down from the 'high' of the birth. Postnatal depression is not the woman's prerogative. Fathers who involve themselves in the lives of their families in such an intimate way often experience the same swings from one emotion to another that women have always been subject to.

The hundred fathers in Jackson's study, of whom the majority had taken time to share the early days of parenting, admitted to some feelings of gloom. They felt they should be happy, but felt perturbed that they were not. Many felt anxious about their new role of parent but found no sympathetic outlet in which to discuss their worries. Some were surprised at their anger and resentment over what seemed like the baby's total domination of their lives, and the feeling that they had been displaced in their partner's affection. But many men felt too embarrassed to voice these feelings, and found no one to discuss them with. Whereas women have a 'free trade' area of support and advice, men, it appears, do not easily respond to their friends in this way.

As a result of this isolation some of the men talked to turned to their own fathers with surprisingly satisfactory results. Grandfathers enjoyed talking to their sons and having contact with their grandchildren in a more intimate way which gratified everyone. It seems as if a woman can only give herself completely to her baby if she feels 'held' by her man, who himself needs supportive parenting. This father told me how he felt: 'Ten minutes after Di came from the hospital, he began to cry! I found it unsettling – I felt the need to escape – go to work or something! I realized that's *my* baby and he's here to stay, and I'm responsible from now on. Around that time I did want to see more of my parents. It was as if now we had shared concerns – I think I felt closer to my father than at any previous time. We talked and I felt that he wanted to talk to me.'

Some men do sail through those early weeks with vigour and enjoyment, but they may be in a minority. But what is true of everyone, mothers and fathers, is that emotions are extremely labile during this initial period of adjustment to parenthood. Many couples have told me they felt totally unprepared for some, if not most, of the demands of parenthood. Perhaps it is better to recognize the impossibility of being prepared for every new challenge and try to take life as it comes, day by day.

POSTNATAL DEPRESSION

Most women, and some men, experience a degree of depression after the birth of their baby and during the early weeks of adjusting to parenthood. Women have a feeling of emptiness; the pleasant glow of well-being that pregnancy induces has gone and in its place a real baby makes demands which far exceed all expectations. Both mind and body are in a state of turmoil and there is never enough time to make sense of what is happening because the baby has to come first. It is hardly surprising that many women have what is called the 'baby blues' which start around the third day after the birth. This mild emotional ripple causes a woman to become tearful, often crying for no apparent reason, but these tears are a pleasant release, and by the next day have disappeared.

But for other women this ripple of sadness develops into a wave of postnatal depression, often lasting many weeks or even months. This particular depression is extremely unpleasant, and may strike a woman quite unexpectedly after one delivery and not another. However it does not appear to be related to any previous history of depression. It can be difficult to cope with if it is ignored, not only for the sufferer herself, but also for her family. A woman who feels postnatally depressed gradually becomes desperate if left to cope alone, 'like living at the bottom of a black pit' was how one mother described it. And in extreme cases the condition becomes a psychotic breakdown which necessitates hospitalization under psychiatric treatment (see Further reading, page 213).

THE NORMAL CHANGES AFTER GIVING BIRTH

If all goes well, having a baby produces a 'high' which lasts for a variable length of time according to the individual woman; coming down to earth is not always easy and often produces a temporary mood swing in the opposite direction. Certainly some of the 'depression' is physiological, due in part to the extraordinary upheaval the woman's body goes through, readapting to its non-pregnant state. The feelings aroused by the sudden hormonal changes after giving birth, coupled with the intense fatigue of recovering from labour, and looking after a newborn baby while trying to maintain some vestige of domestic normality inevitably get labelled postnatal depression.

Every new mother also has her own internal psychological challenges to respond to. Depending on her character and past emotional experience, the adaptation to motherhood will be undertaken willingly or with grave misgivings. Most urgently there is the challenge of matching the fantasy of motherhood – all soft focus cuddles with an adorably cherubic baby dressed in white – with the reality of a crying, red faced infant who has been sick over everything for the sixth time that day! And where there are unresolved fears, lack of family support, problems accepting responsibility, or simply a feeling of events having gone too fast and feeling out of control as a result, a woman will easily feel tearful, emotionally withdrawn or unstable and perpetually stretched to the limit. The unrelenting demands of motherhood, augmented with feelings of acute fatigue, loss of positive body image, financial dependence and temporary loss of job status and colleagues – it would be surprising if a turmoil of such proportions did not evoke a deep response.

'I DIDN'T LOVE MY BABY FOR THE FIRST FOUR MONTHS . . .'

Some women are intensely relieved to know that others have shared this experience. Postnatal depression may also mean a woman cannot feel love for her baby temporarily. Many women feel guilty if there is a mismatch between what they imagine they should feel and what they really do feel. These same woman are intensely maternal and suffer in silence, often only sharing their fears after the problem has receded. But even when they are not yet 'in love', they still care for their baby devotedly. And then suddenly they realize they do love their baby, but it may take weeks or months and is usually related to the baby becoming more responsive. Of course feeling unresponsive can also be a problem for fathers, particularly if they do not have much contact with their child (see Bonding, page 18).

Finally it is important to understand that many women feel the total responsibility of the baby is terribly oppressive, even when they longed to be a mother. Of course if you, as the father, are sharing the 24-hour-a-day care of the baby – really sharing this emotional responsibility, then the woman is far less likely to get depressed or feel overwhelmed. But even with support and domestic help, most women will have periods of feeling odd and out of touch with normality during this initial period of adjustment.

SUPPORT IS ESSENTIAL

If you notice that your partner is depressed, withdrawn, uninterested in the baby, or desperately over-anxious, tearful, does not sleep and is hyperactive, or alternatively wants to sleep all the time, then make sure you get her to seek help sooner rather than later. Usually these symptoms can be alleviated. The suffering woman desperately needs extra help with the baby and with domestic chores. She needs her physical symptoms to be attended to as well as the psychological ones; a practitioner who sees her as a whole person and not just as someone needing to stop feeling depressed will be most helpful. The usually prescribed anti-depressant drugs are often inappropriate for postnatal depression and will only ever be a temporary measure – long-term solutions will not be found by suppressing the symptoms. She needs a chance to evaluate what is happening without feeling guilty or a failure – preferably with the loving support of her partner which will enable her to make a full recovery.

Try and get your partner to talk to you so you can understand what she is going through. Make sure that her GP is sympathetic, ask for an appointment and go together to discuss what treatment would be best. Be as patient and loving as you can – this may be hard if you, too, are feeling depressed with your new role as a father, but rest assured that it is possible to find help and to feel better. If you are unable to be with your partner because of other commitments then be sure to find a replacement support person to take your place temporarily, and be ready to make up for lost time later on. Find out through your local branch of the National Childbirth Trust (see Useful addresses, page 213) where your nearest postnatal support group is and contact them yourself if your partner feels unable to. These informal support groups, run on a mother-to-mother basis, can often arrange for someone to go with your partner in the beginning – everyone remembers the struggles of those first few weeks – or you can take her yourself. Regular contact through postnatal support groups with other mothers who have young babies will provide not only a social network, but also a sharing environment with other people who have had similar experiences. Finally it is essential that you understand the nature of postnatal depression to be able to support your partner fully while she is getting better. Try contacting the Association of Postnatal Illness who will give you information and advice (see page 216).

THE COUPLE'S RELATIONSHIP

In the first few weeks of the new family's life most couples do not have much time to think about their relationship or to find time to be solitary. This has always been a problem for mothers, but now fathers are experiencing it as they involve themselves more in the demands of baby care. Of course some men refuse to alter their usual habits just because a baby comes along. Their work and social commitments remain pretty much unchanged and the traditional parenting roles are adhered to, come what may. These less involved fathers do not suffer from the 'lows' of close fathering, but then neither do they profit from the 'highs'. Men who do become involved in caring for their babies – up to twenty-four hours contact a week as opposed to the minuscule one or two hours of some 'traditional' fathers – say that the benefits outweigh the problems and that the satisfaction and pleasure that they derive from sharing the care of their newborn baby was considerable. Given the opportunity, babies respond and enter into a dialogue immediately after birth. They smile in the first two weeks – a smile that is not just wind! This willingness and capacity to respond gives you and your partner the courage to go on even when exhaustion threatens to overwhelm you both. But however enjoyable and all-absorbing a tiny baby is, you both need a break from time to time to replenish yourselves as a couple – and as individuals following your own pursuits.

Fathers who made huge efforts in the home during the early weeks have told me they often gradually came to feel resentful and frustrated. This they found bewildering because they firmly believed that becoming more involved was the 'right' thing to do; they had freely chosen to take on the role of primary supporter to the mother and baby. Nevertheless frustration developed – expressed through domestic irritations, such as not even being able to find time to mow the lawn. These caring men wanted to respond gladly to the demands made upon them but felt anxious that they would be swamped. Fearing their contribution was being taken for granted they inevitably felt uneasy for needing praise and recognition.

In traditional families the father has his own independent life at work apart from his family. But among couples who share the parenting roles more closely, fathers experience some of the same conflicts that mothers have always felt between family commitments and the adult world. This father told me how he felt. 'I took a week off when Tanya came out of hospital. I did everything I could do, except feed the baby, but I did feel I needed my work, to get away, I couldn't wait to get home to see them both, but I needed that time away to assert my independence. I was aware that Tanya didn't have that chance, she was stuck at that time.'

Although many couples rate the first six months after the birth extremely low in marital satisfaction, others who are sharing the demands have the reverse experience. They are able to appreciate each other's problems more fully when the baby becomes a focal point for the talking and exchange of feelings which has always been a recipe for a successful relationship. Both mother and father feel needed, appreciated and involved – but not overwhelmed or isolated in one particular role within the family.

AMBIVALENCE ABOUT SHARING

There is another challenge related to increased father-participation which is often overlooked until it happens. Some women find it harder to give up the exclusive mother–baby relationship than they had anticipated before the birth. There may be an uneasy feeling that if a woman shares baby care with her man, she is somehow failing as a 'good mother'. Her reluctance or feelings of ambivalence are most often expressed in terms of over-protection of the baby or criticism of the father's methods of baby care. This is naturally more intense during the breastfeeding phase, when a mother feels that very strong link with her baby. Even so this reaction can be unexpected as this father told me. 'Before Clara was born we used to talk about how we'd share looking after the baby . . . Stephanie said she wouldn't do everything, that I had to do my bit too. I got used to the idea, and I thought, well, I'll give it a go. You see my job is flexible because I work for myself. So I can arrange to be home a bit more. But now when I say to Steph "Shall I do that", she says something like, "No, you do it too slowly." I don't really do as much as I could. I wouldn't mind doing a bit more really.' This father had to wait some time before his partner began to let him take care of their baby. Gradually the necessary trust was established between the couple which enabled the mother to feel happy with a more sharing relationship.

Although sharing may seem a logical progression for a committed father it is not always as easy as it sounds to put into practice. Men often feel anxious about their physical awkwardness, and lack of experience in babycare makes them hesitate – a newborn baby appears terrifyingly vulnerable and fragile. Some women also feel threatened because they feel a sense of loss rather than gain as the father moves towards closer involvement with 'her' baby. Unless the couple is determined to involve the man right from the start, hospital arrangements can often lead to the mother becoming an 'expert' during the vital first days. Because of the strength of traditional parenting patterns it is very easy for a mother to become possessive of her exclusive role with the baby. Many women feel powerful and intensely satisfied in their mothering role. Asking them to share this may demand a joint effort from the couple to find ways for the woman to find similar satisfaction in other areas of her life. A man who senses that his partner is unwilling to share their baby may have to examine whether as a couple they are really sharing themselves.

Both people have to lose something as individuals in order to become a couple able to help each other unselfishly share their baby. A woman may express her reluctance to share in practical terms by making it difficult for her partner to do anything very much with their baby. If the father is already hesitant and lacking in self confidence this message that 'mother knows best' will further reduce the father–baby interaction. It may take a conscious effort to reverse this trend and as usual the necessary trust has to be established between the couple in their intimate relationship. Wanting to share your baby can become an extension of the care you give each other as a couple – or it may reflect a competitive power struggle of one partner's unmet, or unexpressed, needs. If they are really to share the subtle demands of their baby a couple should first attend to each other's needs. Only then will both partners be able to put the baby before themselves and still maintain a sense of shared strength and harmony as a couple. If you neglect each other resentment from one or other partner may successfully sabotage everyone's best intentions.

Crossing boundaries is not just a problem for mothers. For a man to allow the nurturing qualities of his personality to come to the surface means he has to be reasonably comfortable with the so-called 'feminine' side of his personality. Caring for a fragile, newborn baby entails sensitivity and a gentle touch. Some men find these demands too threatening to their 'masculine' self image. They prefer to remain firmly in their well established role of traditional, distant fathering and will only gradually venture into the baby's world by more oblique routes, usually when the baby has become a robust toddler.

Other couples do not find sharing a problem and are happy to hand the baby to and fro between them, particularly if the woman wants to continue her own outside work commitments at some point after the birth (see Organizing work schedules, page 172). And fathers who have long working hours can always find a special time to be with their baby. With mutual support anything goes, as this father told me. 'I used to get up after the early morning feed, around six o'clock. I'd give Jeff his bath, we'd both get in, lots of water everywhere, great fun. Hannah went back to bed and pretended to sleep through the noise. Then sometimes in the warm weather we'd go for a walk. Me and my baby and all the joggers!'

INHERITED PATTERNS

Men and women learn from their parents what is appropriate parenting behaviour. The fear of appearing less 'macho' by caring for babies or small children seems to be an inherited attitude to fathering. Men who had fathers who were uninvolved found it difficult to express the gentler parenting characteristics.

Luckily in human behaviour nothing is static; for many of the men I have talked to it was just this distant relationship which inspired them to make drastic changes in their own style of fathering. Whatever your plans, during the first few weeks after the birth it is worth evaluating your feelings, and, if you are attempting fundamental changes, making sure you do not have too many outside negative influences nearby, such as relatives or friends who could undermine your confidence. They should be kept firmly at bay if they are known to be disapproving of your increased involvement until you and your partner are more confidently established in your new roles.

Before the birth most first-time fathers have worries about how successfully they can look after a very young baby. But there is one level of involvement which every father can attempt with no fear of failure and every likelihood of success. It is not a practical skill, and you need nothing except a calm, relaxed atmosphere with your baby in your arms. One man described this fathering activity well: 'I've shared as much as I can, but when you can't feed the baby you have to think along another line. I've tried to develop that special awareness which many men do find hard, but which we all have within us, we all have the capacity for. You have to surrender yourself, really feel where the baby's at. It is hard for some people to stop being frightened and allow the baby just to "be" – so many men feel they have to make faces, or jump about with their babies, to get them to laugh or something. But I try and make time to just sit with her close in my arms and be together.'

Postnatal sex

As one father put it when we talked about postnatal sex, 'I've decided making love soon after having a baby is like good fish and chips – it probably does exist, but never in your own local chippie!' Of course after nine months of pregnancy, giving birth and the immediate postnatal period, your normal sex life may seem a pretty hazy memory anyway. Those Sunday afternoons in bed making love are as hard to believe in as a hot sunny day in the middle of winter. Most couples agree that during the first few weeks after the birth, particularly of a first baby, there are so many things to cope with that making love often becomes temporarily less important. After a second or third baby, however, couples get back into the normal swing of lovemaking much faster.

MEN'S REACTIONS

After a first baby men's reactions when asked how they are enjoying sex vary enormously. 'Sex, what's that, I can't remember what to do, it's been such a long time!' 'During pregnancy I found her very attractive sexually. Now I hope she'll get back to normal quickly. I don't feel she's *un*attractive now, in a way she's more so because she's the mother of our child. Yes I do feel differently about her now, I'm not quite sure how.' 'After the birth we were both high. When Helen came home from hospital we did screw the first week she was back, we were both surprised how randy we felt!'

As usual with sexual responses everyone is different, and it is unwise to anticipate how you, or your partner, will react. Although intercourse may not be top of your list, lots of holding, cuddling and touching are usually what both partners want and enjoy. In fact most couples do experience some temporary setbacks restarting sexual intercourse after having a first baby. Considering all the new challenges you are facing in every area of your lives it would be surprising if sex was completely unaffected. Certainly it helps if you both have a patient, loving attitude and a good sense of humour during those early weeks.

Although your body has not been through the trauma of giving birth you will probably need some time to adjust to your new role as a father. The myth that a man's sexuality is totally uninfluenced by outside stress or intense emotion is a thing of the past. The demands of living through the first few months of family life while trying to be supportive at home and efficient at work reduces many men's libido. Sexuality is still as important as ever, but actual intercourse may seem a less dominant need for the time being. Your sexual relationship is just a part of the wider adjustments you and your partner are making on almost every level of your lives, both inside and outside the family.

Some men do feel differently about sex at this time, even though they may have felt no anxiety before the birth. Some report increased awareness and sensitivity of the woman's enjoyment. They often feel more caring, particularly if the woman has had stitches, and their lovemaking becomes gentler and more considerate than before.

Occasionally a man may be deeply affected by seeing a difficult delivery and find this interferes with his capacity to make love. A sensitive man fears that penetration could damage his partner, and may not trust her to tell him if she is uncomfortable. Things will generally get back to normal as the memory fades. But it is always sensible for the couple to discuss a problem like this to reassure each other and avoid the misunderstanding of feeling rejected. The man needs to be confident that his partner is fully healed, and more important, that she will guide him during intercourse so he need not fear hurting her. Suggest to your partner that you could gently massage her perineum with vitamin E oil, which helps the healing process and reassures you both when everything is back to normal.

THE WOMAN'S FEELINGS

It can take days, weeks or months before a woman feels confident and comfortable about her body after giving birth. Luckily intercourse is not the only way of enjoying sex. This is a time when many women appreciate oral sex and mutual masturbation as a way of keeping up their sexual dialogue. All women need lots of encouragement from their partners that they are still sexually attractive, even while they are still unlike their 'normal' shape.

As if simply giving birth were not enough to cope with, many women these days have the added problem of stitches after an episiotomy, which can be uncomfortable and irritating and sometimes painful for a variable amount of time. And after a Caesarean birth or a forceps delivery a woman may need extra time to recover, and regain her sexual and erotic body image.

RECOVERING SEXUAL AWARENESS

All women, whatever the labour, feel bruised and stretched after childbirth and it will take time to recover full sensitivity and awareness. Daily pelvic floor exercises are essential to aid recovery and revitalize sexual sensitivity. These exercises also increase the blood flow to the bruised or stitched area which helps the healing process.

Doing exercises alone is always rather boring, so once you have resumed regular sexual intercourse you can join in. After penetrating just stay still for a while and suggest your partner practise her pelvic floor exercises so you can let her know how much you appreciate her increased muscle power! Alternatively you can try thrusting slowly, pausing occasionally for her to give you a vaginal 'kiss'. Apart from being pleasurable for you, it will also help her reach a more intense orgasm.

If your partner has any continuing pain or discomfort several weeks after the birth you can help by going with her to see your GP to ask for a thorough check-up. (If this does not seem satisfactory ask to be referred to a specialist clinic or a consultant gynaecologist for a second opinion.) Sometimes stitches given after an episiotomy or tear do not heal satisfactorily and women do not always receive the sympathy and care they require to regain their pre-pregnant health. In fact many women neglect themselves after giving birth because the focus of interest has shifted to the baby's well being. If you can be supportive and encourage your partner to take extra care of herself; find a GP who understands the normal physiological and emotional strains on every mother during the childbearing year, you may avoid the disabling side-effects of having a baby.

FATIGUE AND DISTRACTIONS

For a variety of reasons, hormonal, physiological and psychological, women are slower to become sexually aroused in the first few weeks after having a baby. An intense 'maternal preoccupation' sometimes makes it difficult for a woman to lose herself in abandoned love-making. It is as if she has a third ear which is always listening for the baby, who often reflects this phenomenon by being unusually wakeful and fretting as soon as the couple withdraw their attention and hop into bed! No mother, and very few fathers, can continue to make love if their baby is crying. One couple told me they found a solution by having a babysitter come between feeds at the weekend to take the baby out, so that they could relax undisturbed and make love if they felt like it.

The distraction of a crying baby is not the only problem – fatigue is even more likely to put your libido in the deep freeze. This mother found she was so tired and overwhelmed that lovemaking was the last straw. 'I was so tired, it became unreal. All day and night, every two hours or so I'd feed Danny. Then change him and settle him and so on. I did try to cook and clean and do the shopping. Bob used to get home around eight for his supper, by that time I was like a wet rag, specially as Danny cried a lot in the evenings. I felt like a portable milk bar, I felt weird and unrecognizable. If Bob wanted to have a cuddle or go to bed I used to shrug him off, I couldn't bear the idea of someone else wanting something from me, hanging from me like I was a Christmas tree. I hated the dog too, those sad eyes looking at me needing affection, one more to look after!'

These feelings are not atypical in a woman trying to cope alone during the early postnatal days. Lovemaking is never isolated from the rest of a couple's relationship – it is always an integral part of the wider dialogue. Sharing the responsibilities reduces the fatigue and stress and enables both partners to find comfort and reassurance in each other. Even if 'making love' is centred more in mutual tenderness and caregiving than in genital sex, it can still be satisfying and sensual. Express your feelings about sex and encourage your partner to do the same, that way misunderstanding will be avoided and you will stay in tune with each other.

MAKING LOVE AGAIN

Inevitably after having a baby lovemaking will not be as spontaneous as it once was. Many men try not to express their impatience at the time it takes to get back to normal, but if you are feeling sexually frustrated it is far better to look for a solution together rather than to bottle up resentment. The first few times you attempt sexual intercourse it will help to reduce outside distraction to a minimum. Your baby should be either asleep, or quiet in another room so your partner can relax and concentrate on herself and you. Before attempting penetration make sure your partner is not feeling anxious about her perineum. (If she has had stitches or a tear, it is a good idea to look and feel that everything is back to normal, otherwise she may feel too tense to enjoy herself.) Even if your partner has had a Caesarean birth she will have less natural vaginal lubrication for at least six weeks after giving birth, and possibly longer if she breast-feeds. This means vaginal lubricating jelly is essential, or penetration will be uncomfortable, particularly if you are using a condom.

It is completely normal for a woman to need more time to become aroused after having a baby. You will need to be a more patient and attentive lover. This is the time to use all your powers of seduction as your partner may feel very 'virginal'! At the moment of penetration your partner should consciously relax her pelvic floor towards you. If she lies on top and guides your penis herself this may help her not to tense her pelvic floor. One father who had thoughtfully prepared to make love for the first time after the birth told me, 'Well we did it all, baby at my mother's, bottle of Beaujolais, I did my full Casanova routine, we were really turned on. The moment came and suddenly I could hear Anna doing her breathing for contractions! That was it, we both burst out laughing. We managed – it wasn't wonderful, but once you get over the virgin-first-time feeling things get easier!'

BIRTH CONTROL – THE MAN'S RESPONSIBILITY

Even the most caring and liberated men have been known to feel at a loss when it comes to the question of birth control. The fear of an unwanted pregnancy can be a strong disincentive to lovemaking. A woman who has recently given birth, probably had stitches in her perineum, felt bruised and sore for a time, will welcome a break from the worry of birth control. This is the ideal time for you to take over that responsibility. Most couples do not resume full sexual intercourse before the woman's six-week postnatal check-up. However, if you both feel enthusiastic about making love during the early weeks there is no reason not to as long as your partner has a fully healed perineum. The only safe method of contraception is for you to wear a condom. The pill is not recommended if your partner is breastfeeding and the diaphragm and the intra-uterine device (coil) can only be re-fitted at the first postnatal check-up. Breastfeeding is not a reliable method of birth control, nor are the other 'natural' methods before the woman's body has returned to its normal rhythms.

SEX AND BREASTFEEDING FROM THE MAN'S POINT OF VIEW

It is not unusual for men to have feelings of jealousy or envy which focus on the breastfeeding relationship. Some fathers feel painfully displaced by the baby in the early weeks, particularly if the woman 'falls in love' with her baby and is overly preoccupied with breastfeeding. The love and attention – the breasts themselves – that were available exclusively for him in the past, now have to be shared on a regular and seemingly permanent basis. This causes real pain which is often left untended because these same fathers genuinely love their babies and feel vulnerable expressing emotions which might be misinterpreted. Surprisingly the woman is often unaware of her man's need for a more overt expression of love and affection – even when sexual inercourse has not been resumed. But once a man can acknowledge the nature of his real needs and discuss it freely and without fear of rebuff with his partner, a solution can be found.

SEX AND BREASTFEEDING FROM THE WOMAN'S POINT OF VIEW

Some lucky women find breastfeeding sexually arousing when they recover from the fatigue of the first few months. As this mother said, 'It was great, a big "turn on" every few hours. I couldn't wait for Pete to come through the door!' If a woman enjoys breastfeeding it can make the whole of her body more erotically responsive, which in turn makes lovemaking more enjoyable.

However in the early days many women find that breastfeeding inhibits them sexually. They feel their bodies taken over with maternal feelings and find their libido is dormant for a while. Gradually this changes and they then turn back to their man with increased passion, and tenderness. Some fathers mirror these feelings and feel comfortable with the lull in their normal sex lives. Those who do not inevitably begin to feel frustrated and have to learn to cultivate patience and hold on. Remember breastfeeding does not last for ever!

During the time soon after the birth it will undoubtedly help if you can reassure your partner that you can love her in all her roles, as a sexually attractive woman and as a mother. If you do make love during the phase when the baby is being fed every two or three hours the mother's breasts are extremely tender and so a position for intercourse has to be found where no pressure is put on them. Some women feel inhibited, or fear that you will be disgusted because even the lightest touch may cause the milk to flow. Of course some couples find this exciting and a man can safely suck his partner's breasts – following the rules of supply and demand, all that happens is more milk is produced for the baby's next feed!

Chapter 9

Postnatal practicalities

Paternity leave

It is quite usual in industrialized countries for mothers to take time off work when they have a baby. It is quite unusual for fathers to do the same. Maternity leave recognizes how important it is for mother and baby to have uninterrupted time together for several weeks or even months after the birth. This time is not just to establish the feeding pattern, but also to give the baby the vital experience of a stable relationship, the lack of which, according to authorities like Bowlby and Winnicott, will have devastating and long-term effects.

But although research done here and in the United States over the last fifteen years has clearly demonstrated just how engrossed fathers too can be with their babies; how delighted and involved they become in the very first days after the birth, this is still not officially recognized in the man's other world – his work place. After the birth of his baby, the 'normal' thing for a man to do is to carry on as if nothing has happened. The denial of the father's role in the family, except as breadwinner, not only places an impossible burden on the mother who is expected to meet all the baby's demands single-handed, but it is unfair on the man.

A few enlightened countries such as Sweden have long ago recognized, and funded paternity leave for all fathers. In Britain there is no legal provision for paternity leave and efforts to change the law have been deliberately opposed. There appear to be only about sixty firms who do provide leave for fathers, usually at reduced pay. Some professional trade unions in Britain and in other EEC countries do support the idea of paid paternity leave, but on the whole it is not yet the norm for all fathers.

In Britain social class differences also emerge in the length of time taken to be at home after the birth of a baby. Professional men are more likely to be able to afford to take unpaid, or holiday, leave than non-professional men who simply cannot afford to stop working. In fact research shows that this latter group of fathers often had to resort to other methods to stay at home to support their families. One way was to rely on the goodwill of the family doctor to supply them with some paid 'sick' leave. Given the very real financial difficulties and social pressures against paternity leave for this group of men it is interesting that they in fact managed to be at home for longer than men in other social classes.

So what is the real value of paternity leave? Why should a father take time off from work after his baby's birth? It is the obvious opportunity for him to get acquainted with his baby without the pressures of work coming between them. But is that really so important, and anyway, is there much a man can do, except the cooking, cleaning and shopping – which anyone can do? If men believe that paternity leave is just a chance to do housework, then no wonder they are not clamouring for more time off work!

A FATHER'S PLACE IS IN THE HOME

Before the birth you may have been uneasy about committing yourself to taking an active share in the care of your baby. Are you the 'right' type, will you do the 'right' things at the 'right' time, or will you be hopelessly out of your depth? Your worries are probably similar to your partner's – after all women are meant to know instinctively what to do with babies – men are not! Try approaching the future as an experience where you can pool resources, learning as you go along how best to share the changing demands from the baby, from your work, and each other. One thing is certain, your baby will accept you both uncritically as you are.

From a father's point of view the first weeks with a new baby are unrepeatable. Babies are not just 'blobs' needing food. They are extremely active and interesting; the more time you spend together, the more the baby will respond. It is a myth that babies sleep all the time; in fact some hardly seem to sleep at all and are alert and wakeful right from the start. Each day brings new skills and another revealing facet of your baby's personality. In the past many fathers missed being part of this 'unveiling' of a new human. But this is changing, and as more men take paternity leave and opt to be the primary source of support in the home they are often amazed at how unexpectedly enthralling a newborn baby can be. One father was openly sceptical before his own daughter was born. 'Well, the housework wasn't much fun, it seemed to be endless. But Jessie was amazingly interesting, I wasn't prepared for that really. You know, like when she did her first really big yawn, it was such an achievement. She looked so surprised, we both laughed. Mind you if you'd told me six months ago I'd be raving about a baby yawning, well I'd have said you were daft. But when it's your own I suppose it's different?'

PRACTICAL AND MORAL SUPPORT

Providing practical help after the baby comes home is essential. Before the birth, first-time parents often find it impossible to grasp the sheer hard work involved in the non-stop relentless demands from the baby; the emotional and physical fatigue that may overwhelm one person trying to do everything alone. One person can do it alone – but two people by sharing the highs and lows can actually enjoy it.

During the first week with a newborn your partner will be dominated by two main concerns. First she will have a need to tell the story of her experience of giving birth many times over. She will probably relive the labour in her mind, like a film repeating over and over again; in part to grasp what really happened, but also to place it securely in her memory. You too may want to share your perception of the experience either in words or by writing an account of the birth as you saw and felt it. Usually fathers have a keener sense of the exact sequence of the labour which can help the woman fill in any gaps in her memory.

The other concern is your partner's deepening preoccupation with her baby. It is almost as if the umbilical cord was still intact with mother and baby still attached to each other's inner world. D. W. Winnicott called this 'primary maternal preoccupation' and recognized it as an essential and satisfying part of the mother–baby relationship. It is this free flowing interconnection that every baby needs to experience to grow into a healthy, well-integrated person. This is where the father becomes the key person. Your presence is invaluable; by giving practical support you are also giving the emotional sustenance that every woman needs to feel secure enough to allow this 'preoccupation' to develop. Most men see their function during this phase as a natural extension of their usual role. As the main supporter you are in charge of the 'external' world, protective, practical and ready to encourage your partner to lean on you until she has satisfactorily established herself in her new role and can then re-enter the external world. It has been noticed that where a father is absent or unsupportive, and there is no substitute support network, the woman will be less competent and achieve less satisfaction in the crucial feeding relationship with her baby.

And what about paternal preoccupation? I have observed that some fathers become equally engrossed with their infants – if the environment is encouraging and the desire is there. Remember that during the early days your baby is highly receptive to your attentions, so set aside a time, every day, to be together, preferably during a calm, wakeful period. If you take charge of bath time, or the nappy change half way through a feed, this provides you with an ideal starting point. However you may need some encouragement and support from your partner to get you going. But once you decide to try a specific task just go ahead and 'have a go'.

IF WORK DEMANDS WIN

I talked to several men who had regretted not having taken paternity leave after the birth of their first child; either because they had not appreciated the essential nature of their role at home, or because of unyielding work demands. A woman alone is much more likely to feel overwhelmed by the total responsibility of continuous child care and may become depressed – this inevitably affects the couple's relationship. Cut off from work and the social network it provides, and probably financially dependent for the first time in her adult life – no wonder unsupported motherhood reduces self confidence and enhances resentment. A mother coping unaided begins to feel de-valued by her man if he refuses to become involved in the day-to-day care of their baby. (The baby may also demonstrate through his behaviour some awareness of the mother's unhappiness.)

Paternity leave gives a man the ideal opportunity to establish his family as a strong and harmonious unit. Those men who really cannot find the time to be at home for at least a week after the birth should try to provide an alternative support system – a relative, suitable friend or a professional to take their place. Absent fathers should be fully aware of what they personally are missing while recognizing the need to make up for lost time with their baby and to be ready to repair any strain on their relationship with their partners.

Many of the fathers I talked to agreed that those first few weeks after the birth were some of the most tiring but enjoyable of their lives. Men who do share the physical and emotional demands of those first weeks of family life feel that they personally changed irrevocably from the experience. They acquire a real understanding of housework, and what a deep commitment to satisfying a baby's needs really demands. And they all report feeling a high level of satisfaction about their involvement, even though in some cases going back to work felt like a holiday. But for others going back to work was a wrench, and many were surprised by how much they missed their child. A successful businessman, who stayed at home till his daughter was two weeks old, told me, 'When I went back to work I was suprised to catch myself thinking about her, wondering if she was sleeping or whatever. I used to ring home several times a day, just to see how they were. I suppose I just found work was a bit less important; less "real" in a way.'

Practical arrangements

Couples vary in how they arrange their lives after the birth. Most prefer to have at least a week alone without relatives or too many visitors, to get themselves established. This is often very difficult to arrange, but is a good idea if you want to take over certain responsibilities; bathing, winding, changing the baby are all new skills to be mastered, and you will need time to practise before you feel confident in front of your mother-in-law's quizzical gaze. After the first week or fortnight most couples prefer the father to ease back into work gently rather than suddenly being away all day every day. Unfortunately many men do not have the luxury of free choice, but if you can bear these points in mind you may be surprised how much you can achieve.

ORGANIZING WORK SCHEDULES

If you are contemplating shared parenthood, start making preparations early – preferably during pregnancy. Organizing two peoples' work commitments and giving your baby the care he needs is going to take sensitive and careful planning. Your baby is almost bound to have some difficulty in adjusting to being cared for by two (or more) people. A baby has a different perception of time and his protests about the disappearance of a loved caregiver will vary in intensity according to his developmental stage (see Further reading, page 218). Before six months of age most babies will accept whichever loving adult they are given. But at around that time a baby begins to distinguish more vividly between his parents and will often reject an outside person who is not very familiar and part of his everyday experience. Your baby knows his likes and dislikes; basically he prefers his world to remain stable and unchanging – that is, with both parents within reach day and night! Although this idyllic state of affairs is usually only possible during holidays you should try to make your baby's environment as secure as you possibly can. For example, until he is old enough to understand, you baby will see you or your partner's disappearance to work as a total loss – painful as death is for an adult. So it is probably a good idea to make initial separations brief, extending the length of time gradually. When he is more mature he will see it as a temporary but acceptable 'game' of hiding and reappearance. Your role as parents is to assess your baby's capacity to cope with this 'loss', and make every effort to reassure him verbally and non verbally that it is only temporary.

Never lie when it comes to leaving a child, even for brief periods of time. Get into the habit of explaining what is going to happen well before the time of your departure, even to a pre-verbal child. Babies always sense when you are getting ready to go out. Tell your child exactly when you are leaving, who will be there in your place and what time approximately you will return. If you are not exactly sure when that will be, explain that too with the reassurance that you will come as soon as possible. Describe very simply some of the things that will happen while you are away – mealtimes, walks, bathtime or bedtime. Always stay a little with the person who is to take over from you and when the moment comes, never pretend you are not leaving and creep out when the child is asleep or distracted by someone or something. Better to brave the tears calmly, reassure any expression of fear or anxiety so your baby can learn that although you have to leave you do always return.

Unlike adults, babies who are secure will express themselves pretty directly when they are disturbed or upset about something. This father told me of his early days caring for his nine-month-old daughter. 'For Maria to leave for work was quite a problem in the beginning. I used to dread the moment. We'd all go to the door and say "goodbye Mummy" and then Stephanie would start. She'd hold out her arms and cry and struggle with me. We tried every kind of goodbye routine and in the end we settled on the short version. Maria would kiss her and we would wave and say goodbye, and Maria would leave in spite of the screams. I was left with Stephanie in a state, we'd walk around and I'd talk to her and try to comfort her. It did get better gradually, but I did feel a bit helpless at the beginning, and wondered whether I could cope. Mind you, I think we grew out of it together, I got more confident and she stopped carrying on.' Parents who are having difficulties leaving their baby need to give each other a lot of emotional support and encouragement. And as this father recognized, the more secure he became in his role the easier it was for the baby to accept the changes in her world too.

THE TRANSITION FROM WORK TO HOME

The transition from work to the child-centred world of home is not so simple either. Some fathers say they need time to unwind before taking over full responsibility for the baby. They feel the contrast of demands is very powerful and find a bath or a drink and a few minutes to relax helps them re-enter the family. Women who have been away working all day feel very much the same – everyone needs a short time to recover before starting on their other role. This father described his homecoming, 'I step in the door and it hits me! All day I've been thinking for myself and suddenly I have to suspend "me" and tune in to her. At times I feel too strung up in my world and it takes time to relax into hers. It's like going from Concorde to a pony and trap!' Parents who share this experience rapidly evolve their own methods of helping each other with the change-over period. Although the emotional switch is demanding it is also exciting and stimulating. Physical exhaustion may be a more difficult problem to cope with. Often your baby will make up for the loss of daytime contact with his mother by waking in the night or asking for a night feed. It will be less tiring if you can take the baby into bed with you and as the routine settles down he will probably stop asking for this kind of confort and reassurance and sleep normally again. If you are receptive your baby will tell you how he is feeling about his life. Often you may find his message inconvenient or disturbing – but then no one ever said human relationships were easy!

THE WOMAN'S CONFLICT

Mothers are often painfully anxious about leaving their baby – even with their partner. Because a gradual separation is healthier, aim for flexibility when your partner is planning a return to work and always try and be over-generous with maternity leave. Some women who returned to work early subsequently regretted not sharing enough of the baby-days, which anyway are so transitory. It is also essential to allow plenty of time to make the change-over, especially if the baby is being weaned at the same time. Once the baby is happy and secure with the changes in the family's lifestyle then both parents can turn their attention to their own needs.

Women's enjoyment of shared parenting varies. Some express the timeless conflict of needs between work and children, feel stretched to the limit and unable to enjoy either role in a leisurely fashion. 'Rushed motherhood' was the way one woman described it. She felt her work spilled over into her children's lives and she felt both guilty and resentful of her conflicting preoccupations. But while some women find these challenges irreconcilable many others feel liberated and gain in self esteem when they are free to follow their own pursuits. Feeling surprised at the ease with which they could let go the traditional image of the always available 'ideal' mother, these women felt the time they spent mothering was more creative because it was not their exclusive role.

CONFLICT BETWEEN WORK AND FAMILY WORK

'Work is a continuous thread, it's always with me. Jenny and the baby are temporary breaks – enjoyable, but I'm always aware that I'm going back to my work.'

Women have always had to reconcile the conflict between the disparate areas of 'mother-work' and 'other-work'. Today, as fathers move closer into the family arena, they too are having to reconcile the conflicts and respond to the challenges inherent in this new lifestyle.

As more fathers widen the scope of their fathering the barriers between work and family have begun to break down. Those men who are moving away from traditional 'male' patterns have been called 'androgynous', a new word for all those humans who are unafraid to use all aspects of their personalities – male or female.

Unfortunately changing an established order is never simple and pioneers always encounter unexpected challenges. Studies of British fathers seemed to indicate that class and occupation is a major factor in how a man rated his work–family conflict. Professional work demands time and dedication, and although like this father I talked to, men often feel dissatisfied and regret the lack of time spent in the family, they seem powerless to alter the situation. 'My work is like a clock ticking away in my head. Periodically it can be stopped and then I'm with the family, I feel part of their lives. But unfortunately most of the time I'm just not able to be there – I need an eight-day week to fit it all in . . .' Men like this one recognized the benefits of being more available to their children and the personal satisfaction it would provide. But there remained a mismatch between their public and their private lives which they seemed incapable of solving. They clearly felt themselves to be involved to a far greater degree than fathers of previous generations, and even though the actual time they spent in the family was not enormous, the desire was there.

It may be interesting to note that men in non-professional work reported far less conflict between work and family demands. This group did not regard a high level of involvement with the children as part of their family responsibilities. But paradoxically they actually spent more time in a caregiving role at home than the professional fathers who said they wanted to, but in fact did not! Some of these professional men were in occupations which have been termed 'greedy'. They often voice their sadness that their good intentions to be different from their own fathers have gradually been whittled away. They too saw less of their children than they wished, or deemed acceptable. The fact that they believed in the 'rightness' of shared family and childcare seemed to increase their conflict and anxiety, but not actually to improve their 'performance'.

Work in itself is not enough to explain their absence. In these days of high unemployment lack of work has not caused any dramatic increase in fathers' involvement in the home. Child care and housework are not seen as acceptable alternatives to 'real' work for men obliged to be at home. Men, it seems, do not respond well to being forced into greater involvement in the family. They prefer to offer help and if they do may well see themselves as 'special', and in need of appreciation for their contribution. Those men who really share the parenting role with their partners and take full emotional responsibility for their child have crossed a boundary where they no longer expect gratitude. This is where couples can help each other, by refusing to accept the traditional separation between Love and Work and being equally committed to parenting and to sharing what has been called the 'work of love'.

MEN'S ATTITUDE TO THEIR WORK

The attitude a man has towards his job is an important factor in the way he feels about family involvement. Some men feel their work is for themselves first, and their family second. Others feel the reverse, they see themselves working *for* their families, find less satisfaction in their occupation but also feel less work–family conflict. These were the fathers who found the birth of a baby gave them surprising satisfaction and confirmed a direction in their lives. They often realized that they had been waiting, in a sense, for this chance to use their full potential. Fatherhood brought together a lot of loose threads and made them feel emotionally strengthened. This father said, 'Now I feel more committed to family life. I work to earn money but I feel it's right that work is less important. I want to be all together with my family, they are the central issue now. If I could find a way to work at home with Kate we'd really like that.'

Many men see their work as central to their lives. They do not work to live – they live to work. It represents their membership in the adult world of power and status with a high degree of enjoyable social contact. Men like this see themselves functioning best and feeling happiest responding to the demands from their work which feel clear and unambiguous. 'Be tough', 'think incisively and logic-ally', 'always be on top and never show my true feelings', 'get the other guy before he gets me!' – these are all descriptions men have given me of themselves at work.

Home and family are a refuge from this demanding, cut and thrust, and competitive environment. There they can find restorative peace before returning to the excitement of the world outside. The dilemma is obvious; none of the qualities listed above, which appear essential in the workplace, is even mildly appropriate when applied to baby care. And because the time at home in the family is limited, the underlying personality which includes sensitive caring aspects has little opportunity to be expressed. In fact the man is looking to receive care for himself – he feels needy rather than bountiful. It appears that these men often have a deep reluctance to allow themselves free expression of the softer side of their natures for fear that once the barriers came down 'all would be lost' and their work *persona* would be depleted. That the reverse is true is unimaginable. Men like this see their fathering role as primarily one of giving support and providing help – when work permits. The interest in the baby is expressed primarily through the woman; it is positive and is well integrated into family life – the man himself is absent, but his presence, expressed through the woman, is a strong one. For these men to make the decision to cross over the almost tangible boundary between work and home-work, a man (and his partner) has to be convinced that it is not only 'safe' to do so but that it is ultimately beneficial to himself – as well as to his family.

Inevitably everyone makes certain decisions about priorities – personal and public. If the aim is to bridge the artificial division of the sexes which proclaims that men work and women look after children, and if parents, irrespective of gender want to develop all aspects of their personalities – to blend outside work and parenting, sharing and valuing each as equally creative and beneficial – then closer involvement with their children, particularly when they are babies, provides both parents with an ideal meeting ground.

Most men realize that work can become a devouring, but quantifiable force in their life. Not so with baby-work where the demands and the results are ambiguous, changeable, unstructured and often unquantifiable. All of which makes rather different demands on a man's normal working personality. And a father may feel particularly vulnerable because baby-work involves using those very aspects of himself which, if applied to his outside workplace, would be totally inappropriate. There is also an element of anxiety that once the boundary is crossed it might be impossible to retreat again – emotional involvement is less easy to control than intellectual commitment.

Fortunately babies suffer no such anxieties; they know what they want – undivided energy and attention from whoever cares for them. If you give them your time they will show you the way. As one father explained, 'My work is intensely satisfying to me, but Zoe is quite different. When I'm looking after her I'm engaging with people rather than things. I have to open myself to another world – children do change you.'

BALANCING THE DEMANDS

Many of the fathers I talked to were engaged in a complicated balancing act between the demands of family and work. These men struggled to make time to be with their families – sharing housework, and continuing the normal work schedule as best they could. They were often tired, sometimes frustrated, but felt they were on the 'right track'. All working parents recognize these symptoms, but whereas women tend to support each other, men do not. Research shows that men who engage in a more active fathering role in baby and child care often find themselves isolated from their fellow workers. Men are not usually supportive of each other's commitment to father-work, and prefer to base their social contact on discussions about football or the Stock Exchange, rather than their feelings about fatherhood. Those men who find a like minded colleague tend to go quietly away and discuss family matters out of the mainstream. Some fathers also encounter open hostility over their close involvement, sometimes disguised as accusation of 'shirking' work or responsibility. These comments often mask an older generation's anxiety about change. Working mothers have always had to withstand some hostility about the dual nature of their role – it is a new experience for men, who find it equally uncomfortable. But those fathers who are working inside and outside the family, unless they are single parents (see page 202) will probably have the loving support from their partner which helps them overcome any feelings of isolation and frustration.

The kind of relationship a couple pursues inevitably influences the time a father spends with his baby. Men often give the need to earn more money as a reason for their non-involvement with their children. Parents of a new baby are often anxious about finance, particularly in these days of high unemployment. Women who have worked before having a child do not enjoy being financially dependent after the birth. Studies show that having a baby is a crisis for many women, who do not experience motherhood as the total fulfilment portrayed in TV commercials. Isolated from friends and family, many women who are left alone to care for a young baby quickly become depressed. Often their anger and depression finds expression through financial worries which are off-loaded on the man. If the mother devotes herself to being a 'perfect mother', then the least the man can do is support her 'properly'. When a couple are sharing the responsibilities of child care this polarization is less likely to occur, but frequent communication and negotiation are necessary even so. Some couples decide to mark time, or even drop their standard of living for a while to ensure the man has the flexibility to spend time with his baby. But this does represent a real sacrifice for some men who may indeed be threatened by loss of promotion or expertise if they spend time away from work. In a sensible world which recognized the importance of father-work, no family would suffer economic hardship or loss of status because a man wished to care for his child. Regrettably, at the moment, for the majority of couples, this is a real dilemma.

MAKING THE CHOICE

Working mothers have always realized that choice is the aim for all parents, when it comes to balancing child care with work commitments. Those men who admit to sadness and regret that they are unable to spend enough time with their families ultimately have the power to redefine how fatherhood is recognized in our society. In fact one wonders why they put up with the status quo. Fathers who wish to spend time with their children taking full physical and emotional responsibility – not just as a 'helper' – should be able to do so without anxiety about their jobs suffering or being considered a social oddity. Men and women – parents – have to combine their energies, define their needs and those of their children and, rather than blaming each other, find sensible ways to achieve their aims.

Chapter 10

Baby care

Caring and comforting

Fathers have always cared about their babies – and these days many now care *for* them as well, giving the hour-by-hour attention that used to be thought of as exclusively the mother's responsibility. A baby these days is no longer handed back to the mother when something is wrong, so that babies experience fathers in the role of comforter, and know that men can 'mother' as well as women.

'GOOD ENOUGH' PARENTING

Many first-time expectant fathers express fears about their capacity to care for, and comfort, a newborn baby. A robust toddler seems fine, but a tiny, fragile infant who cannot communicate with words is a daunting prospect. (What many men do not realize, is that it is often just as daunting for a woman!) In our society of small, scattered families, most couples have never even held a young baby until their own is handed to them in the delivery room.

Research shows that when men decide to be the primary caregiver they have all the qualities their children need to enable them to thrive. Men can develop the same caring, intuitive, non-verbal skills that women also have to acquire as mothers. 'Good enough' mothering is not a sex-linked characteristic that only women possess. On the contrary, some couples have found that the man can 'mother' with more enjoyment and satisfaction than women, and in some cases the father has even opted to stay at home full time to be with their child. Mother then becomes the 'helper', after work and at weekends.

You will probably find the first few times you are left alone with your baby rather daunting. The best way to cope with these fears of being inadequate is to just get on and have a go! You and your baby will quickly discover your own methods of feeding, changing, or going to the shops. As your confidence grows so will your enjoyment. Start modestly and you will soon find your days with the baby varied and amusing. Several fathers I have spoken to are rather more adventurous than the mothers, taking regular trips to the swimming pool and trips around the countryside in their stride.

COPING WITH CRYING

'I used to come home and she often had bad colic and was screaming. I eventually found the solution. I used to put her in the car, in the carry cot, take some sandwiches and a drink and then drive up the motorway for about an hour and then back again. This gave Lucy a break. As soon as the car stopped she'd start yelling again, amazing it was. We used to both get into a sort of helpless rage with her, it was a dreadful four or five weeks, I kept saying it'll never be this bad again – never!'

Whether or not they share the day-to-day care of their baby, all parents worry if she cries for long periods. It is a sad fact that we take it for granted that babies will inevitably cry, but in some societies this is just not so. Crying as a way of communicating should ideally be a baby's last resort. Yet often it becomes the method babies most frequently resort to. A baby should never be left alone to cry for long periods. If you respond reasonably quickly you will soon discover there are different noises for different needs. Babies become attached to those people who react to their efforts at communicating. Getting a response helps the baby build up trust; confidence in herself and the outside world. She makes a noise which provokes a reply, and gradually the baby understands she is part of a dialogue which is safe and reliable. A baby who is left to cry alone for long periods does not have the chance to make these vital discoveries. She will probably resort to crying more quickly and frequently, and be harder to pacify, missing the opportunity to try less desperate methods to enter into the dialogue to get what she needs.

WHY DOES YOUR BABY CRY?

'No one told us that babies scream like that, no matter what you do. We went to visit a cathedral with some visiting Americans keen on seeing England. I remember holding this tiny baby in my arms and he was yelling fit to burst. I just held him up in the church and shouted, "Please stop him, please let him stop." No one who hasn't had a crying baby knows how awful it is; it's something you just survive – just!'

Life from a newborn baby's point of view is pretty demanding. Before birth, a baby is securely held, in an ideal temperature, with subdued lighting, surrounded by reassuring rhythmic sounds. At birth all this vanishes. To survive, the baby must suck, swallow, breathe – and is expected to 'ask' for what she wants. No wonder babies resort to crying, and no wonder parents have a struggle to interpret their cries. Do they mean hunger, pain, a wet nappy, fear or need of a cuddle? Both parents will offer everything until eventually the baby responds, or exhaustion takes over and she sleeps.

Even the most confident of parents eventually get to the end of their tether if their baby cries for long periods. If you feel you are in this situation you should seek help and advice from postnatal support groups and special clinics (see Comfort measures (below) and Useful addresses, page 216). Medical reassurance that there is nothing organically wrong with the baby will also be helpful. Usually this persistent crying miraculously stops at around three months and then the baby begins to enjoy life normally.

But even if your baby has an easy-going personality, just caring for an infant is exhausting, demanding and sometimes frustrating. That is why a baby needs two (or more) people to share the parenting. It is normal to need a rest from the 24-hour round-the-clock demands of a young baby. Babies are intensely sensitive to the atmosphere around them. Even if the adults try to hide their feelings, babies often sense what is going on through touch, smell, or the pitch of a voice. They then react by feeling insecure and express it by fretful, 'difficult' behaviour. This is where sharing the baby is the best solution. If the father has been out at work, he will be able to comfort and reassure the baby, simply because he is fresh to the situation. This is of course just as applicable if it is the mother who has been away from home, and comes back to take over.

COMFORT MEASURES

Some babies (like some adults) need a lot of comfort sucking. Mothers can feel drained and irritated by what seems like constant demands on them to give the breast. Often it is not food, but the equally important comfort and reassurance that your baby wants. You can provide this and give the mother a much needed break. Try giving the baby a dummy (pacifier) and then hold her in your arms to settle her. There are specially designed ortho-dentic dummies on sale now which do not distort the baby's mouth. Or put a very clean little finger in her mouth and allow her to suck on that. Sooner or later she will be able to find her own finger or thumb, but in the early weeks she may not be able to comfort herself because she loses her thumb too easily.

COMFORT FOR THE MOTHER

In the first weeks after the birth when many babies are demanding to be fed every two or two and a half hours round the clock, it is very helpful if you are willing to get up sometimes during those endless night feeds. You can bring your partner a drink and provide comfort for her too! You can then take the baby after her feed, change and settle her while your partner goes back to sleep. Alternatively you can give the baby a bottle occasionally if your partner can express enough breast milk for a feed (see Further reading, page 213).

PERSISTENT CRYING

If your baby cries for extended periods there are other comfort measures you can try, too. Massage (see page 185) may help. You may like to try homeopathic remedies or acupressure – there are acupuncturists who will treat young babies and show you how to release painful wind if this is the problem. If your baby has had a difficult birth or forceps delivery, or a Caesarean birth, a gentle treatment called cranial osteopathy may be the solution. Some babies are allergic to cows' milk in the mother's diet so it is worth asking your doctor's advice about testing for this possibility.

Try, too, to help your partner relax and feel more confident about herself as a mother. Many women become depressed after giving birth, and most get desperately tired. Make sure your partner is getting enough support and practical help as well as time away from the baby to recharge herself as an individual. Bear in mind that stress in your working life, moving house, a bereavement in the family or just the newness of family life can all affect the baby, who is intensely sensitive to the atmosphere around her.

CHANGING NAPPIES CAN BE O.K.

When I talk to a group of expectant fathers I always say they should be careful not to be cheated out of their share of the baby's nappy changes. This is usually greeted with incredulous laughter – how could anyone feel cheated of a messy job like that? But think about it for a moment. When you change a baby she lies back and has eye contact with you. You are creating comfort out of discomfort. This is a time for talking and smiling – engaging in those games of imitation that even tiny babies enjoy. Often a baby will be at her most responsive and endearing during and after a nappy change. A good time is half way through a feed when she is not too hungry and not yet too sleepy to be responsive. Breastfed babies smell very sweetly and even their bowel motions, although a spectacular orange/gold colour and of a runny consistency, do not smell unpleasant. Cleaning a baby's bottom needs a gentle touch and when that is finished there is time for a bit of body massage and a 'chat' – even very young babies respond to sounds and emulate facial expressions. Perhaps now you can see why I feel fathers should not be deprived of their share of that particular interaction?

BABY MASSAGE

There are several books on baby massage available (see Further reading, page 213) and you may want to learn specific techniques. A particular problem such as colic/wind pain may require some special technique but generally you and your baby will discover your own 'method' as you go along. Men often worry that they are too clumsy, or rough to be able to massage a fragile baby. But if you enjoy holding and stroking your baby this is not a problem, you will automatically adapt yourself as you extend the touching to massage. Most parents do this kind of stroking entirely without prompting – while you hold your baby, or change him you will instinctively caress and stroke his body. If you want to develop this loving touch into massage choose a time when your baby is relaxed and comfortable – perhaps after the bath (unless he is then ready for a feed) or during a nappy change. Make sure the room is warm and cosy and you are both feeling relaxed. Put the baby on a soft towel on your lap, or on the bed – wherever you are comfortable. Use some baby oil on your hands and begin by just stroking his body, gently opening his arms and legs as if stretching. Do not forget the hands, fingers and feet. Turn the baby on his front and then massage gently up the spine and around the shoulders. Just allow your hands to mould round the baby's body and follow your inclinations as you observe the baby's reactions. Some babies love to have their heads and faces stroked too, always be sensitive to the baby's enjoyment and you will quickly discover what is both pleasurable and comforting to you both.

BATHING YOUR BABY

Try and be at the hospital when the midwife shows parents how to bath a baby. Even if you are not going to take full responsibility right away for bath-time, just being there will be supportive and you will learn how your baby likes things done. Everyone feels nervous the first few times they bath a baby, but confidence comes with practice and eventually you will find it one of the best ways to enjoy time with your baby. Some fathers prefer to take the baby into the bath with them. If you do this make sure the water is not too hot and because babies lose body heat quickly, always have the bathroom really warm before starting to undress them. You should get into the bath first and your partner can then hand the baby to you. Support his head and shoulders and slowly allow him to sink into the water while resting on your body. Always keep hold of the baby with one hand, use the other one to sponge him, this way he will be quite safe. When he has had enough, your partner can lift him out of the bath into a large, warm towel. Many young babies seem to feel safer bathing within the security of your arms rather than in a traditional baby bath. Whichever way you choose, remember to allow yourself plenty of time to enjoy the fun. If you decide that bathing the baby is to be your job, bear in mind that even if you have a hectic working schedule your baby will not mind if he sees you at 6 a.m. or 10 p.m.!

FEEDING THE BABY

However the baby is to be fed it is important for you to be there as much as possible during the first few weeks. If the baby is bottle fed you can take an equal share right away. If your partner is breast-feeding it is also helpful if you can be on hand as hospitals vary in the amount of information and support they give a new mother. Knowing a few basic guidelines means you can help get the process under way independently.

Your partner should be sitting comfortably, or lying down if she prefers (see Further reading, page 213). When sitting use two pillows to raise the baby up to breast level. The baby's abdomen should be touching his mother's, his lower hand tucked under the body, well away from his mouth or it may get tangled up with the nipple. Always make sure the baby is properly 'latched on' – the whole of the nipple and the areola must be in the baby's mouth. Remind your partner to press her breast a little so that the baby can breathe freely as he sucks. Finally help your partner to relax as this facilitates the milk flow. She will appreciate a drink and a snack when she is feeding the baby. Try and create a warm, calm atmosphere for the nursing couple while they are still learning about breastfeeding. Dim lights, soft music and quiet conversation may be helpful. Keep disruptive or demanding visitors to a minimum until everyone is more confident and feeding has become a routine. (This can take four or five weeks.) When the baby has had enough to eat you can take over, to wind, change and settle him back to sleep, or just hold him in your arms while your partner relaxes or has a nap.

THE BABY'S PERSONALITY

From the first meeting your baby has her own personality. There is a vitality and a feeling of 'otherness' which is exciting for the parents, but can also be disturbing. The interaction between the mother and baby – how well their personalities match – plays a part in how easily the feeding relationship develops. Sometimes a baby is 'just not herself' for a few days after the birth. This can be because of a difficult delivery, or because the baby has absorbed drugs administered to the mother during her labour. Sometimes nothing obvious is upsetting the baby, but still she fusses, frets or finds life generally unsettling. Your partner will naturally react, and if this difficult time continues she may become exhausted, depressed and disheartened. Hormonal changes can also be debilitating at this time. Your presence and support can be invaluable. By sharing the problems and seeking the baby's lovable characteristics – while appreciating the struggle your partner is having – you can prevent a pattern of dissatisfaction and tension arising between mother and baby.

BEING AWARE

Caring for a young child's needs, bathing, changing, holding and cuddling are all delightfully sensual experiences for both parent and child – as long as the child's needs are always respected and recognized as completely separate from your own. Most fathers are pleasantly surprised by this aspect of baby care as they find it reflects in a deeper and more fulfilled physical relationship with their partner. Babies and young children thrive in an atmosphere of safe, caring sensuality. However it is absolutely vital for the child's sake that there is never any sexual blurring on the adult's side. As a parent if you encounter any feelings which disturb you or arouse you sexually, stop immediately, and honestly assess yourself. Try and share your feelings with your partner and make sure you seek professional help if you feel you might in any way lose control (see Useful addresses, page 218).

Feeding

PROBLEMS WITH BREASTFEEDING

Many women want to breastfeed but encounter problems in the early weeks. Sometimes these are 'technical' problems (see Further reading, page 213) but more frequently it is tension or anxiety which is disturbing either the mother or the baby. It is clear from research that if the man is absent or has a negative attitude the breastfeeding relationship deteriorates. Your encouragement, support and appreciation of her as a mother create what has been called the mother and baby's 'social security' – the harmony between you and your partner that enables her to devote herself to the baby (see Caring for each other, page 150). Your pleasure is at one remove – your body is not directly involved, but the ensuing mutual satisfaction of the mother and baby is in part yours too. It is a bit like making love and 'giving' your partner a satisfying orgasm – for her sake, just for her own enjoyment. Her pleasure is her own, but would be diminished or non-existent without your care and tenderness.

Sometimes a woman refuses even to consider this method of feeding – she dislikes her breasts being touched and finds the idea of a baby sucking vigorously on her nipples completely repugnant. There are couples who consider breasts as 'belonging' only to their sexual relationship, and others who find the sexual feelings aroused by feeding a baby become confused with infidelity or even incest. You and your partner should aim to be as honest with each other as possible about these very basic issues, and having put the baby's needs first look for a compromise solution.

DECIDING TO BOTTLE FEED

In most hospitals these days, women are encouraged to breastfeed even if only for a short time. Besides being best for the baby this is more comfortable for the mother, as drugs to suppress the milk are no longer given because of their side effects. But if a woman is really not happy to continue breastfeeding, she should be free to stop as soon as she wishes. As one expert in infant care said, it is not enough for the baby to want to feed, the woman has to want to give her breast.

Feeding a baby, whether by breast or bottle, is not just a question of getting food from a 'container' into the baby's stomach. Food, its preparation, how it is eaten, where and with whom – all form part of one of our greatest pleasures. Eating is often a part of adult social, sensual and romantic rituals. Babies are considered by some experts to be even more acutely sensitive to touch, smell, taste and environment than adults are. And feeding, by whatever method, provides parents with the opportunity to give their baby a pleasurable experience many times each day for several months. But from the baby's point of view, it is the quality of the handling and holding which are more important than the fact that she is breastfed. Sensitive bottle feeding can include all these facets and it is something a father can do just as successfully as a mother. In the end, it is the quality of the relationship which develops between the giver-of-food and the baby that is of paramount importance. It is the willingness to participate – the wanting to be involved in the give and take – that turns each feed into the unfolding of a relationship between two loving people.

MAKING TIME WITH YOUR BABY

Sharing the day-to-day care of the baby with your partner is important, but simply spending time with the baby is vital too. Even if you
are not able to make any changes in your work commitments you can
arrange to have a special time with your baby every day. This may
mean a bath at 10 p.m., or an early morning walk in the park.
Looking at and touching objects, going outside to feel the wind or
rain, become pleasurable events because of how the baby reacts to
each new experience. Even just being together with your baby,
sitting or lying somewhere warm and relaxing is fun. Choose a time
when she is feeling comfortable and sociable and you may be
pleasantly surprised at the range of communication that is possible,
even with a young baby. Just as with all relationships, taking time
to listen and respond is one of the best ways to show love and
affection. Your baby will quickly learn ways to return this attention
and show you just how special this time together can be.

Weaning

'I always thought weaning was a simple matter, that one day Dan
would be put on a bottle and eat food, and that would be that. For us
it was a very different story. Karen wanted to go back to work three
days a week and so she wanted Dan to take a bottle as well as breast
night and morning. But Dan had his own ideas and they turned out to
be very different from ours! Talk about diplomacy and breakdown
of talks between East and West. Those guys had nothing on us – we
could teach them a thing or two about compromise!'
   The dictionary defines weaning as 'to cause to desert former
habits', and anyone who has resolved to do just that knows how
difficult it can be, particularly if the 'habit' was a pleasurable one. We
will look mainly at weaning from the breast, rather than the bottle,
because an older baby or toddler sucking a bottle seems more socially
acceptable than a baby of the same age at the breast. There are two
interrelated aspects to think about when weaning a baby from the
breast – the simple nutritional needs of a growing child, and the
infinitely more complex readiness of mother and baby to be weaned
from each other.
   The father's role is as important during this, the first move towards
independence between mother and child, as it was in the previous

phase of establishing the dependence of the feeding relationship. As we have seen, to feed an infant sensitively a parent has to identify strongly with the baby's needs. As the time for weaning approaches, the mother must let go her identification with the infant, but only if, at the same time, the baby shows herself ready to become more separate. Usually the child's growing up coincides with the mother's resumption of her own independence and weaning will be resolved quite smoothly. If possible allow your baby to lead the way; when she is ready she will show you.

THE MOTHER'S FEELINGS ABOUT WEANING

After about six months of continuous breastfeeding many women begin to feel that it would be pleasant to have their bodies back for themselves – to be a free agent again. The timing of this gradual disengagement is very individual and no one should feel guilty or abnormal if they take longer or begin earlier. You can help by confirming your partner's feelings of self-confidence; encouraging her to talk honestly about her feelings and involving yourself in her attempts to interpret the baby's needs and signals. And your objectivity means you become an important anchor for both mother and baby. You can also contribute by taking a more active share in caring for the baby – it is always easier to leave her with you than anyone else. Once your partner and the baby have tried this time apart, and enjoyed it, you can take the lead in making time together as a couple. It is not always easy to find a suitable 'parent' substitute, but if you have looked after your baby you will be better equipped to judge sensitively how long you and your partner can safely be away.

As the baby shows signs of independence, your partner may feel a strong need to be valued in another area of her life. You are the best person to show her the positive side of weaning and encourage her to look forward to the next stage of parenting. After so many months of being in an intensely demanding and richly rewarding relationship, it is no wonder that some women suffer depression when their babies are weaned if they do not get enough support from their partners to enable them to experience comparable satisfaction outside the breastfeeding relationship.

RECOGNIZING THE BABY'S READINESS TO WEAN

If you can, it is better to postpone weaning until your baby shows you that she is ready to begin the gradual move away from her hitherto primary source of satisfaction, her mother's breast. Of course weaning is not like painting a room – it does not start on Monday and finish on Saturday. Emotional growth is unpredictable and never proceeds in a straight line; weaning is just one of the many changes in your child's life which should not be hurried if it is to be what Winnicott called 'meaningful'.

Winnicott believes that a baby shows her emotional readiness to wean by playing the game all babies adore – dropping objects over the edge of their pram or cot. The baby is demonstrating her ability to 'let go' and still feel safe. Fathers often worry about what is normal for babies at a particular stage, but where weaning is concerned every baby is different and there are no rules. If your partner wants to go on feeding and the baby agrees, and you are happy, then it is nobody's business to disapprove. The ideal pace is your baby's, although this is often impossible because of other family or work commitments. If you can be supportive and take a more active part in your baby's life at this time you can provide the security for both mother and baby that will enable them to feel confident that this 'separation' is an inevitable part of life – and far from being a loss of babyhood is a positive move towards maturity.

If your baby seems ready to drop a breastfeed, encourage your partner to allow her to do so. You will notice that at a particular feed – often where there are other people around – your baby spends more time staring round and wanting to see what is happening than sucking. If this happens over several days and she is already enjoying tasting 'real' food and will drink either from a bottle or a cup, there is your cue to suggest dropping that breastfeed (see Further reading).

When she has dropped one feed, you can expect your baby to gradually lose interest in the others, one by one over the next few months. But an illness, or some disturbance like moving house, or your being away on a business trip, may mean a return to the breast for a bit longer. If your partner starts to go out to work that may also prolong the weaning process, as mother and baby will need to enjoy their special closeness as a way of re-establishing contact for a while longer. Babies vary in their individual weaning style; just as they do in pot training or learning to talk, and no parent should worry about their baby being different from the child next door.

Apart from recognizing the signals from your baby and supporting your partner you can also increase your own practical involvement. Now you can feed the baby and share this central part of the baby's life. Your baby will now be at an age when you can start to play games with her, and she will enthusiastically join you and your partner in more wide ranging exploration of the outside world. Many fathers have told me they found the weaning phase extremely satisfying as far as their own relationship with the baby was concerned. Babies at this stage are very good company and great fun. You will find new ways of extending what has always been traditionally seen as the father's role – playing and doing things together. But remember to include your partner if she wants to join in, she may feel a bit redundant as she adjusts to no longer being the centre of the baby's world.

BABIES WHO NEED TO SUCK

Right from the start some babies do seem to need a lot more comfort sucking than others. Those babies who do not suck their own finger or thumb will often use the breast for comfort or to fall asleep. Some mothers are happy to go on providing this particular and necessary contact for their babies, while others gradually find they have had enough. If your baby needs this 'comfort sucking' she may be placated with a bottle, but you will probably have to give this – the baby will see little point in taking a bottle if the 'real' thing is close at hand!

If your partner becomes pregnant again while breastfeeding she will probably want to wean the first baby. You may need to support your partner in this decision if she feels guilty about not allowing the child to take her own time. Make sure the baby is provided with an abundance of substitute comfort and extra love to see her through any distress she might feel through separating from the breast.

EXTERNAL PRESSURES TO WEAN

These days many mothers have to go back to work well before the baby is six months old. There are several ways of mixing bottle and breastfeeding and each couple must find what suits them and their lifestyle – for example, giving breastfeeds morning and night and a bottle during the day.

Some fathers are impatient for the baby to be weaned so they can take more responsibility for the day-to-day care of their baby. This father told me: 'I couldn't wait for the time when he came off the breast. As soon as I could feed him too, well I felt an equal then with Pam. Now we could really share everything.'

Some toddlers do find weaning difficult. Your child may still demand a feed at night when she clearly does not need food. Your partner may have tried everything, but the baby always wins the battle for the breast. One solution is for you to take over and get up when the child cries in the night – possibly every night for a week – give her a cuddle, a drink of juice or water and then put her firmly back to bed (or even sleep in the same room with her for a while if she seems frightened). Gradually she will accept that she has to give up the breast – it may be temporarily painful for everyone, but your presence and care will help both mother and baby take this inevitable step.

TODDLERS WHO REFUSE TO BE WEANED

Some toddlers do find weaning difficult. Like many other points of change in a child's life there do seem to be 'magic' moments when they are ready, and can move on to a more mature stage given the right support. However if something goes wrong on either side, then often a toddler gets stuck and may cling to an outdated position like a record stuck in a groove. If this happens your child may continue to demand a feed at night when she clearly does not need food. The mother tries everything, but the baby always wins the battle, for that is what it has become, for the breast. It seems that if the baby senses any ambivalence in the parents, particularly the mother, about weaning (or the other common problem of getting toddlers to sleep in their own beds) a struggle is almost inevitable.

I have found the solution which works best, whether it be to solve sleep problems or weaning, is for the father to step between the two protagonists and act as peacemaker. But first you must make sure that your partner will be fully supportive of your role. It is absolutely no good, or help to anyone if, having staggered into the crying child and started to pacify her yourself, your partner suddenly arrives and gives in. If this happens your child quickly senses the atmosphere and will get even more anxious. Before you start, make absolutely sure that your partner will leave you to deal with the toddler and not interfere unless you request her help. You have to be willing to devote yourself to getting up every night for quite an extended period, perhaps a week or more to reach a comfortable solution.

Chapter 11

The changing role of fatherhood

In 1980 it was calculated that there were at least 115,000 single-parent families in Britain headed by a man, with 200,000 children in their care. Divorce rates are rising every year, and it seems safe to assume that this number has risen at the accepted growth rate of 6 per cent per annum. Although there is far less data available on single fathers it has been estimated that 90 per cent of children in their care are of school age and on average, these 'lone' fathers remarry within two years of becoming single parents through separation, divorce or death of a spouse.

A single parent of either sex faces some obvious problems. However there is one stark difference so far as single fathers are concerned – they have also to contend with all the fundamental attitudes about the structure of 'good' families. Society at large still clings to the belief that a mother's presence is vital for a child to develop into a healthy person. The attitude reflected in the old Victorian motto hung above the mantelpiece 'What is a home without a Mother?' still persists, making it difficult for single-parent families headed by the father to be fully accepted. Single parenting involves undeniable challenges and stress – but it is not all gloom and doom by any means. Many one-parent families grow to be proud and well pleased with themselves and relish their independent and flexible lifestyle. The children in these families need not be indiscriminately pitied or assumed to be tomorrow's human casualties or delinquents in the making. The fantasy of the 'real' family, composed of mother, father, 2.4 children and a dog in the back of the family car ignores the needs of the families who no longer fit that narrow parameter. Single parents have special needs and difficulties which could be overcome if they were given more positive support. They need appreciation for doing a good job and less pity. While the condemnation, which can appear for having failed as a 'real' family, is always destructive.

The circumstances which create a single father, whether through divorce or bereavement, and whether he has chosen his role or has had no alternative, will all affect the way in which he and his child adapt to their new family status.

Fathers and divorce

Those who have not lived through a divorce may sometimes see it as a single dramatic event. This is far from the truth – divorce is just one part of a crisis which effects every member of the family over a long period of time. It is not within the scope of this book to deal with anything but a few important issues surrounding the break-up of a family, and as this book is primarily for fathers the emphasis will be on them and the importance of their role.

Coming to terms with the end of a relationship is a long, hard and painstaking business, very similar to coping with a bereavement. If you have a child you are inevitably faced with an additional dimension to the problem. When a couple separates each person searches for ways to put themselves together again as individuals, and a lengthy and often painful process of self assessment takes place. Every aspect of personal life comes under review, inside and outside the marriage. But amidst the chaos of disintegration there is the possibility of regeneration. Having to re-establish their own domestic arrangements impels many fathers to define consciously the depth and scope of their relationship with their child. For the majority of work-dominated men that interaction has included an unspoken assumption; children need fathers. Many men, faced with the loss of everyday contact with their child because of divorce, come face to face with an often previously unacknowledged need of their own; fathers need children too.

When you have a child, divorce is a re-arrangement, not a total dissolution of the previous relationship with your spouse; you are only dissolving part of your interaction – the parental part has to continue, with certain obvious mutations, until the child is fully independent. How individual mothers and fathers resolve these problems, which continue with ups and downs over the years, depends to a large extent on the strength of both parents' commitment to unselfish, child-centred parenting. Whatever your pain and anguish, however angry and combative you may feel towards your ex-spouse, your child's need for both parents remains constant. The breakdown of a marriage should not be allowed to mean the breakdown of the child's contact with either parent. Your child is always the 'innocent party' no matter what.

SEEKING OUTSIDE HELP

Finding sensible solutions, or even working compromises to these major adjustments is often too difficult for a couple to do. Their own pain and confusion severely diminishes the capacity to parent in the normal way – there is often not enough emotional, or physical energy available to do anything more than simply stay alive. Every couple going through divorce has raw and needy feelings which often make it impossible to plan for their child's immediate future, let alone take decisions which will influence the next few years. Trying to reach an amicable arrangement, for sharing your child after separating may be one of a series of problems that you have to resolve. If you and your partner cannot agree about child access, try consulting a Conciliation Service (see Useful addresses, page 216) where the emphasis will be on finding solutions in the child's best interest while in no way attempting to interfere in the parents' decision to separate. It has been shown that the damaging after effects on the child of divorce can be dramatically reduced if both parents put the child's needs first and studiously avoid the easy temptation of continuing marital warfare through the child.

PREPARING YOUR CHILD

Try and prepare your child for the separation before this major upheaval takes place. For many parents, even the idea of talking to a child in a way he will understand is just too difficult at a time when they are wrestling with their own acute problems of disbelief and distress. Most children are left totally unprepared for the bombshell of their parents' separation. Feelings of guilt and an inability to face the child's anger or sadness seem to prevent even the most loving of parents being able to talk to their children at this time. Whatever the situation honesty is the best policy. Try and talk to your child in language he will understand to prepare him for the future separation, even if he does not appear to want to listen. Always reassure him that he is in no way responsible for the divorce and emphasize that continuing love and support will always be available to him from both his parents. If you know there will be a period when you will not see your child, be truthful, while searching for ways to retain some form of contact through letters or phone calls. Try not to allow adult turmoil to upset your dialogue – the message is; 'this is hell for us both, but we will survive and continue to love each other no matter what'.

These reassurances assume that you have made maintaining contact with your child one of your top priorities. In 90 per cent of divorces it is the mother who retains custody, although if the child is of school age this is not now a foregone conclusion. All parents who live through a divorce suffer from diminished self esteem and self confidence. This disorientation can make a man reluctant to persevere with the problems of seeing his child, particularly if the child has been caught up in the battle between the couple during the divorce. But somehow divorcing couples must make it a priority to take their child's need for access to *both* parents out of the arena of marital warfare. Your child is not an extension of yourself – he is an entirely independent being when it comes to maintaining the love he has for both his parents. Lawyers are not always helpful on this subject, and often do not encourage their clients to consider the long-term results of decisions taken at a time when most people are unable to think clearly. If divorcing parents want to maintain contact with their child it is advisable where possible, to have joint custody so that both parents have a legal right to be involved in the child's future life.

YOUR CHILD NEEDS YOU

After divorce a child's need for regular contact with both parents remains urgent and constant. Once a father has moved out of the family home the problem of maintaining this connection becomes a matter for the whole family's attention. It is essential, as soon as the separation is definite, that arrangements are made for the child to spend enough time with you on a regular basis for the easy familiarity between parent and child to be unbroken. Although it is inevitably traumatic for everyone when one or other parent leaves home, luckily where children are concerned, even the most painful experiences of divorce have been shown not to be permanently damaging. However the length of time it takes for this turmoil to subside will depend largely on how well each adult copes with the new experience of being a parent who happens to be divorced, rather than a parent who is married.

In the long term a father's presence and support is essential to stabilize the child's life, and his absence has been shown to restrict the child's social and developmental growth severely. A child has to preserve his basic non-alignment to survive – to be happy he needs to feel a degree of respect and tolerance between his parents which may take a long time to re-establish after a divorce. And it is not only the children who benefit from the continued connection between father and child; custodial mothers with boys also find life easier when their ex-partner has frequent access to the boy. It sounds obvious in principal, in reality it is frequently a complex and hard struggle, but if both parents recognize their child's needs honestly and generously they will find a way. But even where everyone is trying hard, for many fathers financial and geographical considerations can also severely hamper regular access. However, the basic need is unalterable; contact between non-custodial parent and child must be maintained if the child is to flourish normally. It is important to realize that divorce need not remain a sad, painful 'death' of a family – in the long term it is possible for parents to find ways to resurrect the best of their parenting skills for their own, and their child's benefit and satisfaction.

SHARED PARENTING AND DIVORCE

As shared parenting becomes more common, it seems likely that men who have practised it, if faced with divorce, will not be willing automatically to give up their children's daily care to their ex-wife. Fathers who have shared caregiving during their marriage have a clearer idea of what it means to take full responsibility for a child and so are more able to take up the role of single fathering. By contrast a man who takes over the care of his children out of revenge, or after a bitter struggle with an ex-partner, who has no experience of running a house and has to give up his job to look after his child, will be in a very different state. How difficult the transition is will depend on how the man arrived at his single-father status. If he has made an active choice to take on this role it has been shown that the change-over is easier. Men who had no alternative are often angry and resentful for long periods of time. If both adults make an effort on each other's behalf for the good of the child there will be less wasted energy, if nothing else! One father decided that as he had been very involved with his son before the marriage was dissolved, he wanted to take on full responsibility; the idea of being a 'Sunday' visitor to his child was abhorrent to him. He and his partner were able to suspend their personal animosity to make the best possible arrangements for their child. 'I just felt it was impossible not to go on living every day with Leon. As Yvonne had been studying and I had been full time "mother" it seemed the best for Leon that we kept his routine as much the same as before. I'm not saying it hasn't had its problems, but in some way I feel this is the most important thing I've ever done in my life.'

'Lone' fathers – widowers

It is not easy to compare the situation of men who are separated with men who are widowers. Some of the practical challenges are the same, but the emotional adaptation needed is very different. The circumstances at the time of the death, and the quality of the subsequent support given to the husband, will affect his capacity to cope as a 'lone' father. And it is precisely there that these fathers are different – they are alone; never again, in any way, can they share their parenting with their spouse. Coming to terms with this loss, the process by which both adults and children learn to live without spouse or parent has been well documented (see Further reading, page 213). Divorced single fathers may initially be offered less sympathy, but although they have 'lost' their marriage its dissolution involves them in emotional activity. They are putting a lot of energy into re-framing their relationship with the ex-partner, trying to adjust to being apart, while facing the inevitable contact over their child. This may mean that they will tend to suffer less depression and long-term desolation. By contrast a widower will usually be given a lot of short-term sympathy and support which will help him over the initial shock of the bereavement. But because their loss is final and complete, these fathers often do become very depressed and their sense of desolation lasts much longer than for men who are divorced. The desolation of these 'lone' fathers often leads to a growing sense of isolation as friends and relatives settle back into their own lives, hoping everything is now 'back to normal'.

The universal themes of single parenting

Gradually over a period of time the lives of all single parents begin to share some common themes. Financial problems are universal, as all single parents will tell you. The feeling that you are under constant financial pressure, have to watch where every penny goes, is not calculated to make a relaxed atmosphere in the family. For a single father it may not be the loss of his partner's supplementary income which is the cause of his financial problems. He may find that his own earnings drop too. He may have to refuse overtime, or promotion, even if it is available, because of child care commitments. The lack of government day-care facilities makes the pressure exerted on single fathers to remain in full-time employment even more perplexing; single mothers are expected to remain at home with their child, single fathers definitely are not. In Britain it is estimated that five-sixths of single fathers continue working, although 35 per cent of these will probably give up work temporarily at some point to care full time for their child. Single fathers lack status in the eyes of society and often find this particularly difficult at a time when they are making a double adjustment – becoming a single man once again and becoming the sole major parent to their child.

Closely related to the struggle to make ends meet, are the conflicts that arise through rarely having enough time to relax and enjoy the pleasanter aspects of parenting, many of which also cost money! Rushing from work to housework and child care leaves many single parents with little time or energy for themselves. Once he has met his child's needs a father may be too exhausted and often lacking in confidence to go out and find adult companionship. But many fathers are surprised to find they enjoy this fully extended lifestyle. 'I had to learn to cook – nothing too complicated, it's quite nice to be able to eat "junk food" and not feel guilty! Housework is all right, I find it quite relaxing in some ways, the mindless repetition is quite therapeutic for me. Mind you I let it all go during the week and I do get ratty that it just sits there and waits for me. There's no one to blame or moan at – it's all up to me. That's the hard bit I suppose, the lack of chat, I do miss adult conversation sometimes . . .'.

Fathers who continue to work and care for their child will find themselves with very little spare time. But those who give up their work may regret it. Many men do not fully appreciate that their work place also provides them with an essential element of social contact. Becoming a full-time house-worker is no substitute, and studies of single fathers show that they often get depressed and lethargic. Some of them also develop 'aggressive frustration' which may spill over on to their children. There is no readily available support system for single fathers and the occasional man in a playgroup, for example, may find he is viewed as an oddity and not easily included in the cosy social world of the other mothers.

PERSONAL PROBLEMS

Although research shows that men get more sympathetic attention than women when they care singlehandedly for their child, many did not find this particularly helpful. Several fathers would have preferred less sympathy and more positive encouragement and appreciation for their efforts. Men often find it hard to ask for help, or admit personal difficulties. Single fathers frequently worry that they cannot 'come up to scratch' in homemaking and creating a 'mothering' atmosphere for their child. These feelings of personal inadequacy may stem from what has been called the 'tyranny of the two-parent model' – the notion that the only proper environment for the healthy development of a child contains a mother and a father. And although the fear that their children may have more problems than other children is one shared by all single parents, it is worth noting that no research has been able to show that this is so. In fact, even where there are opposite sex pairings – a father looking after a daughter, a mother looking after a son – studies show there need be no problem if the parent plans appropriate strategies to counteract any difficulties during adolescence. Sadly it seems that many fathers do not receive the kind of help they most need, although research shows that they succeed even so. There is, in short, no evidence that lone fathers cannot create a healthy environment both for themselves and for their children's development. There is a good deal of evidence that we, the community, make it extremely hard for them to do so.

Support groups such as Gingerbread (see page 216) can be very helpful in enabling single fathers to share a common experience of these and other problems. But as one father told me, it's not always the problems that need sharing. 'It's not so much the crises which get to me – I always manage somehow. It's the nice things I miss sharing with someone. You know, like when Sharon was an angel in the nativity play at her playgroup. Well my "ex" and I did both go, but she sat on one side and I on the other. That's when you feel it. We do talk about business and things, but it's not the same somehow.'

Stepfathers

The growing number of divorces has meant that another role is emerging for an increasing number of men – stepfathering. Many divorced men may have been denied custody of their own children but through re-marriage have assumed the responsibility for another man's child instead. The latest figures show that in America one in two children live in a step family, while in Britain the estimate is at least one in five, and probably rising. But in spite of the in-built problems facing what are known as 'reconstituted' families, a majority of children felt satisfied with their relationships within the step family. How successfully a child accepts a step parent seems to depend upon the child's age at the time of re-marriage. A very young child will adapt much more easily than an adolescent to a new 'father'.

For the stepfather, this new role may be very stressful at first. This father described it as a make or break situation in which he felt everything was up to him. 'When I married Lyn I told everyone I was happy to "take on" her two kids. Looking back I realize I did it rather like "taking on" a house with dry rot – a sense of foreboding and not knowing where it would all lead to. Eventually I came to feel that it's been OK – a tremendous challenge to me personally. I've really had to look at myself which hasn't been easy at times.'

Although in this section special attention will be paid to men who become stepfathers and want to share parenting, the following guidelines are equally applicable whoever is becoming the step parent. Becoming a step parent is a challenge – but it is wise not to anticipate problems or look for them. Let things happen slowly, at their own pace. One study of stepfathers suggested that they often moved too fast, not giving themselves or the children enough time to adapt before moving in with rather traditional 'heavy' paternal demands. Try and relax and not feel pressured by the new situation – all relationships take time. Remember too that you and the child have not actively chosen each other and that feeling obliged to care for someone is not an ideal way to start a relationship. Allow the child to express his feelings and try not to feel rejected by any initial negative reactions. Pay attention to your own feelings and always discuss them as openly as possible with your partner. It is never a good idea to let resentment build up, and where step parenting is concerned it is even more vital to keep the lines of communication open. So in the beginning as a stepfather, tread slowly and tactfully – as you and the child form your own special bond your role will become clearer.

MAINTAINING SPECIAL LINKS

One of the biggest problems for a child is to maintain contact with an absent parent while at the same time forming a relationship with a stepfather. And one of the most important things you can do is to encourage the child's relationship with his biological father. You should not see this tie as a threat to your own relationship with the child – you are an additional father, not a replacement for the real thing. An American study by Wallerstein and Kelly found that in happily re-married families children do not find this a problem or a source of conflict. The biological father does not fade from the picture and the children just enlarge their view of the family to embrace three parents. But a child does suffer intensely if the new family expect him to renounce his love of the biological father as a price of love and acceptance in the new family circle. Both fathers have a close role to play and those children who are given the space in which to develop their lives will flourish.

Your stepchild will usually also have other long-standing emotional ties – grandparents, relatives and friends who will want to maintain contact. Here too your acceptance of and encouragement in maintaining these special links will be helpful and appreciated. Remember this is not a completely new family, you are the new addition and as such will need to feel your way in carefully. There will be times when you may feel outnumbered, or an outsider to established 'family' jokes and traditions. This will gradually change to include you, but initially you may feel uncomfortably like the odd man out.

THE KEY TO SUCCESS

As a newly married couple you will have none of the usual time and space to establish yourselves which a first-time marriage enjoys. You are 'on show', having to share your partner with her child right from the start. If you have never had a child yourself this may come as a shock and put an additional strain on the relationship. Conflicting needs may make it difficult for you to find time alone as a couple without provoking divided loyalties. As the adult you will probably often have to contain your needs in the beginning. The success of the new family depends on your relationship with your partner. This is where your attention should be centred. If you are a strong unit the family will become equally sturdy too. It takes time and patience to find a comfortable way of life as a couple and it is not easy to balance your needs with those of a demanding, possibly insecure child, but in the long term there is no reason why everyone should not feel content. Children often benefit from a direct approach and simple explanations can help to create an atmosphere of trust. You can explain that all couples need regular time alone, but that this does not mean that you do not care for the child, or that you are taking his mother away. All children ultimately benefit from living with happy, close parents even if this closeness is hard for them to accept at the beginning. Your partner may also need your support to 'wean' herself away from the very close bonds that may have been established if she has lived alone with her child for a time. If you are already a father and have your own child's needs to consider as well, you will be well aware of the problems. But however many children are involved, the basic requirement for a stable couple relationship will remain the same. (For further reading about step families, see page 213.)

Whether you are already a parent or not, you may be tempted at the outset to be a 'super' parent – or expect your partner to be one! There is no such person; we all have our off days and our children have to learn our personal inconsistencies. It is a show of strength, not weakness, to admit you cannot cope, or feel overwhelmed by some aspect of the new family's life. It is unrealistic to expect everyone to be happy all the time and places an unfair burden on yourself and the rest of the family. You may not be the only one trying desperately hard; the children may also be making tremendous efforts to be 'good' to try and please you. Some children take the opposite line, start off hostile and uncooperative but relax slowly as they feel more secure, until with luck the relationship settles down. You can help this process by being natural and spontaneous – this will help to establish a family culture where feelings are fully expressed and no one has to be the 'goody' or the 'baddy'.

IMPOSING DISCIPLINE

In many new marriages where there are children, discipline becomes an issue. Codes of behaviour in the family should be the natural parent's responsibility – you are there to support. It is best to avoid confusing the child with contradictory rules – a child will very quickly learn to play you off against each other (this happens in every family!) if you and your partner do not present a united front. This does not mean you must adopt a rigid attitude to discipline; the best solution is for you and your partner to work out your own code together. But in the beginning it is wise not to interfere too actively. Discuss these issues in private with your partner and then give her the support she needs to maintain a secure working framework. This does not mean that you should tolerate misbehaviour, or be unresponsive if you are directly challenged by your stepchild: all children can be irritating and badly behaved, not just those who have gone through periods of insecurity or instability. As a stepfather you must gradually assume responsibility in the family and as one man I spoke to found out, it is not always a bad thing to do so. 'It was tough going in the beginning. I felt Pat was testing me a lot of the time. I was trying hard not to be the "heavy" father, I was worried she would resent me even more if I told her off. Finally one day I couldn't stand her behaviour any more and I gave her a really good dressing down. Much to my amazement she took it all in and was a changed child. She told me long afterwards that she remembers that day as a turning point for her, she felt I became a real father when I told her to stop behaving badly!' It is probably unnecessary to add that all discipline has to be within a loving atmosphere, so that everyone can feel more, not less, secure and cared for.

Financial problems are a very real source of anxiety and potential conflict in many re-married families. Money, or the lack of it, can be a continuing area of friction, not only between you and your partner, but for the children as well. Every couple has to find their own solutions, but it is a good idea if money is kept as an adult concern and not used as a way of arousing a child's already racing anxiety. A very young child will only sense the adults' heightened emotional state – an older child will need some clear explanation and all will need reassurance. A child will often worry about being a financial burden, or feel responsible for a situation clearly beyond his control. Here again it is the couple's joint concern to find a workable and realistic way of life on the finances available. But it does help if everyone is quite clear about who is responsible for who, and who is paying for what, and how! Re-married couples probably have to be more than usually careful to discuss, not only the actual financial facts, but also the feelings that these limitations and obligations provoke.

It takes time and a sense of commitment for a new family to become securely blended. Grandparents and friends can help by accepting and supporting the new family, especially in the early stages when any step parent is in an essentially vulnerable position. But you are probably not alone in feeling vulnerable; your partner, however much she loves you, may also be finding her new role quite a challenge. A woman who has learned to live alone as a single parent has had to develop some pretty independent characteristics. However much she loves you, she will also have some feelings about her new status as your wife, and it may take her a while to realize that she once more has a loving presence which can be relied upon.

There is no doubt that re-marriages do come under a lot of pressures, from inside and outside the family itself. Statistically, second marriages are even more likely to collapse than first. If more help and guidance were available early on some of these second divorces might be avoided. There are now books and organizations which attempt to provide some of this support. Remember that asking for help is not an admission of failure on anybody's part – rather it shows your commitment to the new family and your desire to put it on a happier footing. Stepfathers who overcome any early difficulties and persist in trying to make a good relationship with their stepchild are usually happy with the result. Children often form affectionate, long-term relationships with their step parents and grow to value their presence in their lives as they mature. The early years may be challenging, but the satisfaction of contributing to the all-round development of the child within a family setting will more than compensate for the effort involved.

Chapter 12

The growing child and the outside world

Fathers who try shared parenting are often pleasantly surprised to discover unexplored personal talents when they care for their baby. Traditional parenting tends to apportion mother and father particular roles. Mothers nurture and are expressive, fathers are the bridge to the child's perception of the outside world. A father will play, stimulate and draw the child gradually away from the intensely close initial relationship with the mother, towards maturity. Shared parenting means a willingness to share all these activities. Where the couple feels secure, it is possible for a father to discover he is naturally more nurturing than the mother. Couples may reverse roles, or find they are each fulfilling whatever role seems to be appropriate at the time. In fact both partners are free to develop their full potential, and the baby draws what he needs from whoever is present. The differences between the parents arise less from any 'roles' they play in or out of the home, but from the personalities of the two people concerned. A fallen, weeping toddler can expect the outstretched arms to belong to whichever parent is nearest and responds instinctively and confidently to his need for comfort.

WHAT HAPPENS TO THE 'SHARED' BABY?

If couples experience difficulties in the practical and psychological organization of shared parenting, how does the baby, recipient of so much care and thought, cope? Fears for a baby's welfare, emotional stability, or sex identification all seem to be groundless. Babies are usually happy if their needs are correctly interpreted – whether it is Dad or Mum who interprets them seems unimportant. Experts now agree that a baby will 'bond' successfully and happily with two, or more, key people. In fact it may even be preferable from the baby's point of view that the intense emotions of the exclusive and often

problematical mother–baby relationship are more widely distri-
buted. Intimate and early familiarity with both mother and father
makes it easier for the child to define his separateness from both
parents and enables him gradually and naturally to learn their
strengths and fallibilities. Through everyday contact with both
parents the child can develop his own balanced perspective of them
so that in later years neither parent can be fixed on, blamed, idealized
or totally rejected. Adult personality problems, so often rooted in
unsatisfactory mother–baby relationships, may be avoided if the
father is actively and emotionally involved from infancy onwards. In
this way shared parenthood offers the possibility of emotional
growth and harmony for each member of the family.

As the baby grows he becomes aware that both his parents have a
life inside and outside the family circle. He learns through living it
that this is the natural way of life for both men and women, so that
when the time comes he will be free to live the same way if he desires.
This healing of the split – father in the outside world, mother inside
the family – enables the child to learn and take what he needs from
both his parents. He makes the distinctions himself on the basis of
the real differences between his parents and not from culturally
supported stereotypes.

WHAT THE 'EXPERTS' SAY

Studies of young children who have had a 'highly participant' father
show them to be as 'normal' as other children but with a few
interesting differences (Russell). In Sweden these young pre-school
children were found to be more sociable than those from traditional
families. Another study in 1979 found children aged between four
and twelve who had 'sharing' parents had more flexible attitudes
about parenting roles and a less rigid sex-stereotyped view of life in
general. These same children were no different from any other
children in their choice of male–female interests or activities. But
they did express a higher degree of independence in thought and
action; they felt they had more control over their own lives.

Parents who wonder about the effect of this altered balance in the
family on their daughter's development might be interested in a study
done in Israel in 1981, which found that girls who had highly
involved fathers scored higher on the so-called 'masculine' traits –
they tended to be more assertive and outgoing, for example. A

similar study of shared parenting in Sweden also showed that girls had more interaction with their fathers than those brought up in traditional homes.

Although research programmes like these are fascinating, they all involve young children and it is probably difficult to assess the long-term benefits for children of shared parenting. Unless society also changes its views of what men and women 'should' do, the established pressures to conform which come from schools and the peer group will be hard to resist. The need to be like other families, not to be different, is very strong in adolescence when children are more likely to fall back on traditional sex-role stereotypes. Parents have to accept this as all part of the child's need to become independent and live his own life. But at least these children can fall back on their own vivid experiences and will be ultimately freer to choose their own solutions when in their turn they become parents.

A CONCLUSION . . .

The aim of this book has been to encourage men and women who are entering parenthood to open themselves to alternative ways of being a mother or a father. Not to step blindly into the pen of traditional parenting; but rather to climb to the top of the nearest hill and take a good look around before finding their own path into family life. Becoming a parent is probably the most important single step we take in our adult life and as such deserves our full attention. The nine months of pregnancy is a time of creativity for both parents who will inevitably re-assess their own childhood experiences in the light of hopes and fears for their child's future. This emotional 'homework' is an integral part of becoming a parent for both sexes but is often harder for the man to achieve unless it is harnessed to a definite task. Bearing in mind the conflict between work and home interests that exists within many of today's fathers, this book has tried to facilitate the man's involvement with his partner's pregnancy leading to an active participation with the labour and birth of their baby. By establishing the father's practical involvement during the pregnancy an emotional empathy has the chance to evolve between the couple which strengthens and enlivens their relationship at this crucial time.

Then, having forged this direct link, the hope is that both parents will see the endeavour of shared parenthood as a natural extension of the father's now tangible involvement within the family. Neither parent is stuck in a pre-ordained role – both are free to develop their strengths and support each other's vulnerabilities inside and outside the family.

But why should any man decide to take on the unknown challenges of involved fatherhood while continuing the ongoing demands of his work? Quite simply to take the ideal opportunity to develop himself as a fully rounded human being – to heal the split between masculine and feminine within his personality and to enable his partner to do the same for herself. Every father will personally benefit from a closer involvement with his family – this two way traffic of give and take is not just for the good of the child, or the relief of the mother, it irrevocably liberates the father from the chains of patriarchy.

Once the process is established, both partners are free to draw upon every aspect of their personalities without fear – there is a harmonious blending of strengths where before there was anxiety and the threat of chaos unless rigid boundaries were maintained. Neither parent becomes isolated or over-burdened within a pre-ordained role, both can move as the situation demands within and without the family – work and 'love-work' have equal status and respect.

And finally it is my hope that this book will contribute to the security of the children of shared parenting. As they mature these children will carry with them into the outside world first-hand knowledge of the intrinsic qualities and differences within each parent, not based on gender but rather on individual aptitude. Parenting in the future becomes a state of being for which all people are fully equipped regardless of gender – all children are then loved and cherished as society's shared responsibility and its most treasured gift.

Further reading and bibliography

If conception is a problem:
Joseph Bellin & Josleen Wilson, *The Fertility Handbook*, Penguin, 1985.

Preparation for Childbirth:
Sally Inch, *Birthrights – A Parent's Guide to Modern Childbirth*, Hutchinson, 1983.
Barbara Dale & Johanna Roeber, *Exercises for Childbirth*, Century, 1982.
Sophy Hoare, *Yoga and Pregnancy*, Unwin Paperbacks, 1985.
Sheila Kitzinger, *Pregnancy and Childbirth*, Michael Joseph, 1985.
—— *Giving Birth: Parents' Emotions in Childbirth*, Gollancz, 1971.
—— & L. Nillson, *Being Born*, Dorling Kindersley, 1986.
Janet Balaskas, *The Active Birth Partner's Handbook*, Sidgwick & Jackson, 1984.
Michel Odent, *Entering the World, The Way to Gentle Loving Birth*, Penguin, 1985.

Postnatal concerns:
Amelia D. Auckett, *Baby Massage, The Magic of Loving Touch*, Thorsons, 1982.
Maire Messenger, *The Breastfeeding Book*, Century, 1982.
Anne Price & Nancy Bamford, *The Breastfeeding Guide for the Working Woman*, Century, 1984.
Penelope Leach, *Baby and Child*, Penguin, 1985.
Vivien Welburn, *Postnatal Depression*, Fontana Paperbacks, 1980.
Martin Richards, *Infancy*, Harper and Row, 1980.
Jo Douglas & Naomi Richman, *My Child Won't Sleep*, Penguin, 1985.

Books about fathering:
Brian Jackson, *Fatherhood*, Allen & Unwin, 1983.
Charlie Lewis, *Becoming a Father*, OUP, 1986.
Ross D. Parke, *Fathering*, Fontana, 1981.
Graeme Russell, *The Changing Role of Fathers*, OUP, 1983.
Robin Skynner / John Cleese, *Families and How to Survive Them*, Methuen, 1983.

Special Needs:
Anne Hooper, *Divorce and Your Children*, Unwin Paperbacks, 1983.
Bryan M. Knight, *Enjoying Single Parenthood*, Von Nostrand Reinhold, 1980.
Diana Davenport, *Going it Alone, One Parent Families*, Pan Books, 1982.
Elizabeth Hodder, *The Step-Parents Handbook*, Sphere Books, 1985.
Jill Krementz, *How it Feels When a Parent Dies*, Camelot Press, 1981.

BIBLIOGRAPHY

Apgar, V. and Beck, J., *Is My Baby All Right?*, Trident Press, 1974.
Appleton, W. S., *Fathers and Daughters*, Papermac, 1982.
Arcana, J., *Every Mother's Son*, The Woman's Press, 1983.
Beail, N. and McGuire, J. (eds), *Fathers' Psychological Perspectives*, Junction Books, 1982.
Bibring, G. L., 'Some considerations of the psychological processes in pregnancy' in Eissler, R. S. and Freud, A. (eds) *The Psychoanalytic Study of the Child*, New York Universities Press, 1959.
Bittman, S. and Rosenberg Zalk, S., *Expectant Fathers*, Hawthorn Books, 1978.
Bowlby, J., *Childcare and the Growth of Love*, Pelican, 1965.
Breen, D., *The Birth of a First Child*, Tavistock Publications, 1975.
Colman, A. and L., *Earth Father, Sky Father*, Spectrum Books, 1981.
Daley, E. A., *Father Feelings*, Morrow and Co., New York, 1978.
Dinnerstein, D., *The Rocking of the Cradle: the Ruling of the World*, Condor Books, 1979.
Dunn, J. and Kendrick, C., *Siblings – Love, Envy and Understanding*, Grant McIntyre, 1982.
Fein, R. A., 'Men's experiences before and after the birth of a first child', PhD thesis, Cambridge, Mass., 1974.
—— 'Factors contributing to first time fathers' readiness for fatherhood: an exploratory study', Family Relations, 1982.
Greenberg, M. and Morris, N., 'Engrossment: the newborn's impact upon the father', *American Journal of Orthopsychiatry* 44, 1974.
Hodder, E., *The Step-Parents' Handbook*, Sphere Books, 1985.
Inch, S., *Birthrights: A Parents' Guide to Modern Childbirth*, Hutchinson, 1982.
Ingham, M., *Men*, Century, 1985.
International Childbirth Education Association, 'Diagnostic ultrasound in obstetrics', 1984.
Jackson, B., *Fatherhood*, Allen and Unwin, 1983.
Journal of Allergy and Clinical Immunology, Vol. 16, 6, 1986.
Kitzinger, S., *Pregnancy and Childbirth*, Michael Joseph, 1985.

—— The Experience of Breastfeeding, Penguin, 1984.
—— Giving Birth: The Parents' Emotions in Childbirth, Gollancz, 19/11
—— and Davis, J. A. (eds), The Place of Birth, OUP, 1978.
—— Women's Experience of Sex, Dorling Kindersley, 1983.
Klaus, M. H. and Kennell, J. H., Parent Infant Bonding, second edition, C. V. Mosby Co., 1982.
Leboyer, F., Birth Without Violence, Fontana Collins, 1983.
Lewis, C., Becoming a Father, OUP, 1986.
Lynn, D. B., The Father: His Role in Child Development, Brookes Cole, 1970.
Macfarlane, A., The Psychology of Childbirth, Fontana, 1977.
McCluggage, D., The Centred Skier, Bantam, 1983.
Mead, M., Growing up in New Guinea, Pelican, 1963.
Montagu, A., Touching, Harper (Colophon Books), 1978.
—— Life Before Birth, Signet Books, 1977.
Noble, E., Childbirth with Insight, Houghton Mifflin Co., 1983.
Oakley, A., Women Confined, Martin Robertson, 1974.
Oakley, A. and McPherson, A. and Roberts, H., Miscarriage, Fontana, 1984.
Odent, M., Genèse de l'homme écologique, L'instinct retrouvé, Epi, 1979.
Owen, U. (ed.), Fathers Reflections by Daughters, Virago, 1983.
Parke, Ross D., Fathering, Fontana, 1981.
Pincus, L., Death in the Family: the Importance of Mourning, Faber, 1981.
Rapoport, R. & R. N. & Strelitz, Z., Fathers, Mothers and Others, Routledge and Kegan Paul, 1977.
Rich, A., Of Woman Born, Virago, 1981.
Richards, M. P. M. (ed.), The Integration of a Child into a Social World, Cambridge University Press, 1974.
Russell, G., The Changing Role of Fathers, OUP, 1983.
Skynner, R., One Flesh Separate Persons, Constable, 1976.
—— and Cleese, J., Families and How to Survive Them, Methuen, 1983.
Verney, Dr T. & Kelly, J., The Secret of the Unborn Child, Sphere Books, 1977.
Walczak, Y. & Burns, S., Divorce: the Child's Point of View, Harper & Row, 1984.
Wallerstein, J. & Kelly, J. B., Surviving the Break-Up, Grant McIntyre, 1980.
Winnicott, D. W., The Child, the Family and the Outside World, Pelican, 1985.
—— The Maturational Process in the Facilitating Environment, Hogarth Press, 1979.

Useful names and addresses

National Childbirth Trust,
9, Queensborough Terrace,
London W2 3TB
(01-) 221 3833
Organizes antenatal classes and network of postnatal supporters including breast feeding counsellors nationwide.

Association of Radical Midwives,
Lakefield,
8a, The Drive,
Wimbledon.
London, SW20.

AIMS – Association for Improvements in Maternity Services,
163, Liverpool Road,
London N1 ORF.
Pressure group that campaigns for the rights of parents.

The Birth Centre,
101, Tufnell Park,
London, N7.
(01-) 609 7466
Provides information, antenatal classes and support for those who seek a non-mechanized birth.

Society to Support Home Confinements,
17, Laburnam Avenue,
Durham DHY 4HA
(0385) 61325
Help about home birth.

British Acupuncture Association,
34, Alderney Street,
London, SW1.
Can provide list of qualified practitioners.

British Homeopathic Association,
Basildon Court,
27a, Devonshire Street,
London WIN 1RJ.
Will provide list of qualified practitioners.

La Leche League (Great Britain),
Box 3424. London, WC1 6XX.
(01-) 404 5011
Help and support to breastfeeding mothers.

The Meet-A-Mum Association,
Mary Whitlock,
26a, Cummor Hill,
Oxford OX2 9HA.
Support for parents after birth.

Marie Stopes House Family Planning Clinic,
108, Whitfield Street,
London W1T 6BE.
(01-) 388 0662

Community Health Group for Ethnic Minorities,
28, Churchfield Road,
London W3 6EB.
(01-) 993 6119
Advice on nutrition and support with interpreting and translating.

Foresight, The Association for the Promotion of Pre-Conceptual Care,
The Old Vicarage,
Church Lane, Witley,
Surrey GU8 5PN.
(please enclose a S.A.E. for reply)
Information on nutrition before and during pregnancy.

Twin Clubs Association,
'Porthladd', 27, Woodham Park Road,
Woodham, Weybridge,
Surrey.
Self help organization, support before and after with multiple births.

Caesarean Support Groups,
c/o Lynne Hallet,
9, Nightingale Grove,
London SE13 6EY.
(01-) 318 2820
Information and support to those who have a Caesarean birth.

Gingerbread,
35, Wellington Street,
London WC2 7BN.
(01-) 240 0953
Mutual support network for one parent families.

National Council for One Parent Families,
255, Kentish Town Road,
London NW5 2LX.
Information and advice.

National Childminding Association,
204/206, Bromley High Street,
Bromley BR1 1PP.
(01-) 464 6164
Aims to improve facilities for childminders and children.

National Association for the Childless,
318, Summer Lane,
Birmingham B19 3RL.
(021-) 359 4887
Support and information about fertility problems.

Microtens Obstetric Hire Service,
Neen Pain Management Systems,
Barn Lodge, Gooseberry Hill,
Swanton Morley,
Dereham, Norfolk NR20 4NR.
036283 – 767
TENS Hire Co.

General Council of Registered Osteopaths,
21, Suffolk Street,
London SW1 Y4H9.
(01-) 930 3889
Will provide a list of qualified osteopaths – you may have to be persistent to find out which practise Cranial Osteopathy.

If There is a Problem

Institute of Family Therapy,
43, New Cavendish Street,
London W1.
(01-) 935 1651
Provides counselling and therapy
for couples and families whatever
the crisis.

The Miscarriage Association,
Dolphin Cottage,
4, Ashfield Terrace,
Thorpe,
Wakefield, West Yorks.
(0532) 828946
Support and advice for those who
have had a miscarriage.

Society after Termination due to
Fetal Abnormality,
c/o ASBAH
22, Upper Woburn Place,
London WC1H OEP.
(01-) 288 1382

Parents Anonymous,
6 Manor Gardens,
London N7 6LA.
(01-) 263 8918
24-hour line for stressed parents.

Stillbirth & Neonatal Death
Society,
37, Christchurch Hill,
London NW3 1LA.
(01-) 794 4601
Information and support nationwide for bereaved parents.

Down's Children Association,
4 Oxford Street,
London W1N 9FL.
(01-) 580 0511
Advice on the care of Down's children.

Contact a Family with a Handicapped Child,
16 Strutton Ground,
London SW1 2HP.
(01-) 222 2695
Introduces parents of handicapped
children to each other to give support.

The Foundation for the Study of
Infant Deaths,
5th Floor, 4 Grosvenor Place,
London SW1.
Research into cot death, support for
parents who have lost a baby.

The Association for Postnatal
Illness,
7, Gowan Avenue,
London SW6 6RH.
Advice from those who have experi-
enced similar problems.

Addresses of Conciliation Services,
Try local branch of Citizens Advice
    Bureau, or probation offices.
Counsellor works with both
    parents to find best solutions for
    child in access and related
    problems after separation or
    divorce.

Families Need Fathers,
97c, Shakespeare Walk,
London N16 8TB.
(01-) 953 8932
Group of men and women who
fight for the rights of fathers where
custody has been granted to the
mother.

Index

paternity leave 50, 151, 169–72
  and father's role in home 169–70
  practical and moral support
    170–1
  and work demands 171–2
patience, needed by father
  in postnatal period 157
  in pre-natal period 115
pediatricians 141, 142
pelvic floor exercises 93–6, 100–1,
    104, 163–4
pelvic inflammatory disease 31
perineal stitches 79, 163–4, 165
persistent crying 184–5
  see also under babies
personality, baby's 187–8
personal problems, of single parents
    201–2
pethidine 67
photograph of baby
  in special care 141
  after termination 63
physical pleasuring 42
pill, birth 166
placenta
  delivery of
  praevia 68, 125
planning future pregnancies
  after Caesarean 130
  after death of child 146–7
playgroups 203
playing, baby's 192
positions for birth 120–21
  practising 65–6, 77
positive affirmation 104–5
post-mortem, after termination 64
postnatal feelings 153–61
  ambivalence about sharing
    159–60
  depression 53, 153–5, 171, 179,
    184
  exhaustion 151, 172, 174
  happiness and excitement 170,
    171, 172
  high 150

hostility
  between couple 152
  between fathers and work
    colleagues 179
  resentment and frustration 158
  temporary disinterest in baby
    156
postnatal period
  caring for partner in 150–67
  couple's relationship in 157–8
  first few weeks 169–70, 172
  inherited parenting patterns in
    161
  normal changes in 155
  support essential in 156–7
postnatal practicalities 168–80
  arrangements 172–80
  balancing demands 179–80
  father's role in home 169–71
  making the choice 180
  men's attitude to their work
    177–8
  and moral support 170–1
  organizing work schedules
    172–4
  paternity leave 168–72
  and work demands 171–2
  transition from work to home
    174
  woman's conflict 175
  work vs family work 175–7
postnatal sex 161–7
  birth control as man's
    responsibility 166
  fatigue and distractions 164–5
  making love again 165–6
  men's reactions 162–3
  recovering sexual awareness
    163–4
  sex and breastfeeding
    from man's point of view
    166–7
    from woman's point of view 167
  woman's feelings 163
postnatal support groups 157, 183